POWER OF
ATTORNEY
HANDBOOK

POWER OF ATTORNEY HANDBOOK

with forms

Edward A. Haman
Attorney at Law

Sphinx Publishing
A Division of Sourcebooks, Inc.
Naperville, IL • Clearwater, FL

Third Edition, 1998

Published by: **Sphinx® Publishing, a division of Sourcebooks, Inc.®**

Naperville Office
P.O. Box 372
Naperville, Illinois 60566
(630) 961-3900
FAX: 630-961-2168

Clearwater Office
P.O. Box 25
Clearwater, Florida 33757
(813) 587-0999
FAX: 813-586-5088

Interior Design and Production: Shannon E. Harrington, Sourcebooks, Inc.

This publication is designed to provide accurate and authoritative information in regard to the subject matter covered. It is sold with the understanding that the publisher is not engaged in rendering legal, accounting, or other professional service. If legal advice or other expert assistance is required, the services of a competent professional person should be sought.

From a Declaration of Principles Jointly Adopted by a Committee of the
American Bar Association and a Committee of Publishers and Associations

Library of Congress Cataloging-in-Publication Data
Haman, Edward A.
     Power of attorney handbook : with forms / Edward A.Haman.—
3rd ed.
         p.   cm.
     Includes index.
     ISBN 1-57071-348-0 (pbk.)
     1. Power of attorney—United States—Popular works.   2. Power of
attorney—United States—Forms.   I. Title.
KF1347.Z9H35   1998
346.7302'9—dc21   98-15492
                                                                                              CIP

CONTENTS

USING SELF-HELP LAW BOOKS. 1

INTRODUCTION. 3

CHAPTER 1: WHAT IS A POWER OF ATTORNEY AND WHO NEEDS ONE?. 5

CHAPTER 2: LAWYERS 9
  Do You Want a Lawyer?
  Selecting a Lawyer
  Working With a Lawyer

CHAPTER 3: THE LAW CONCERNING POWERS OF ATTORNEY. 15
  In General
  The Law in Your State
  Legal Research

CHAPTER 4: FINANCIAL POWER OF ATTORNEY. 19
  In General
  Real Estate
  Durable Financial Power of Attorney

CHAPTER 5: HEALTH CARE POWER OF ATTORNEY 29
  Durable Power of Attorney for Health Care
  Living Wills

CHAPTER 6: OTHER POWER OF ATTORNEY FORMS 35
  Power of Attorney for Child Care
  Revoking a Power of Attorney

APPENDIX A: STATE LAWS 39

APPENDIX B: FORMS 57

INDEX 211

USING SELF-HELP
LAW BOOKS

Whenever you shop for a product or service, you are faced with various levels of quality and price. In deciding what product or service to buy, you make a cost/value analysis on the basis of your willingness to pay and the quality you desire.

When buying a car, you decide whether you want transportation, comfort, status, or sex appeal. Accordingly, you decide among such choices as a Neon, a Lincoln, a Rolls Royce, or a Porsche. Before making a decision, you usually weigh the merits of each option against the cost.

When you get a headache, you can take a pain reliever (such as aspirin) or visit a medical specialist for a neurological examination. Given this choice, most people, of course, take a pain reliever, since it costs only pennies, whereas a medical examination costs hundreds of dollars and takes a lot of time. This is usually a logical choice because rarely is anything more than a pain reliever needed for a headache. But in some cases, a headache may indicate a brain tumor, and failing to see a specialist right away can result in complications. Should everyone with a headache go to a specialist? Of course not, but people treating their own illnesses must realize that they are betting on the basis of their cost/value analysis of the situation, they are taking the most logical option.

The same cost/value analysis must be made in deciding to do one's own legal work. Many legal situations are very straight forward, requiring a simple form and no complicated analysis. Anyone with a little intelligence and a book of instructions can handle the matter without outside help.

But there is always the chance that complications are involved that only an attorney would notice. To simplify the law into a book like this, several legal cases often must be condensed into a single sentence or paragraph. Otherwise, the book would be several hundred pages long and too complicated for most people. However, this simplification necessarily leaves out many details and nuances that would apply to special or unusual situations. Also, there are many ways to interpret most legal questions. Your case may come before a judge who disagrees with the analysis of our authors.

Therefore, in deciding to use a self-help law book and to do your own legal work, you must realize that you are making a cost/value analysis and deciding that the chance your case will not turn out to your satisfaction is outweighed by the money you will save in doing it yourself. Most people handling their own simple legal matters never have a problem, but occasionally people find that it ended up costing them more to have an attorney straighten out the situation than it would have if they had hired an attorney in the beginning. Keep this in mind while handling your case, and be sure to consult an attorney if you feel you might need further guidance.

INTRODUCTION

This book is designed to enable you to prepare your own power of attorney without hiring a lawyer. It will explain the different types of powers of attorney, guide you in deciding which type you need, and show you how to prepare it. Be sure to read the previous section on "Using Self-Help Law Books."

The difficulty in covering any area of law on a national scale is that the law is different (and ever changing) in each state. However, the general type of information found in most powers of attorney is very similar in each state. Appendix A of this book will give you some information about the specific laws of your state. Many states have officially approved forms. These forms and forms for use in states without official forms are located in appendix B.

The old saying that knowledge is power is especially true in the law. Lawyers have worked hard for many years to make the law complicated, so that only they have the knowledge and the power. This book will give you a fair amount of knowledge so that you can take back some of the power. By reading this book, you will be able to know as much about powers of attorney as most recent law school graduates, and know more than many.

Read this entire book (including the listing for your state in appendix A) before you prepare any papers. This will give you the information you need to decide what forms you need and how to fill them out. You may also want to visit your local law library to get more information. Chapter 3 will help you with this.

To complete the necessary forms, you will need to use the general instructions in the main part of this book, consult the listing for your state in appendix A, and use the information from any additional reading and research you do. Many of the official state forms also contain detailed instructions and valuable information. If you need to refer back to this book for answers to specific questions, use the Table of Contents and the Index to help locate the answers you need.

WHAT IS A POWER OF ATTORNEY AND WHO NEEDS ONE?

1

A power of attorney is simply a paper giving another person the legal authority to represent you and act on your behalf. This is necessary when some third person is asked to rely on that authority. Of course, a power of attorney is not necessary every time someone does something for you. For example, if you ask me to get a gallon of milk for you from the supermarket, I can do it without a power of attorney. I will be paying for it with cash at the time I get it, and the grocer has no concern about our arrangement.

It is an entirely different matter, however, if you ask me to go to your bank and borrow $2,000 in your name. The bank will want to be sure that you are legally obligated to repay the loan, and they won't just take my word for it. The bank will want to protect itself, so it will require some kind of proof that you have authorized me to obligate you to repay the money. A power of attorney could provide the bank with the assurance it needs.

TERMINOLOGY To understand a power of attorney, it is necessary to know a few terms:

agent. A person who is given authority by a power of attorney.

attorney-at-law. A person who is licensed to practice law before state or federal courts. The term has no relationship to a power of attorney.

attorney-in-fact. A person who is given authority by a power of attorney. This is another term for *agent*, and is used in many statutes.

durable power of attorney. A power of attorney that continues after the principal becomes incapacitated.

execute. To sign a legal document, thereby making it effective.

general power of attorney. A power of attorney that gives the agent very broad powers, generally to conduct all kinds of business on behalf of the principal.

limited power of attorney or **special power of attorney.** A power of attorney that limits the agent's authority to certain specific areas or actions.

power of attorney. A document that gives one person (the *agent*) authority to act on behalf of another person (the *principal*). The plural is *powers of attorney*.

principal. A person who signs the power of attorney, and thereby gives someone the authority to act on his or her behalf.

springing power of attorney. A power of attorney that does not become effective until a certain event occurs, such as the incapacity of the principal.

An example of how some of these terms are used is: "The principal executed a limited power of attorney, giving his agent the power to handle the sale of his car." In general, you need a power of attorney whenever you want someone else to act on your behalf in a matter of legal significance. Next, we will discuss the more common uses of powers of attorney.

FINANCIAL POWER OF ATTORNEY

A financial power of attorney gives a person you designate the authority to act on your behalf in financial matters. This can be limited to one financial transaction, certain types of transactions, or can include all types of transactions. You will need a financial power of attorney if you want someone to be able to act for you in some or all of your financial dealings. This is usually done when you have distant or numerous financial matters to attend to and cannot be there personally to transact all of the business. Chapter 4 will discuss the financial power of attorney in more detail.

HEALTH CARE
POWERS OF
ATTORNEY AND
LIVING WILLS

Health Care Power of Attorney. A health care power of attorney is a special type of power of attorney that allows the agent to make decisions about the medical treatment for the principal. This can only occur if the principal is unable to make such decisions for himself. A health care power of attorney is most often used by a husband and wife, or close family members. Without a health care agent, doctors and hospitals may be reluctant to provide certain medical care if you are unable to give consent or make decisions about treatment options. Chapter 5 will discuss these in more detail.

Living Wills. A living will is somewhat similar to a health care power of attorney, but it is limited to the refusal of certain medical treatment in the event of a terminal illness or injury. Without a living will, doctors or hospitals may decide they are legally obligated to perform certain procedures which you may not desire, in the event you become seriously ill and are unable to communicate your desires. A living will tells others what you want to happen in certain circumstances. You may see this called by other names, such as a *declaration regarding life-prolonging procedures* or an *advance directive.*

A few states have developed a living will that includes a provision for appointing an agent. However, such an agent only has authority to act on the principal's behalf if the principal has a terminal illness or injury, or is permanently unconscious. In such a situation, the agent can only make decisions regarding the use of life-prolonging procedures. If the principal is not in terminal condition or permanently unconscious, the agent does not have any authority.

The Difference. The difference between a health care power of attorney and a living will may be explained by the following example. Suppose you are in an automobile accident. You are brought to your local hospital emergency room, treated, stabilized, and admitted to the hospital. You are unconscious, but are expected to recover (i.e., you are neither in a terminal condition nor permanently unconscious). If all you have is a living will, it will not be of any help, because a living will only becomes active if you are in a terminal condition or permanently unconscious. A question arises as to your treatment: Would your recovery be more complete by (1) having immediate surgery, or (2) waiting until you are awake and going through physical therapy? Obviously, you are unable to listen to the doctors explain the pros and cons of each course of treatment, and make a decision. Depending on the law in your state and the hospital policy, the doctors and the hospital may wait until you wake up (when it may be too late to opt for surgery), or allow a relative of yours to make the decision (possibly a relative you would rather not have decide for you). If you have a health care power of attorney, a person whom you trust would have the authority to make the decision. Living wills are covered in more detail in *How to Write Your Own Living Will*, by Edward A. Haman (Sphinx Publishing).

POWER OF
ATTORNEY FOR
CHILD CARE

A power of attorney for child care allows someone to make decisions regarding the care of your minor child or children. You may want to have this type of power of attorney if your child will be spending prolonged periods of time living with a friend or relative, where you may not be able to be reached in an emergency. Doctors or hospitals may be reluctant to give medical treatment to a child without the consent of the parent. A power of attorney authorizing your friend or relative to consent to medical treatment for your child may resolve this problem. Also, if your child will be living with someone else, that person may need a power of attorney in order to enroll your child in school.

LAWYERS 2

Do You Need a Lawyer?

The answer to this question will depend upon whom you ask. If you ask a lawyer, he or she will probably say that you definitely need one. However, by the time you are finished reading this book you will know almost as much as most lawyers about powers of attorney.

The purpose of a power of attorney is to allow someone you trust to act on your behalf when you are unable to do so. A power of attorney needs to accurately reflect your wishes, and meet the legal requirements for it to be honored by others. The way most lawyers would approach this would be to consult your state laws, possibly a book such as this one, look at examples of other powers of attorney (that either he or other lawyers have prepared), and prepare a document to fit your situation. That is exactly what this book will enable you to do for yourself.

One of the first questions you may have about a lawyer, and most likely the reason you are reading this book, is: How much will an attorney cost? Attorneys come in all ages, shapes, sizes, sexes, racial and ethnic groups—and price ranges. For a very rough estimate, you can probably expect an attorney to charge anywhere from $75 to $300 per hour. Some may prepare a power of attorney for a flat fee, which may typically range anywhere from $50 to $500.

If you decide to hire a lawyer, the remainder of this chapter will help you to select and work with him or her more effectively. (**Note:** This chapter is designed to help you select an attorney for any type of legal problem, therefore, a few of the suggestions may be unnecessary for a relatively simple power of attorney.)

SELECTING A LAWYER

Selecting a lawyer is a two-step process. First you need to decide which attorney to make an appointment with, then you need to decide if you want to hire that attorney.

FINDING LAWYERS

Selecting a lawyer is somewhat like choosing a doctor or dentist. The following suggestions will help you get started.

- ☛ Ask a friend to recommend a lawyer he or she has used and was happy with.

- ☛ Lawyer referral service. You can find one by looking in the yellow pages phone directory under "Attorney Referral Services" or "Attorneys." This is a service, usually operated by a bar association, which is designed to match a client with an attorney handling cases in the area of law the client needs. The referral service does not guarantee the quality of work, the level of experience, or the ability of the attorney.

- ☛ Yellow pages. Check under the heading for "Attorneys" in the yellow pages phone directory. You may also find display ads here indicating attorneys' areas of practice.

- ☛ Ask another lawyer you know, or have used in the past for some other matter, if he or she handles powers of attorney, or could refer you to an attorney who does.

EVALUATING A LAWYER

From your search you should select three to five lawyers worthy of further consideration. Your first step will be to call each attorney's office, explain that you are interested in having a power of attorney prepared, and ask the following questions:

- ☞ Does the attorney (or firm) handle preparation of powers of attorney (or handle whatever type of assistance you need)?

- ☞ How much can you expect it to cost?

- ☞ How soon can you get an appointment?

If you like the answers you get, ask if you can speak to the attorney. Some offices will permit this, but others will require you to make an appointment. Make the appointment if that is what is required. Once you get in contact with the attorney (either on the phone or at the appointment), ask the following questions:

- ☞ How much will it cost, and how will the fee be paid?

- ☞ How long has the attorney been in practice?

- ☞ Has the attorney prepared many powers of attorney (or handled your type of legal situation)?

- ☞ How long will it take to have a power of attorney prepared (or complete the particular type of case)?

If you get acceptable answers to these questions, it's time to ask *yourself* the following questions about the lawyer:

- ☞ Do you feel comfortable talking to the lawyer?

- ☞ Is the lawyer friendly toward you?

- ☞ Does the lawyer seem confident in himself or herself?

- ☞ Does the lawyer seem to be straight-forward with you, and able to explain things so that you understand?

If you get satisfactory answers to all of these questions you probably have a lawyer you'll be able to work with. Most clients are happiest using an attorney with whom they feel comfortable.

WORKING WITH A LAWYER

In general, you will work best with your attorney if you keep an open, honest and friendly attitude. You should also consider the following suggestions.

Ask questions. If you want to know something or if you don't understand something, ask your attorney. If you don't understand the answer, tell your attorney and ask him or her to explain it again. There are points of law that many lawyers don't fully understand, so you shouldn't be embarrassed to ask questions. Many people who say they had a bad experience with a lawyer either didn't ask enough questions, or had a lawyer who wouldn't take the time to explain things to them. If your lawyer isn't taking the time to explain what he's doing, it may be time to look for a new lawyer.

Give your lawyer complete information. Anything you tell your attorney is confidential. An attorney can lose his license to practice if he reveals information without your permission. So don't hold back information.

Accept reality. Listen to what your lawyer tells you about the law and the legal system, and accept it. It will do you no good to argue because the law or the system doesn't work the way you think it should. And remember: It's not your attorney's fault that the system isn't perfect, or that the law doesn't say what you'd like it to say.

Be patient. Don't expect your lawyer to return your phone call within an hour. He may not be able to return it the same day either. Most lawyers are very busy, and over-worked. It is rare that an attorney can maintain a full caseload and still make each client feel as if he is the only client.

Talk to the secretary. Your lawyer's secretary can be a valuable source of information. Often the secretary will be able to answer your questions and you won't get a bill for the time you talk to him or her.

Keeping your case moving. Many lawyers operate on the old principle of the squeaking wheel gets the oil. Work on a case tends to get put off until a deadline is near, an emergency develops, or the client calls. There is a reason for this: Many lawyers take more cases than can be effectively handled in order to make the income they desire. Your task is to become a squeaking wheel that doesn't squeak so much that the lawyer wants to avoid you. Whenever you talk to your lawyer ask the following questions:

- ☞ What is the next step?

- ☞ When do you expect it to be done?

- ☞ When should I talk to you next?

If you don't hear from the lawyer when you expect, call him the following day. Don't remind him that he didn't call; just ask how things are going.

How to save money. Of course you don't want to spend unnecessary money for an attorney. Here are a few things you can do to avoid excess legal fees:

- ☞ Don't make unnecessary phone calls to your lawyer.

- ☞ Give information to the secretary whenever possible.

- ☞ Direct your question to the secretary first. You will be referred to the attorney if the secretary can't answer it.

- ☞ Plan your phone calls so you can get to the point, and take less of your attorney's time. Write down an outline if necessary.

- ☞ Do some of the leg work yourself. Pick up and deliver papers yourself, for example. Ask your attorney what you can do to assist him or her.

- ☞ Be prepared for appointments. Have all related papers with you, plan your visit to get to the point, and make an outline of what you want to discuss and what questions you want to ask.

Pay your attorney bill when it's due. No client gets prompt attention like a client who pays his lawyer on time. However, you are entitled to an itemized bill, showing what the attorney did and how much time it took. If your attorney asks for money in advance, you should be sure that you and the lawyer agree on what is to be done for this fee.

Firing your lawyer. If you find that you can no longer work with your lawyer, or don't trust your lawyer, it is time to either go it alone or get a new attorney. You will need to send your lawyer a letter stating that you no longer desire his services, and are discharging him from your case. Also state that you will be coming by his office the following day to pick up your file. The attorney does not have to give you his own notes or other work he has in progress, but he must give you the essential contents of your file (such as copies of papers already prepared and billed for, and any documents you provided). If he refuses to give you your file, for any reason, contact your state's bar association about filing a complaint or *grievance* against the lawyer. Of course, you will need to settle any remaining fees owed. For more information, see *Legal Malpractice and Other Claims against Your Lawyer*, by Suzan Herskowitz (Sphinx Publishing).

THE LAW CONCERNING POWERS OF ATTORNEY 3

IN GENERAL

The basics of the law concerning powers of attorney are fairly simple. By signing a power of attorney you are giving another person the authority to act on your behalf. Your power of attorney can give your agent broad powers, or it can limit him or her to specific actions.

The law provides that other people may rely on your power of attorney in doing business with your agent, so you will be bound by what your agent does through the power of attorney. This means that you had better have a great deal of trust in the person you select as your agent.

The big problem: The real reason for giving someone a power of attorney is to get some third party to believe that your agent really has authority to act on your behalf. Traditionally, and in many states even today, a third party can be left "holding the bag" if the agent does not really have authority. Therefore, many people and businesses are reluctant to honor a power of attorney. Some states have taken care of this problem by making the following three laws:

1. Creating an official form in the state law.

2. Eliminating liability of a third party who relies on the power of attorney in the official form.

3.   Making it illegal for a third party to refuse to honor a power of attorney in the official form.

In other states, however, it may be difficult to get a bank, stock broker, or any others to do business based upon a power of attorney. The law for specific types of powers of attorney will be discussed in more detail in later chapters of this book.

THE LAW IN YOUR STATE

Many states have established approved forms for powers of attorney. First, refer to the listing for your state in appendix A of this book, which will tell you about the power of attorney laws in your state, and where to locate your state's laws. You will then locate the proper form in appendix B and complete it. More information about how to use appendix A is found in later chapters. Generally you should not need to go beyond the information in this book, however, if you wish to study your state's law on powers of attorney, the next section of this chapter will give you more information about using the law library.

LEGAL RESEARCH

After this book, you may want to visit a law library. One can usually be found at your county courthouse, or at a law school. Ask the law librarian to help you find what you need. The librarian cannot give you legal advice, but can show you where to find your state's laws and other books on powers of attorney. Some typical sources are discussed below.

STATUTES OR CODE   The main source of information is the set of books containing your state's laws. These are the *statutes*, or *code*, of your state (e.g., *Florida Statutes, Mississippi Code*). The title of the books may also include words such as *revised*, or *annotated*. (e.g., *Annotated California Code, Kentucky Revised Statutes*). The word *revised* means updated, and the word *annotated* means the books contain information which explains and interprets the laws. Titles may also include the publisher's name, such as *Purdon's Pennsylvania Consolidated Statutes Annotated*. The listing for your state in appendix A gives the title of the set of laws for your state. A few states have more than one set of laws, by various publishers (e.g., *Michigan Statutes Annotated* and *Michigan Compiled Laws Annotated*).

Each year the legislature meets and changes the law, therefore, it is important to be sure you have the most current version. The most common way to update laws is with a soft-cover supplement, found in the back of each volume. There will be a date on the cover to tell you when it was published (such as "1998 Cumulative Supplement"). Other ways laws are updated is with a supplement volume, which will be found at the end of the regular set of volumes; or a looseleaf binding, in which pages are removed and replaced, or changes are placed in a supplement section. Checking the most current law is probably all you will need to do. But if you want to go further, the following sources may be helpful:

PRACTICE
MANUALS

Practice manuals are books containing detailed information about various areas of the law. They usually include forms for all different situations.

DIGESTS

A digest is set of books that give summaries of appeals court cases. A digest for your state is best (e.g., *Florida Digest*, *California Digest*), as the national digest is difficult to use. Look in the index for the subject, such as "Power of Attorney," "Principal and Agent," "Agency," "Health Care Power of Attorney," "Life-prolonging procedures," etc.

CASE
REPORTERS

Case reporters contain the full written opinions of the appeals court cases. There will often be a set of case reporters specifically for your state (e.g., *Michigan Reports*). There are also regional reporters, which include cases from a number of states in the same geographical area (e.g., *Southern Reporter*, *Northwestern Reporter*). Furthermore, many of the reporters are divided into two or more series. Rather than continue numbering volumes, at some point in time the publisher decided to label the volumes as the second series or third series, and started over with volume 1. For example, *Northwestern Reporter, Second Series* (abbreviated *N.W. 2d.*).

LEGAL
ENCYCLOPEDIA

A legal encyclopedia is like a regular encyclopedia—you look up the subject you want (such as "Power of Attorney," "Principal and Agent," or "Agency"), in alphabetical order. *American Jurisprudence* (abbreviated *Am.Jur.*) and *Corpus Juris Secundum* (*C.J.S.*) are the major sets, and some states have their own, such as *Florida Jurisprudence.* As with the reporters, you may find legal encyclopedias with a second series, such as *American Jurisprudence, Second Series* (abbreviated *Am.Jur. 2d*).

Financial Power of Attorney 4

In General

A financial power of attorney authorizes the agent to act on your behalf in financial matters (as opposed to health care matters). This may include such things as buying and selling real estate or other property, entering into contracts, investing, banking transactions, operating a business, and making decisions regarding lawsuits.

Traditionally, a power of attorney was a long document that explained in detail all of the powers given to the agent. Such a power of attorney is found in appendix B as Form 1. To simplify things, some states have created shortened financial power of attorney forms. In these states, the state law spells out the details for each power, which are only generally referred to in the power of attorney document itself. Appendix B contains specific state forms if you live in one of the following states: Alaska, California, Colorado, Connecticut, Georgia, Illinois, Indiana, Maine, Minnesota, Montana, Nebraska, New Mexico, New York, North Carolina, Tennessee, Texas, and Wisconsin. Instructions for these statutory forms are found in the forms themselves. If you do not live in one of these states, you will need to use Form 1 in appendix B. Instructions for completing Form 1 can be found later in this chapter under the heading "Durable Financial Power of Attorney."

Sometimes you may need a power of attorney for someone to do a very specific thing for you. **Example:** You have agreed to sell your boat. The buyer will pick it up and pay you on the following Saturday, but you will be out of town then. You could execute a power of attorney to give your friend the authority to sign a bill of sale or any title transfer documents, and accept payment. This is a *limited power of attorney*. Form 61 in appendix B may be used in such situations. To complete the LIMITED POWER OF ATTORNEY (Form 61):

1. Type in your name and address on the first line in the first paragraph, and your agent's name and address on the second line.

2. In the blank space after the second paragraph, type in a description of what your agent is being authorized to do on your behalf. In our example above, you might type in: "To whatever is necessary to complete the sale to John Smith of my 1994 Tracker bass boat, Serial Number 1994837590, Registration Number FL 39920-C; including delivery of said boat, accepting payment, and executing any documents necessary to transfer title and ownership."

3. Fill in the date, and signature lines at the bottom. (**Note:** You may or may not need to attach a notary provision, depending upon what state you live in. Also, many states have their own forms for a power of attorney to transfer title to a motor vehicle or boat, so check with the state agency that handles such title or registration transfers before using the form in this book.)

REAL ESTATE

A somewhat unique type of financial power of attorney is one concerning real estate. You may need such a power of attorney if you are purchasing or selling property in another state (or even in a distant area of your state) and you will not be able to be there to sign the necessary papers.

Often you will need to comply with the requirements of the title insurance company or the lender, and they will usually provide you with the form they require. For example, while there is no good reason why a general power "to purchase or sell any and all real estate as my agent sees fit" can't be used, most lenders will require the power of attorney to specifically describe the particular piece of property being bought or sold.

You will note that many of the power of attorney forms in various states include a general provision for real estate. However, this form may not be satisfactory to a lender. States which have such statutory forms usually provide in the law that the form is valid, and some states even make it illegal for the lender or title company to refuse to accept the approved form. You could argue that the lender is violating the law if it doesn't accept the form, but it would probably not be worth your time to fight this out in court while your real estate deal waits.

A power of attorney granting the power to buy or sell real estate will need to be executed in the same manner as required for a deed in the state where the property is located. This may require a certain number of witnesses, notarized signatures, and space requirements for recording information. Therefore, check with an attorney or real estate professional as to what is required for your particular property.

Form 2 is a POWER OF ATTORNEY FOR REAL ESTATE, which relates to a specific piece of property. Be sure to refer to your state's listing in appendix B when completing this form. To complete Form 2, you need to:

1. Type in your name and address on the first two lines in the first paragraph.

2. Type in the name, address and relationship to you, if any (i.e., wife, husband, brother, etc.) of your agent on the third line.

3. In the space following the first paragraph, type in the legal description of the property. The legal description is the same as

will appear on the deed. If you don't have the legal description, type in as specific of a description as possible, which may simply be the street address.

4. If you wish to limit your agent's authority in any way, type in the limitations on the lines in paragraph 5.

5. In paragraph 6 there is a line for you to fill in the date on which your agent's authority will end. If you do not wish to end this authority on any particular date, just cross out the words "or until _____, whichever occurs first."

6. Sign before a notary on the line above the words "Signature of Principal." The notary will complete the rest of the form. Spaces are also provided for witnesses, which may be required in your state. Be sure to follow your state's requirements as to how a deed must be executed.

DURABLE FINANCIAL POWER OF ATTORNEY

A *durable* financial power of attorney is the same as any other financial power of attorney, with one difference. A traditional (non-durable) power of attorney will end if you become incapacitated, whereas a durable power of attorney will continue to be effective. This can be important where you would want your agent, especially your spouse, to be able to conduct business for you if you become unable to do so yourself.

STATUTORY FORMS

Several states have created an approved durable power of attorney form in their statutes. These statutory forms have some standard language, and a list of the various types of powers you may give to your agent. If you live in one of the states with a statutory financial power of attorney form, use the specific form for your state found in appendix B. These forms are fairly similar, and many contain detailed instructions, information, and disclosure statements. Be sure to read each form carefully, and be sure you understand all of the provisions and instructions. If your state does not have a statutory form, use Form 1 in appendix B, which is discussed in the next subsection of this chapter, titled GENERIC FORM.

Statutory forms are usually one of two types: (1) where you place a check-mark or your initials on a line to indicate the powers you are giving to your agent, and (2) where you place a check-mark, your initials, or cross out a line to indicate the powers you are *not* giving your agent. In the second type, you are automatically giving all possible powers to your agent, unless you indicate those you *don't* want him or her to have.

The following states have forms that give agents only the powers designated: California, Colorado, Minnesota, Montana, Nebraska, New Mexico, New York, North Carolina, and Wisconsin. The forms in appendix B for Indiana and Tennessee are also this type of form, but they are not official statutory forms.

The following states have forms that give agents all powers unless otherwise indicated: Alaska, Connecticut, Illinois, and Texas.

If you live in one of these states, use the form for your state in appendix B (see the table at the beginning of appendix B). If you do not live in one of these states, you can use Form 1 in appendix B.

The following provides some basic information to help you with the statutory forms for the states listed:

- Alaska (Form 7): You need to cross out and initial any power you *don't* want to give your agent. If you don't cross out and initial item (L), this becomes a health care power of attorney.

- California (Form 9): You need to initial only the powers you want to give your agent.

- Colorado (Form 11): You need to initial only the power you want to give your agent.

- Connecticut (Form 12): You need to cross out and initial any power you *don't* want to give your agent. If you don't cross out and initial item (L), this will become a health care power of attorney (cross out all others to make this *only* for health care).

☞ Georgia (Form 16): The directions on the form say: "To give the Agent the powers described in paragraphs 1 through 13, place you initials on the blank line at the end of each paragraph. If you **do not** want to give a power to the Agent, strike through the paragraph or line within the paragraph and place your initials beside the stricken paragraph or stricken line." It appears that your initials go in different places depending upon whether you do or do not want to give a particular power to your agent. If you are giving a power, you are instructed to place your initials "on the blank line at the end" of the paragraph. However, if you are not giving a power, you are instructed to place your initials "beside the stricken paragraph." You are also allowed to give a power, but cross out part of it. A portion of the statutory form is set forth below, showing paragraphs 5, 6, and 7. In paragraph 5, the power of Stock and Bond Transactions has been given, except that it has been modified to delete the authority to vote at meetings. The power has not been granted for paragraph 6. The full power has been given for paragraph 7.

> **5. Stock and Bond Transactions:** To purchase, sell, exchange, surrender, assign, redeem, ~~vote at any meeting~~, or *JRS* otherwise transfer any and all shares of stock, bonds, or other securities in any business, association, corporation, partnership, or other legal entity, whether private or public, now or hereafter belonging to me. ___*JRS*___
>
> ~~6. Safe Deposits: To have free access at any time or times to any safe deposit box or vault to which I might have access.~~ _____ *JRS*
>
> **7. Borrowing:** To borrow from time to time such sums of money as my Agent may deem proper and execute promissory notes, security deeds or agreements, financing statements, or other security instruments in such form as the lender may request and renew said notes and security instruments from time to time in whole or in part. ___*JRS*___

On the last page of the Georgia form is a place for the agent to formally accept the appointment. This <u>ACCEPTANCE OF APPOINTMENT</u> must be completed and signed by your agent before the power of attorney will be valid and effective.

☛ Illinois (Form 20): You need to cross out any power you *don't* want to give your agent. This form is designed to be a three-page, fill-in-the-blank form, with the statutes on the back of the first two pages. Therefore, in appendix A, the statutes jump from page 112 to page 114. Be sure to include the statute pages if you use this form. You may want to make a two-sided photocopy of it, so that what is on pages 112 and 114 appears on the back of pages 111 and 113 respectively.

☛ Indiana (Form 22): You need to initial only the powers you want to give your agent. By initialing item p., this becomes a health care power of attorney. There is not a statutory form, but Form 22 meets the requirements of the Indiana statute.

☛ Maine (Form 25): All that is included in appendix B is the notices that are required by Maine law. There is not a statutory form. Use Form 1 and attach it to Form 25.

☛ Minnesota (Form 30): You need to place an "X" on the line in front of only the powers you want to give your agent.

☛ Montana (Form 33): You need to initial only the powers you want to give your agent. As this form is written, the power of attorney is effective immediately and is a durable power of attorney. If you want to make it a springing power of attorney, on the lines under the heading SPECIAL INSTRUCTIONS, type or print the following: "This power of attorney…" If you don't want it to continue indefinitely, you will need to type or print an ending day on the SPECIAL INSTRUCTIONS lines, such as: "This power of attorney shall terminate at 11:59 p.m., on December 31, 2001." If you don't want the power of attorney to be durable (i.e., to continue after you become disabled, incapacitated, or incompetent), you need to cross out that provision at the top of the second page of the form.

☛ Nebraska (Form 34): You need to place an "X" in front of the powers you want to give your agent.

☛ New Mexico (Form 38): You need to initial only the powers you want to give your agent. This form also has an affidavit for the agent to sign, swearing to the validity of the power of attorney. Blank copies of this affidavit should be made for the agent to use each time it is needed. This affidavit is signed at the time the agent seeks to use the power of attorney—not when the power of attorney is signed by the principal. By initialing items 14 and 15, this becomes a health care power of attorney.

☛ New York (Forms 40, 41, and 42): Instead of creating a single form with spaces to indicate when the power of attorney becomes effective and whether it is durable, New York has a separate form for each situation. On any of these forms you need to initial only the powers you want to give your agent. Form 43 is an affidavit for the agent to sign, swearing to the validity of the power of attorney. Blank copies of this affidavit should be made for the agent to use each time it is needed. This affidavit is signed at the time the agent seeks to use the power of attorney—not when the power of attorney is signed by the principal.

☛ North Carolina (Form 45): You need to initial only the powers you want to give your agent.

☛ Tennessee (Form 51): You need to initial only the powers you want to give your agent. By initialing item p., this becomes a health care power of attorney. There is not a statutory form, but Form 51 meets the requirements of the Tennessee statutes.

☛ Texas (Form 53): You need to cross out any power you *don't* want to give your agent.

☛ Wisconsin (Form 59): You need to initial only the powers you want to give your agent.

GENERIC FORM   Form 1 is a general DURABLE POWER OF ATTORNEY for those states that don't have a specific form in their statutes. It is primarily a financial power of attorney, but also includes a section on health care decisions in Article II. Be sure to refer to your state's listing in appendix A before completing this form. To complete Form 1:

1. Type in your name on the first line in the first paragraph, and your address on the second line.

2. Type in the name of your agent on the third line. You will also find spaces to designate successor agents in the event your first choice is unable to act.

3. Check only one of the three boxes below the first paragraph, whichever reflects your wishes. If you want to give your agent authority immediately, check the first box (for a "durable" power of attorney). If you don't want your agent to have authority unless you become disabled or incapacitated, check the second box (for a *springing* power of attorney).

   Warning: Be sure to read the listing for your state in appendix A. Under the heading "Financial," you will find a notation for many states that says either "Durable or springing," or "Durable." If it only says "Durable," a springing power of attorney is not specifically authorized in your state. The law of the following states provides *only* for durable powers of attorney: Florida, Louisiana, Missouri, New Hampshire, Ohio, Oregon, Pennsylvania, and Virginia. If you live in one of these states, check the first or third box only; *do not* check the second box. The following states do not say one way or the other: Alabama, Arizona, Hawaii, Nevada, and Utah. If you live in one of these states and want to make a springing power of attorney, it would be a good idea to check the current status of the law (either by research on your own, or by asking a lawyer if a springing power of attorney is permitted).

4. On the last page, type in the date in the last paragraph beginning, "IN WITNESS WHEREOF."

5. Type in the name and addresses of yourself and two witnesses, and your social security number, on the lines where indicated. If you intend to use this form to allow your agent to buy or sell real estate, remember to be sure it is executed in the manner required for a deed in the state where the property is located.

6. You, your agent, and the witnesses sign before a notary, who will then complete the rest of the form.

HEALTH CARE POWER OF ATTORNEY 5

DURABLE POWER OF ATTORNEY FOR HEALTH CARE

A durable power of attorney for health care allows someone to make medical care and treatment decisions if you are unable to do so. This is more broad than a living will, which only expresses your desires if you become terminally ill or permanently unconscious, and are unable to express your wishes regarding the use of life-prolonging procedures. A living will does not authorize someone to make decisions for you. A durable power of attorney for health care authorizes someone to make all kinds of health care decisions for you, even if you are not in a terminal condition or permanently unconscious. See chapter 1 for more discussion on the difference between a living will and a health care power of attorney.

Unless you live in a state that legally recognizes health care powers of attorney, you may have difficulty getting one accepted by doctors and hospitals. However, on the chance that one would be honored, it would still be better for you to have one. You can also ask your doctor or local hospital administrator whether they accept and honor health care powers of attorney.

STATUTORY
FORMS

The following states have created health care powers of attorney in their laws: Alabama, Alaska (included in a general financial power of attorney), Arizona, California, Connecticut (included in a general financial power of attorney), Delaware, District of Columbia, Florida, Georgia, Hawaii, Idaho, Illinois, Indiana (included in a general financial power of attorney), Iowa, Kansas, Maine, Maryland, Massachusetts, Minnesota, Mississippi, Nebraska, Nevada, New Hampshire, New Mexico (both as part of the general financial power of attorney, and as a separate form), New York, North Carolina, North Dakota, Oklahoma, Oregon, South Carolina, Tennessee, Texas, Utah, Vermont, Virginia, West Virginia, and Wisconsin. Forms specific for these states are found in appendix B. A few states have forms with titles that appear to be health care powers of attorney, but the content of these forms shows that they are really living wills that merely designate someone to communicate your living will desires to health care providers.

Health care authority is also provided as part of a general power of attorney form in Alaska, Connecticut, Indiana, and New Mexico. You can use these forms for health care alone, either by only selecting the health care provisions in the Indiana and New Mexico forms, or by deleting all other provisions in the Alaska and Connecticut forms.

If you live in one of the states listed above as having a specific health care power of attorney form, locate the form for your state in appendix B. All of the forms are fairly simple to complete. They all require you to fill in your name, and identify your agent. Any other places to check or fill in information are very clear as to what is needed. Some forms include provisions for a living will, to state your desires regarding an autopsy and the donation of organs, and to designate your primary physician. Some also contain detailed information about who may and may not serve as witnesses. In any case, be sure to carefully read your state's form, because many include detailed information and instructions to help you fill in the blanks. The following comments may help you with some specific forms:

☞ Alaska (Form 7): You do not need to do anything to give your agent authority to make health care decisions as stated in item "(L)." The Alaska form gives the agent all powers listed, unless you delete them by drawing a line through the item and initialing the box opposite the item.

☞ Connecticut (Form 12): You do not need to do anything to give your agent authority to make health care decisions as stated in item "(L)." The Connecticut form gives the agent all powers listed, unless you delete them by drawing a line through the item and initialing the "box" opposite the item.

☞ Florida (Form 15): In Florida, the agent is called the *surrogate*. The fourth paragraph is used to designate other people who will have a copy of your power of attorney for health care, so that other family members will be aware that someone has been given the power to make decisions for you.

☞ Georgia (Form 17): Paragraph 6 allows you to suggest a person you want to be your guardian if a court is asked to appoint one for you. The last part of this form is to provide sample signatures of your agents. This is so the signatures may be compared to be sure the person claiming to be your agent is really your agent.

☞ Illinois (Form 21): This form is designed to be a two-page, fill-in-the-blank form, with the statutes on the back of each page. Therefore, in appendix A, the statutes jump from page 118 to page 120. Be sure to include the statute pages if you use this form. You may want to make a two-sided photocopy of it, so that the statutes on pages 118 and 120 appear on the back of pages 117 and 119 respectively.

☞ Indiana (Form 22): Check item "p." Also read the paragraph regarding withholding health care and check the box if you agree with its provisions. The language of this paragraph must be in any health care power of attorney in Indiana if you want your agent to have the ability to refuse medical care on your behalf.

☛ New Mexico (Form 38 and Form 39): Form 38 is an all-encompassing power of attorney. To give your agent authority to make health care decisions, initial the "boxes" opposite items 12 and 13. The last page is an affidavit for your agent to sign before a notary, to certify that he or she is not aware of anything that would make the power of attorney invalid. This affidavit should not be signed until it is needed in connection with a particular action your agent is taking on your behalf. Your agent may want to make several blank copies of the affidavit to be filled in and used at later dates. Form 39 is a specific power of attorney for health care, which would be better to use if you only want to give your agent health care decision authority.

☛ Oklahoma (Form 48): This form requires signatures after each provision you select.

☛ Oregon (Form 49): Part E is a provision for your agent to sign accepting the appointment as your agent.

GENERIC FORM

If you do not live in a state with its own form, you may use Form 3, which is a health care power of attorney with living will provisions.

To complete the POWER OF ATTORNEY FOR HEALTH CARE (Form 3) you need to:

1. Type your name on the first line in the first paragraph, and your agent's name, address, and phone number on the second line.

2. If you wish to appoint an alternate agent, in case your first choice is unable or unwilling to act, type in the alternate's name, address, and telephone number on the third line.

3. If you have any special instructions or limitations for your agent, type them in on the lines at the end of paragraph 3. You may want to read the powers of attorney for health care for the other states to get some ideas about what you may want to include here. If there are no instructions or limitation, type in the word "none."

4. In paragraph 4, select one of the three choices that expresses your desires. Check the box in front of your choice, and sign your name on the line after it. Note that choices 1 and 2 also have a box to check regarding the artificial delivery of food and water. This is a special issue because food and water are not automatically included in most definitions of *life-prolonging procedures*, and the withholding of food and water for a certain length of time can cause great pain and discomfort. You may want to discuss this matter with your doctor or another health care professional.

5. In item 6, type in the name of your state on both lines.

6. Type in the date and sign your name on the signature line, before two witnesses and a notary public.

7. Have two witnesses sign where indicated before the notary, and type in their names and addresses.

LIVING WILLS

Although not covered in detail in this book, some discussion of living wills was provided earlier in this chapter, as well as in chapter 1. For detailed coverage of living wills, including the forms adopted by several states, see *How to Write Your Own Living Will*, by Edward A. Haman (Sphinx Publishing). A living will is simply a written statement of your wishes in the event you become terminally ill and are unable to express your desires regarding the use of specifically defined *life-prolonging procedures*. As with a health care power of attorney, unless you live in a state that legally recognizes living wills, you may have difficulty getting one accepted by doctors and hospitals. Paragraph 4 in Form 3 is essentially a living will.

Other Power of Attorney Forms 6

Power of Attorney for Child Care

A power of attorney for child care authorizes someone to make decisions regarding your child when you are not present to do so. This will usually be necessary if your child is going to live with a relative or friend, or will be on a prolonged visit to a relative or friend who lives far away from you.

People send their children to live with someone else for a variety or reasons, including:

- Making the child eligible for enrollment in a desired school.

- Assuring adequate care for the child while the parent is working long hours, or must be "on the road" for business.

- Assuring adequate care for the child during the parent's serious illness.

- Sending a difficult child to someone better able to handle disciplinary problems.

- Keeping the child away from an abusive parent.

- Allowing the child a prolonged visit (e.g., summer vacation) with a friend or relative.

For whatever reason the child goes to live elsewhere, you will probably want that friend or relative to be able to enroll the child in school, sign permission slips for field trips, give consent to emergency or other medical care, and do whatever else is necessary for your child that would require parental consent. To accomplish this, a power of attorney may be needed. Such a form is provided in appendix B of this book.

Form 4 is a LIMITED POWER OF ATTORNEY FOR CHILD CARE. To complete Form 4 you need to:

1. type in your name, your address, your child's name, and the name of the person you want as your agent on the lines in the first paragraph.

2. type in the date, time period, or other provision for when the power will end on the line in the last paragraph. If you want it to continue indefinitely, simply cross out the last line.

3. fill in the date where indicated, then sign on the signature line before a notary.

If you live in Michigan, use Form 29, which also has provisions for extending the power of attorney for an additional period of up to six months.

REVOKING A POWER OF ATTORNEY

As mentioned earlier, your agent will have the authority to bind you by what he or she does on your behalf. To guard against your agent getting out of control, you must have the ability to end his or her right to represent you. There are specific ways to go about revoking a power of attorney.

Some powers of attorney provide that they end on a certain date. If such a provision is not part of your power of attorney, the agent's authority continues until you take some action to end it. Generally, you must sign another document revoking the power of attorney, and give a copy of it to anyone who knows about, or has relied on the power of attorney.

Anyone who is aware of the power of attorney and has conducted business with your agent, may continue to assume your agent has authority until you notify them otherwise. Therefore, be sure to give them a copy of the revocation, preferably either by return receipt mail or having them date and sign a copy so you have proof it was received.

Some of the power of attorney forms in appendix B contain a provision for when the power of attorney terminates. These have optional provisions for termination, and you will check the box for the provision you desire, or write in a provision. The options are: (1) termination upon written revocation by the principal, (2) termination upon a particular date, and (3) termination upon a particular event.

In the case of a financial power of attorney, you need to notify those people with whom your agent has conducted business on your behalf. In the case of a power of attorney for health care (or a living will), you need to notify your doctor, hospital, or other health care provider. Some state laws allow you to notify health care providers orally, although a written revocation is still the best way.

Form 5 is a general REVOCATION OF POWER OF ATTORNEY form. Be aware that this form has not been made a part of the law of any state. To complete Form 5 you need to:

1. Type in your name and address on the first line in the main paragraph.

2. Type in the title of the power of attorney you are revoking on the second line. This will be the title as it appears on the document, such as "Power of Attorney for Health Care," "Advance Health Care Directive," "Statutory Power of Attorney," etc.

3. Type in the date of the power of attorney you are revoking on the third line.

4.   Type in the name of your agent on the fourth line.

5.   Type in the date on the line indicated, and sign on the signature line (sign before a notary if the power of attorney you are revoking was also signed before a notary). Provisions are also included for two witnesses.

Appendix A
State Laws

This appendix lists each state alphabetically, and gives information about each state's laws concerning powers of attorney. You will find one or more of these three categories under each state as follows:

- ☞ "In General." This contains any general power of attorney provisions which do not fall under one of the other categories.

- ☞ "Financial." This gives the reference to state laws concerning a financial power of attorney. Whether a durable or springing powers of attorney are authorized by the state law is also indicated, along with the language suggested in the statute.

- ☞ "Health Care." This gives the reference to state laws concerning powers of attorney for health care, or living wills.

The first category will also give information about finding the state laws, including the full title of the set of law books, with an example of how it is abbreviated. Ask the librarian if you have any difficulty.

ALABAMA

Financial: *Michie's* Code of Alabama 1975, or Code of Alabama 1975, Title 26, Chapter 1, Section 26-1-2 (C.A. §26-1-2). Volume 15A No form or statutory language. Can include a health care power of attorney if it meets the statutory requirements.

Health Care: C.A. §§22-8A-1. "Natural Death Act." Volume 14. Health care power of attorney is part of the living will form found at C.A. §22-8A-4.

ALASKA

Financial: Alaska Statutes, Title 13, Section 13.26.332 (A.S. §13.26.332). Volume 4. Statutory form.

Health Care: Health care is included in the statutory financial power of attorney form. Power of attorney for mental health treatment: A.S. §47.30.950; form at A.S. §47.30.970. Volume 10. Living Will: A.S. §18.12.010. Titled "Rights of Terminally Ill." Volume 5.

ARIZONA

Financial: Arizona Revised Statutes, Section 14-5501 (A.R.S. §14-5501). Durable or springing; "this power of attorney shall not be affected by disability of the principal," or "this power of attorney shall become effective upon the disability of the principal." No statutory form. To be valid, must: (1) clearly show intent to make a power of attorney and clearly designate an agent, (2) be dated and signed; (3) be notarized; and (4) be witnessed by 1 person other than the agent, the agent's spouse, or the agent"s children. A.R.S. §14-5503.

Health Care: Health Care: A.R.S. §36-3224. Volume 11B.

Living Will: A.R.S. §36-3262. (There is also a "Prehospital Medical Care Directive" found at A.R.S. §36-3251.) Volume 11B.

ARKANSAS

Financial: Arkansas Code of 1987 Annotated, Title 28, Chapter 68, Section 28-68-201 (A.C.A. §28-68-201). Volume 29. Durable or springing: "This power or attorney shall not be affected by subsequent disability or incapacity of the principal," or "This power of attorney shall become effective upon the disability or incapacity of the principal," or similar language. Also see A.C.A. §28-68-301. Titled "Powers of Attorney for Small Property Interests." This is limited to (1) property with a gross value up to $20,000, not including homestead or capitalized value of any annual income; or (2) annual income up to $6,000.

Health Care: No form, but the appointment of a proxy in a living will can arguably operate as a power of attorney for health care. Living will form states proxy is appointed only to carry out the living will, but the definition in §20-17-201 appears to be more broad. Living Will: A.C.A. §20-17-201. Volume 20A. Form found at A.C.A. §20-17-202.

CALIFORNIA

In General: *West's* Annotated California Probate Code, Section 4000 et seq. (A.C.P.C. §4000 et seq.). See *California Power of Attorney Handbook,* by John J. Talamo, Douglas Godbe, and Edward A. Haman (Sphinx Publishing).

Financial: A.C.P.C. §4124. "Uniform Durable Power of Attorney Act." Durable or springing: "This power of attorney shall not be affected by subsequent incapacity of the principal," or "This power of attorney shall become effective upon the incapacity of the principal," or similar language. Form may be found at A.C.P.C. §4401.

Health Care: Health Care: A.C.P.C. §4700. "Durable Power of Attorney for Health Care." Form may be found at A.C.P.C. §4771.

COLORADO

Financial: *West's* Colorado Revised Statutes Annotated, Title 15, Section 15-1-1301 (C.R.S.A. §15-1-1301). "Uniform Statutory Form Power of Attorney Act." Form found at C.R.S.A. §15-1-1302. Durable: "This power of attorney will continue to be effective even though I become disabled, incapacitated, or incompetent," or similar language. "Uniform Durable Power of Attorney Act," C.R.S.A. §15-14-501, provides for durable or springing: "This power of attorney shall not be affected by disability of the principal" or "This power of attorney shall become effective upon the disability of the principal," or similar language.

Health Care: Health Care: C.R.S.A. §15-14-506. Authorizes a "medical durable power of attorney," but no form is provided.

Living Will: C.R.S.A. §15-18-101. "Colorado Medical Treatment Decisions Act." Form may be found at C.R.S.A. §15-18-104.

CONNECTICUT

Financial: Connecticut General Statutes Annotated, Title 1, Section 1-42 (C.G.S.A. §1-42). Volume 2. "Connecticut Statutory Short Form Power of Attorney Act." Ignore "Chapter" numbers. Durable power of attorney for bank accounts is found at C.G.S.A. §1-56b. Springing powers of attorney authorized by C.G.S.A. §1-56h. Affidavit for agent to certify that power of attorney is in full force and effect is found at C.G.S.A. §1-56i.

Health Care: Living Will: C.G.S.A. §19a-570. Titled "Removal of Life Support Systems." Form may be found at C.G.S.A. §19a-575 in the 1993 Cumulative Annual Pocket Part.

DELAWARE

In General: Delaware Code Annotated, Title 25, Section 171 (D.C.A. 25 §171). Volume 13. This applies to real estate.

Financial: D.C.A. 12 §4901. Volume 7. Durable or springing: "This power of attorney shall not be affected by the subsequent disability or incapacity of the principal," or "This power of attorney shall become effective upon the disability or incapacity of the principal," or similar language.

Health Care: D.C.A. 16 §2501. Volume 9. Form found at D.C.A. 16 §2505. Requires two witnesses, who may not be related to the declarant, not be entitled to a share of the estate, not have any claims against the declarant, not have any financial responsibility for the declarant's medical care, and not be an employee of the hospital or other facility where the declarant is a patient. The witnesses' must state in writing (this can be incorporated into the living will above their signature lines) that they "are not prohibited from being a witness under D.C.A. 16 §2503(b)."

DISTRICT OF COLUMBIA

Financial: District of Columbia Code, Title 21, Section 2081 (D.C.C. §21-2081). Volume 5, 1981 Edition. The spine of the book reads: "D.C. Code." "Uniform Durable Power of Attorney Act." Durable or springing: "This power or attorney shall not be affected by subsequent disability or incapacity of the principal, or lapse of time," or "This power of attorney shall become effective upon the disability or incapacity of the principal," or similar language.

Health Care: Health Care: D.C.C. §21-2201. Volume 5. Titled "Health-Care Decisions." Form found at D.C.C. §21-2207.

FLORIDA

In General: See *Florida Power of Attorney Handbook,* by Edward A. Haman (Sphinx Publishing) for more detailed information.

Financial: Florida Statutes, Chapter 709, Section 709.08 (F.S. §709.08). Durable: "This durable power of attorney is not affected by incapacity of the principal except as provided in s. 709.08, Florida Statutes," or similar language. Springing powers of attorney are not permitted. Must be executed and witnessed in the same manner as documents to transfer real estate. Can incorporate provisions for health care surrogate.

Health Care: F.S. Chapter 765. Health Care Surrogate form found at F.S. §765.203. Living Will form found at F.S. §765.303.

GEORGIA

Financial: Official Code of Georgia Annotated, Title 10, Chapter 6, Section 10-6-1 (O.C.G.A. §10-6-1). Volume 8. This is titled "Agency," and deals with powers of attorney in general. Durable or springing options in official form. O.C.G.A. §10-6-6 authorizes springing power of attorney, and provides that principal can designate any person or persons to have the power to conclusively determine when the disability or other event has occurred that will make the document effective. Such persons must execute a declaration swearing that the event has occurred. Form may be found at O.C.G.A. §§10-6-141 and 10-6-142. (This is not the "Georgia Code," which is a separate and outdated set of books with a completely different numbering system.)

Health Care: Health Care: O.C.G.A. §31-36-1. Volume 23. "Durable Power of Attorney for Health Care Act." Form found at O.C.G.A. §31-36-10.

HAWAII

In General: Hawaii Revised Statutes, Section 501-174 (H.R.S. §501-174) and §502-84, concern requirements for filing a power of attorney for real estate with the land court and the bureau of conveyances. Ignore "Title" numbers.

Health Care: Health Care: H.R.S. §551D-1. Volume 12. "Uniform Durable Power of Attorney Act." Form found at H.R.S. §551D-2.6.

Living Will: H.R.S. §327D-4. A physician's form for certifying disability is found at H.R.S. §327D-10.

IDAHO

Financial: Idaho Code, Title 15, Chapter 5, Section 15-5-501 (I.C. §15-5-501). Volume 3. "Uniform Durable Power of Attorney Act." Durable or springing: "This power or attorney shall not be affected by subsequent disability or incapacity of the principal," or "This power of attorney shall become effective upon the disability or incapacity of the principal," or similar language.

Health Care: Health Care: I.C. §39-4501. "Natural Death Act." Volume 7A. Form found at I.C. §39-4505.

Living Will: I.C. §39-4504

ILLINOIS

In General: Illinois has two sets of statutes, with different numbering systems. One is "Smith-Hurd Illinois Annotated Statutes," (abbreviated "I.A.S."), and the other is *West's* Smith Hurd Illinois Compiled Statutes Annotated (abbreviated "ILCS"). References are given to both sets. The ILCS has a better index. General power of attorney laws are found in the "Illinois Power of Attorney Act," at Illinois Annotated Statutes, Chapter 110 1/2, Section 801-1 (110 1/2 I.A.S. §801-1); and Illinois Compiled Statutes Annotated, Chapter 755, Article 45, Section 1-1 (755 ILCS 45/1-1). The following are actually subparts of this general law.

Financial: 110 1/2 I.S.A. §802-1; and 755 ILCS 45/2-1. "Durable Power of Attorney Law." There is also a "Statutory Short Form Power of Attorney for Property Law," found at 110 1/2 I.S.A. §803-1; and 755 ILCS 45/3-1. Statutory form provides durable or springing options. Form found at 110 1/2 I.S.A. §803-3; and 755 ILCS 45/3-3.

Health Care: Health Care: 110 1/2 I.A.S. §804-1; and 755 ILCS 45/4-1. "Powers of Attorney for Health Care Law." Form is found at 110 1/2 I.A.S. §804-10; and 755 ILCS 45/4-10.

INDIANA

Financial: *West's* Annotated Indiana Code, Title 30, Article 5, Chapter 1, Section 30-5-1-1 (A.I.C. §30-5-1-1). Durable or springing authorized by A.I.C. §30-5-4-2, but no specific language in statute. Statute does not provide a form, but states that a form can be used that refers to the descriptive language in A.I.C. §§30-5-5-2 to 30-5-5-19 (these sections define each power that is generally referred to, and referenced, in the form). Form 22 in appendix B is not an official form, but it complies with the statutory requirements. Statute provides that a power of attorney must be notarized.

Health Care: Health Care: A.I.C. §16-36-1-1. Titled "Health Care Consent." Allows appointment of a "health care representative," but no form is provided. This can also be accomplished with the general power of attorney pursuant to A.I.C. §30-5-5-1, which includes a provision for health care powers.
Living Will: A.I.C. §16-36-4-1. Form for refusing life-prolonging procedures found at A.I.C. §16-36-4-10. Form for requesting life-prolonging procedures found at A.I.C. §16-36-4-11.

IOWA

Financial: Iowa Code Annotated, Section 633.705 (I.C.A. §633.705). Volume 47. Titled "Powers of Attorney." Durable or springing: "This power of attorney shall not be affected by disability of the principal," or "This power of attorney shall become effective upon the disability of the principal," or similar language.

Health Care: I.C.A. §144B.1. Volume 9. Forms may be found at I.C.A. §144B.5 (Durable Power of Attorney for Health Care), and I.C.A. §144A.3 (Living Will).

KANSAS

In General: Kansas Statutes Annotated, Section 58-610 (K.S.A. §58-610). You may find these volumes as either "*Vernon's* Kansas Statutes Annotated," or "Kansas Statutes Annotated, Official." The supplement is a pocket part in *Vernon's* and a separate soft-cover volume in the "Official." Both sets have very poor indexing systems.

Financial: K.S.A. §58-610. "Uniform Durable Power of Attorney Act." Durable or springing: "this power of attorney shall not be affected by subsequent disability or incapacity of the principal," or "this power of attorney shall become effective upon the disability or incapacity of the principal," or similar language.

Health Care: K.S.A. §58-625. Called a "Durable Power of Attorney for Health Care Decisions." Form found at K.S.A. §58-632.

KENTUCKY

Financial: Kentucky Revised Statutes, Chapter 386, Section 386.093 (K.R.S. §386.093). Volume 14. Durable or springing: "This power of attorney shall not be affected by the disability of the principal," or "This power of attorney shall become effective upon the disability of the principal," or similar language. For recording a power of attorney for the conveyance of real estate, see K.R.S. §382.370.

Health Care: No form, but the designation of a "surrogate" in the living will form can arguably authorize more general health care decision-making. K.R.S. §311.620. "Kentucky Living Will Directive Act." Form found at K.R.S. §311.625. Volume 12.

LOUISIANA

In General: *West's* Louisiana Statutes Annotated. The set of Louisiana statutes is divided into topics, such as "Civil Code," "Revised Statutes," etc., so be sure you have the correct topic. For example, for the Civil Code, the book spines read "West's LSA Civil Code," and front covers read "Louisiana Civil Code." In Louisiana a power of attorney is also called a "mandate," "procuration," or "letter of attorney." The agent is also referred to as the "proxy," or "mandatary." Louisiana allows a "bearer" power of attorney, where no agent is named, whomever has the document in his or her possession has the power of attorney. L.S.A., Civil Code, Art. 2993. Certain powers must be expressly given. L.S.A., Art. 2996 & 2997.

Financial: Automatically durable unless otherwise stated. L.S.A. Civil Code, Art. 3027. Volume 17.

Health Care: No form for health care power of attorney. Living Will: L.S.A. Revised Statutes §40:1299.58.1. Volume 22C. "Natural Death Act." Form may be found at L.S.A. Revised Statutes §40:1299.58.3; special form for military personnel stationed in the state may be found at L.S.A., Revised Statutes §40:1299.61.

MAINE

Financial: Maine Revised Statutes Annotated, Title 18-A, Section 5-501 (18-A M.R.S.A. §5-501). Durable or springing: "This power of attorney is not affected by subsequent disability or incapacity of the principal or lapse of time," or "This power of attorney becomes effective upon the disability or incapacity of the principal." No statutory form. Notice requirements found at 18-A M.R.S.A. §5-508(c).

Health Care: Health Care: 18-A M.R.S.A. §5-801. "Uniform Health-Care Decisions Act." Form found at 18-A M.R.S.A. §5-804. Also provided for in 18-A M.R.S.A. §5-506, but no form in that statute.

MARYLAND

In General: Annotated Code of Maryland, Real Property, Section 4-107 (A.C.M., RP §4-107). Requires that a power of attorney for conveying real estate must be executed in the same manner as a deed, and must be recorded before or with the deed. These volumes are arranged by subject, so be sure you have the volume marked "Real Property," or whatever other volume is listed below.

Financial: A.C.M., Estates & Trusts §13-601. Durable or springing: "This power of attorney shall not be affected by disability of the principal," or "This power of attorney becomes effective upon the disability of the principal," or similar language. Be sure you have the volume marked "Estates and Trusts."

Health Care: A.C.M., Health-General §5-601. Titled "Health Care Decision Act." Living Will and Power of Attorney form may be found at A.C.M., HG §5-603). Be sure you have the volume marked "Health-General."

MASSACHUSETTS

Financial: Annotated Laws of Massachusetts, Chapter 201B, Section 1 (A.L.M., C. 201B, §1). "Uniform "Durable Power of Attorney Act." Durable or springing: "This power of attorney shall not be affected by subsequent disability or incapacity of the principal," or "This power of attorney shall become effective upon the disability or incapacity of the principal," or similar language.

Health Care: A.L.M., C. 201D. Form may be found at A.L.M. C. 201D, §4.

MICHIGAN

In General: Michigan has two official sets of laws, each from a different publisher. One is Michigan Statutes Annotated, (abbreviated M.S.A.) and the other is Michigan Compiled Laws Annotated, (abbreviated M.C.L.A.). Each has a completely different numbering system. References are given to both sets as most libraries will only have one set. Ignore the volume and chapter numbers, and look for the section numbers. You may also find it referred to as a "letter of attorney." Child care power of attorney provisions may be found at M.S.A. §27.5405; M.C.L.A. §700.405.

Financial: M.S.A. §27.5495; M.C.L.A. §700.495. Durable or springing: "This power or attorney shall not be affected by disability of the principal," or "This power of attorney shall become effective upon the disability of the principal," or similar language.

Health Care: M.S.A. §27.5496; M.C.L.A. §700.496. Discusses "Designation of patient advocate," however, no statutory form is provided.

MINNESOTA

Financial: Minnesota Statutes Annotated, Section 523.07 (M.S.A. §523.07). Volume 31. Durable or springing: "This power of attorney shall not be affected by incapacity or incompetence of the principal," or "This power of attorney shall become effective upon the incapacity or disability of the principal."

Health Care: Health Care: M.S.A. §145C.01. Volume 11. Titled "Durable Power of Attorney for Health Care." Form found at M.S.A. §145C.05.

Living Will: M.S.A. §145B.01. Volume 11. "Minnesota living will act." Form found at M.S.A. §145B.04. Living will can be noted on a driver's license. M.S.A. §171.07.

MISSISSIPPI

Financial: Mississippi Code 1972 Annotated, Section 87-3-9 (M.C. §87-3-9), for real estate. M.C. §87-3-13. Financial power of attorney: M.C. §§87-3-101 to 87-3-113. Titled "Uniform Durable Power of Attorney Act." Durable or springing: "This power of attorney shall not be affected by subsequent disability or incapacity of the principal, or lapse of time" or "This power of attorney shall become effective upon the disability or incapacity of the principal," or similar language.

Health Care: Health Care: "Durable Power of Attorney for Health Care Act" is found at M.C. §41-41-151, with forms at §§41-41-159 and 41-41-163. Volume 11.

Living Will: M.C. §41-41-101, referred to as "Withdrawal of Life-Saving Mechanism." Form at M.C. §41-41-107. Revocation form at M.C. §41-41-109.

MISSOURI

Financial: *Vernon's* Annotated Missouri Statutes, Chapter 404, Section 404.700(A.M.S. §404.700). Volume 21. "Durable Power of Attorney Law of Missouri." Specifies which powers must be specifically stated at §404.710, but no form is provided. Durable power of attorney created by either titling the document "Durable Power of Attorney," or by including provision: "THIS IS A DURABLE POWER OF ATTORNEY AND THE AUTHORITY OF MY ATTORNEY IN FACT SHALL NOT TERMINATE IF I BECOME DISABLED OR INCAPACITATED, OR IN THE EVENT OF LATER UNCERTAINTY AS TO WHETHER I AM DEAD OR ALIVE," or "THIS IS A DURABLE POWER OF ATTORNEY AND THE AUTHORITY OF MY ATTORNEY IN FACT, WHEN EFFECTIVE, SHALL NOT TERMINATE OR BE VOID OR VOIDABLE IF I AM OR BECOME DISABLED OR INCAPACITATED OR IN THE EVENT OF LATER UNCERTAINTY AS TO WHETHER I AM DEAD OR ALIVE." A.M.S. §404.705. It must also be executed in the same manner as a deed.

Health Care: Health Care: A.M.S. §404.800. Volume 21. "Durable Power of Attorney for Health Care Act." No form provided.

Living Will: A.M.S. §459.010. Form found at A.M.S. §459.015. Volume 25.

MONTANA

Financial: Montana Code Annotated, Title 72, Chapter 31, Section 72-31-201 (M.C.A. §72-31-201). Form found at M.C.A. §72-31-201. Volume 9. The Code is in gray, paperback volumes, and the annotations are in a separate set of dark brown binders. Durable: "This power of attorney will continue to be effective if I become disabled, incapacitated, or incompetent." (M.C.A. §72-31-222.)

Health Care: No health care power of attorney form. Living Will: M.C.A. §50-9-103. Volume 8.

NEBRASKA

Financial: Revised Statutes of Nebraska, Chapter 49, Article 15 , Section 49-1501 (R.S.N. §49-1501). Volume 3B. "Nebraska Short Form Act." Form found at R.S.N. §49-1522. Durable or springing: "This power of attorney shall not be affected by subsequent disability or incapacity of the principal," or "This power of attorney shall become effective upon the disability or incapacity of the principal," or similar language. R.S.N. §30-2664. Volume 2A.

Health Care: R.S.N. §30-3401; form found at R.S.N. §30-3408. Volume 2A.

NEVADA

Financial: Nevada Revised Statutes Annotated, Chapter 111, Section 111.460 (N.R.S.A. §111.460). Volume 4. Durable or springing: "This power of attorney is not affected by disability of the principal," or "This power of attorney becomes effective upon the disability of the principal," or similar language. If used to convey real estate, must be executed and recorded in accordance with N.R.S.A. §111.450 (i.e., signed, acknowledged, notarized, and recorded).

Health Care: N.R.S.A. §449.800. Volume 12. Form found at N.R.S.A. §449.830. Form for living will found at N.R.S.A. §449.610.

NEW HAMPSHIRE

Financial: New Hampshire Revised Statutes Annotated 1997, Chapter 506, Section 506:6 (N.H.R.S.A. §506:6).. Ignore "title" numbers; look for "chapter" numbers. Durable only: "This power of attorney shall not be affected by the subsequent disability or incompetence of the principal."

Health Care: Health Care:N.H.R.S.A. §137-J:1. Form found at N.H.R.S.A. §137-J:14 & 15.

Living Will: N.H.R.S.A. §137-H:1. Form found at N.H.R.S.A. §137-H:3.

NEW JERSEY

Financial: NJSA (for New Jersey Statutes Annotated), Title 46, Chapter 2B, Section 46:2B-8 (N.J.S.A. §46:2B-8). Durable or springing: "This power of attorney shall not be affected by disability of the principal," or "This power of attorney shall become effective upon the disability of the principal," or similar language.

NEW MEXICO

Financial: New Mexico Statutes 1978 Annotated, Chapter 45, Section 45-5-501 (N.M.S.A. §45-5-501). Volume 7. Supplement is found at the end of each chapter. Durable or springing: "This power of attorney shall not be affected by subsequent incapacity of the principal, or lapse of time," or "This power of attorney shall become effective upon the incapacity of the principal." Form found at N.M.S.A. §45-5-602.

Health Care: N.M.S.A. §24-7-1. "Right to Die Act." Volume 5. Form found at N.M.S.A. §24-7A-4. Must be executed in the same manner as a will (with two witnesses and notarized).

NEW YORK

In General: See *New York Power of Attorney Handbook,* by William P. Coyle and Edward A. Haman (Sphinx Publishing).

Financial: *McKinney's* Consolidated Laws of New York Annotated, General Obligation Law, Article 5, Title 15, Section 5-1501 (C.L.N.Y, Gen. Ob. §5-1501). This set of books is divided in subjects, so be sure you have the correct volume, such as "General Obligation Law" or "Public Health." Durable or springing: "This power of attorney shall not be affected by my subsequent disability or incompetence," or similar language (C.L.N.Y., Gen. Obl. §5-1505). Instead of one statutory form with options for various effective dates, New York has created separate forms for each type: Springing durable (C.L.N.Y., Gen. Ob. §5-1501, 1); springing non-durable (§5-501, 1-a.); effective at a future date (§5-1506).

Health Care: C.L.N.Y., Public Health §2980. Called "Health Care Agents and Proxies." Form found at §2981(d). A living will provision may not be included in a general power of attorney. C.L.N.Y., Public Health §2981(e).

NORTH CAROLINA

Financial: General Statutes of North Carolina, Chapter 32A, Section 32A-1 (G.S.N.C. §32A-1). Durable or springing: "This power of attorney shall not be affected by my subsequent incapacity or mental incompetence," or "This power of attorney shall become effective after I become incapacitated or incompetent," or similar language (G.S.N.C. §32A-8). G.S.N.C. §32A-9(b) requires the power of attorney to be registered in the office of the register of deeds upon the principal becoming incapacitated or incompetent. G.S.N.C. §32A-11 also requires reporting to the court clerk with periodic accountings, unless this is waived in the power of attorney. Statutory form found at G.S.N.C. §32A-1.

Health Care: G.S.N.C. §32A-15; form found at G.S.N.C. §32A-25.

NORTH DAKOTA

Financial: North Dakota Century Code Annotated, Title 30.1, Chapter 30, Section 30.1-30-01 (N.D.C.C. §30.1-30-01). UDPAA. Volume 6. Durable or springing: "This power of attorney is not affected by subsequent disability or incapacity of the principal or by lapse of time," or "This power of attorney shall become effective upon the disability or incapacity of the principal."

Health Care: N.D.C.C. §23-06.5-1. Titled "Durable Power of Attorney for Health Care. Form found at N.D.C.C. §23-06.5-17. Volume 4A.

OHIO

Financial: *Page's* Ohio Revised Code Annotated, Section 1337.09 (O.R.S. §1337.09). Durable only: "This power of attorney shall not be affected by disability of the principal," or "this power of attorney shall not be affected by disability of the principal or lapse of time," or similar language.

Health Care: Health care: Discussed at O.R.S. §1337.11, including provisions required signature and date, two witnesses, and setting forth who can be an agent, but no form provided. Also see O.R.S. §2133.01. Titled "Modified Uniform Rights of the Terminally Ill Act."

OKLAHOMA

Financial: Oklahoma Statutes Annotated, Title 58, Section 1071 (58 O.S.A. §1071). "Uniform Durable Power of Attorney Act." Durable or springing: "This power of attorney shall not be affected by subsequent disability or incapacity of the principal, or lapse of time," or "This power of attorney shall become effective upon the disability or incapacity of the principal," or similar language.

Health Care: 63 O.S.A. §3101. "Oklahoma Rights of the Terminally Ill or Persistently Unconscious Act." Form found at 63 O.S.A. §3101.4. Do-not-resuscitate consent form found at 63 O.S.A. §3131.5.

OREGON

Financial: Oregon Revised Statutes Annotated, Chapter 127, Section 127.005 (O.R.S. §127.005). A power of attorney is durable unless specifically limited.

Health care: O.R.S. §127.505. Mandatory form found at §127.530.

PENNSYLVANIA

Financial: *Purdon's* Pennsylvania Consolidated Statutes Annotated, Title 20, Section 20-5601 (Pa.C.S.A. §20-5601). A power of attorney is durable unless otherwise stated. Pa.C.S.A. §5601.1. Durable only: "This power of attorney shall not be affected by disability of the principal," or similar language.

Health Care: No health care power of attorney provisions. Living Will: Pa.C.S.A. §20-5401. "Advance Directive for Health Care Act." Living will (called "Declaration") form found at Pa.C.S.A. §20-5404. This allows the appointment of a "surrogate," but only to make decisions if the principal is terminally ill or permanently unconscious, therefore it is not a true power of attorney for health care.

RHODE ISLAND

Financial: General Laws of Rhode Island, Section 34-22-6.1 (G.L.R.I. §34-22-6.1) Ignore "Title" and "Chapter" numbers. Volume 6. Durable or springing: "This power of attorney shall not be affected by the incompetency of the donor," or "This power of attorney shall become effective upon the incompetency of the donor," or similar language.

Health Care: G.L.R.I. §23-4.10-1, "Health Care Power of Attorney Act." G.L.R.I. §23-4.11-1, "Rights of the Terminally Ill Act." Form found at G.L.R.I. §23-4.11-3. Volume 4B.

SOUTH CAROLINA

Financial: Code of Laws of South Carolina, Title 62, Section 62-5-501 [C.L.S.C. §62-5-501]. Volume 20B. Durable or springing: "This power of attorney is not affected by physical disability or mental incompetence of the principal which renders the principal incapable of managing his own estate," or "This power of attorney becomes effective upon the physical disability or mental incompetence of the principal," or similar language.

Health Care: C.L.S.C. §62-5-504. Form found at §62-5-504(D). Volume 20B.. Also see "Adult Health Care Consent Act," at C.L.S.C. §44-66-10 which discusses consent for medical treatment and states that this subject can be included in a durable power of attorney, but no form is provided. Living wills covered in the "Death With Dignity Act," C.L.S.C. §44-77-10; living will form found at C.L.S.C. §44-77-50.

SOUTH DAKOTA

Financial: South Dakota Codified Laws, Title 59, Section 59-7-2.1 (S.D.C.L §59-7-2.1). Volume 16B. Durable or springing: "This power of attorney shall not be affected by disability of the principal," or "This power of attorney shall become effective upon the disability of the principal," or similar language.

Health Care: Authorized by S.D.C.L. §§59-7-2.5 to 59-7-2.8, and 34-12C-3, but no forms are provided. Volume 16B.

TENNESSEE

Financial: Tennessee Code Annotated, Title 34, Section 34-6-101 (T.C.A. §34-6-101). Volume 6A. "Uniform Durable Power of Attorney Act." Durable or springing: "This power of attorney shall not be affected by subsequent disability or incapacity of the principal," or "This power of attorney shall become effective upon the disability or incapacity of the principal," or similar language (T.C.A. §34-6-102). No statutory form, but statute provides that a power of attorney may refer generally to the powers listed in the statute (T.C.A. §34-6-109) without re-stating them. To completely understand what powers are included, and what limitations are placed on an agent, you should read the most current version of T.C.A. §§34-6-108 and 34-6-109. If you want to give your agent full powers over all of your financial matters, you can use Form 51 in appendix B. If there are a few specific things you don't want your agent to do, you may list them on the lines in paragraph 2. You may also use Form 1.

Health Care: T.C.A. §34-6-203. Titled "Durable Power of Attorney for Health Care." No statutory form. Volume 6A.

TEXAS

Financial: *Vernon's* Texas Civil Statutes, Probate Code, Section 481 (T.C.S., Probate Code §481). "Durable Power of Attorney Act." The T.C.A. is divided into subjects, so be sure you have the proper subject volume. Durable or springing: "This power of attorney is not affected by subsequent disability or incapacity of the principal," or "This power of attorney shall become effective on the disability or incapacity of the principal." T.C.A., Probate Code §482. Form found at T.C.A., Probate Code §490.

Health Care: Texas Codes Annotated, Civil Practice & Remedies §135.001 (T.C.A., Civ. Prac. & Rem. §135.001). Titled "Durable Power of Attorney for Health Care." Form and required notices found at §§135.015 and 135.016. There is also a mental health directive form at §137.011, to be used only if you have been diagnosed with a mental disorder. Living wills are covered in the "Natural Death Act" T.C.A., Health and Safety §672.001; form found at §672.004.

UTAH

Financial: Utah Code Annotated 1953, Title 75, Chapter 5, Section 75-5-501 (U.C.A. §75-5-501). Volume 8A. Durable or springing: "This power of attorney shall not be affected by disability of the principal," or "This power of attorney shall become effective upon the disability of the principal," or similar language.

Health Care: No provisions for a general health care power of attorney. Living will provisions at U.C.A. §75-2-1104 (volume 8A) are confusing. A living will may only be executed if you are currently suffering from a terminal injury, disease, or illness. However, under U.C.A. §75-2-1106, you can execute a "Special Power of Attorney" that allows you to appoint someone to execute a living will for you if you are incapacitated (this form is provided in appendix B).

VERMONT

In General: Vermont Statutes Annotated, Title 27, Section 305 (27 V.S.A. §305). Ignore "Chapter" numbers. A power of attorney to convey real estate must be signed, have at least one witness, be acknowledged, and be recorded where a deed would be recorded. 27 V.S.A. §305.

Financial: 14 V.S.A. §3051. Durable or springing: "This power of attorney shall not be affected by disability of the principal," or "This power of attorney shall become effective upon the disability or the principal," or similar language.

Health Care: Health care power of attorney: 14 V.S.A. §3451. Titled "Durable Power of Attorney for Health Care." Form and required notices are found at 14 V.S.A. §§3465 and 3466. Living wills are covered at 18 V.S.A. §5252, referred to as a "terminal care document." Living will form at 18 V.S.A. §5253.

VIRGINIA

Financial: Code of Virginia 1950, Title 11, Section 11-9.1 (C.V. §11-9.1). Volume 3. Ignore "Chapter" numbers, and look for "Title" and "Section" numbers. Found in chapter on "Contracts." Durable only: "This power of attorney (or his authority) shall not terminate on disability of the principal."

Health Care: C.V. §54.1-2981, form found at C.V. §54.1-2984.

WASHINGTON

Financial: *West's* Revised Code of Washington Annotated, Title 11, Chapter 94, Section 11.94.010 (R.C.W. §11.94.010). Found in chapter on "Power of Attorney." Durable or springing: "This power of attorney shall not be affected by disability of the principal," or "This power of attorney shall become effective upon the disability of the principal," or similar language.

Health Care: Health care power of attorney authorized by R.C.W. §11.94.101(3), but no form is provided. Living wills covered at R.C.W. §70.122.010, "Natural Death Act."

WEST VIRGINIA

Financial: West Virginia Code, Chapter 39, Article 4, Section 39-4-1 (W.V.C. §39-4-1). Volume 12. Durable or springing: "This power of attorney shall not be affected by subsequent disability or incapacity of the principal," or "This power of attorney shall become effective upon the disability or incapacity of the principal."

Health Care: W.V.C. §16-30-3, and the "Medical Power of Attorney Act, W.V.C. §16-30A-1 (form found at §16-30A-18). Also see "Health Care Surrogate Act," W.V.C., §16-30B-1. All of these are in volume 5A.

WISCONSIN

Financial: *West's* Wisconsin Statutes Annotated, Section 243.01 (W.S.A. §243.01). Ignore "Chapter" numbers. Statutory form found at W.S.A. §243.07. Durable or springing: "This power of attorney shall not be affected by subsequent disability, incapacity or incompetency of the principal or "this power of attorney shall become effective upon the subsequent disability, incapacity or incompetency of the principal."

Health Care: W.S.A. §155.01, titled "Power of Attorney for Health Care." Form found at W.S.A. §155.30. Living wills are covered in W.S.A. §154.01.

WYOMING

In General: Wyoming Statutes Annotated, Title 34, Chapter 1, Section 34-1-103 (W.S.A. §34-1-103). Volume 7. Referred to as "letter of attorney." For powers of attorney in general see W.S.A. §§34-1-103 & 3-5-101. Husband and wife may give each other power of attorney, W.S.A. §34-1-129.

Financial: W.S.A. §3-5-101. Volume 1. Durable or springing: "This power of attorney shall not become ineffective by my disability" or "This power of attorney shall become effective upon my disability."

Health Care: Health Care: W.S.A. §3-5-201. Volume 1. Titled "Durable Power of Attorney for Health Care." No form, but does contain execution requirements. Must be signed by at least 2 witnesses, both of whom must sign declaration stating: "I declare under penalty of perjury under the laws of Wyoming that the person who signed or acknowledged this document is personally known to me to be the principal, that the principal signed or acknowledged this durable power of attorney in my presence, that the principal appears to be of sound mind and under no duress, fraud or undue influence, that I am not the person appointed as attorney in fact by this document, and that I am not a treating health care provider, an employee of a treating health care provider, the operator of a community care facility, an employee of an operator of a community care facility, the operator of a residential care facility, nor an employee of an operator of a residential care facility." At least one witness must also sign the following statement: "I further declare under penalty of perjury under the laws of Wyoming that I am not related to the principal by blood, marriage, or adoption, and, to the best of my knowledge, I am not entitled to any part of the estate of the principal upon the death of the principal under a will now existing or by operation of law."

Living Will: W.S.A. §35-22-101.

APPENDIX B
FORMS

This appendix includes both statutory forms approved by the various states, and generic forms which may be used in any state not having an approved statutory form.

The table on the next page will give you the number of the form to use for your state (this is the *form* number—not the *page* number). Find your state, then read across to find which numbered form to use for the type of power of attorney you need ("FIN." for financial power of attorney, or "H.C." for health care power of attorney). For numbers are found at the upper, outside edge of each form. For example, suppose you live in Texas and are looking for a form for a health care power of attorney. Find Texas on the table on the next page, then read across to the column titled "H.C." This will tell you to use Form 54. You would then locate Form 54 in this appendix and fill it out. Remember, however, that the law and forms may change at any time.

STATE	FIN.	H.C.
Alabama	1	6
Alaska	7	3/7
Arizona	1	8
Arkansas	1	3
California	9	10
Colorado	11	3
Connecticut	12	12
Delaware	1	13
District of Columbia	1	14
Florida	1	15
Georgia	16	17
Hawaii	1	18
Idaho	1	19
Illinois	20	21
Indiana	22	22
Iowa	1	23
Kansas	1	24
Kentucky	1	3
Louisiana	1	3
Maine	25 + 1	26
Maryland	1	27
Massachusetts	1	28
Michigan	1	3
Minnesota	30	31
Mississippi	1	32
Missouri	1	3

STATE	FIN.	H.C.
Montana	33	3
Nebraska	34	35
Nevada	1	36
New Hampshire	1	37
New Jersey	1	3
New Mexico	38	38/39
New York	40-43	44
North Carolina	45	46
North Dakota	1	47
Ohio	1	3
Oklahoma	1	48
Oregon	1	49
Pennsylvania	1	3
Rhode Island	1	3
South Carolina	1	50
South Dakota	1	3
Tennessee	51	52
Texas	53	54
Utah	1	3/55
Vermont	1	56
Virginia	1	57
Washington	1	3
West Virginia	1	58
Wisconsin	59	60
Wyoming	1	3

The table on the following page is a listing of all of the forms in this appendix, including the form number, the name of the state to which it applies (if any), and the page number where the form may be found. You can also find the forms by referring to the form number in the upper, outside corner of the page. Just be sure you are using the correct form for your state. For example, refer to Form 7 listed below. The listing for this form is as follows:

FORM 7 Alaska: ALASKA GENERAL POWER OF ATTORNEY (financial). 76

This tells you that Form 7 is for Alaska and is titled ALASKA GENERAL POWER OF ATTORNEY. As it may not be completely clear from the title what type of form this is, the notation "(financial)" tells you it is a financial power of attorney form.

TABLE OF FORMS

FORM 1   DURABLE POWER OF ATTORNEY 61

FORM 2   POWER OF ATTORNEY FOR REAL ESTATE. 67

FORM 3   POWER OF ATTORNEY FOR HEALTH CARE. 68

FORM 4   LIMITED POWER OF ATTORNEY FOR CHILD CARE 70

FORM 5   REVOCATION OF POWER OF ATTORNEY 71

FORM 6   Alabama: ADVANCE DIRECTIVE FOR HEALTH CARE 72

FORM 7   Alaska: ALASKA GENERAL POWER OF ATTORNEY (financial) 76

FORM 8   Arizona: HEALTH CARE POWER OF ATTORNEY 78

FORM 9   California: UNIFORM STATUTORY FORM POWER OF ATTORNEY (financial). 80

FORM 11   California: STATUTORY FORM DURABLE POWER OF ATTORNEY
          FOR HEALTH CARE. 82

FORM 12   Colorado: COLORADO STATUTORY POWER OF ATTORNEY
          FOR PROPERTY (financial). 86

FORM 13   Connecticut: CONNECTICUT STATUTORY SHORT FORM DURABLE POWER OF
          ATTORNEY (financial) 89

FORM 14   Delaware: ADVANCE HEALTH-CARE DIRECTIVE 91

FORM 14   District of Columbia: POWER OF ATTORNEY FOR HEALTH CARE 96

FORM 15   Florida: DESIGNATION OF HEALTH CARE SURROGATE 98

FORM 16   Georgia: FINANCIAL POWER OF ATTORNEY. 99

FORM 17   Georgia: GEORGIA STATUTORY SHORT FORM DURABLE POWER OF ATTORNEY
          FOR HEALTH CARE. 104

FORM 18   Hawaii: DURABLE POWER OF ATTORNEY FOR HEALTH CARE DECISIONS 106

FORM 19   Idaho: A DURABLE POWER OF ATTORNEY FOR HEALTH CARE 107

FORM 20   Illinois: ILLINOIS STATUTORY SHORT FORM POWER OF ATTORNEY FOR PROPERTY. . 111

FORM 21   Illinois: ILLINOIS STATUTORY SHORT FORM POWER OF ATTORNEY FOR
          HEALTH CARE. 117

FORM 22   Indiana: POWER OF ATTORNEY (financial & health care) 121

FORM 23   Iowa: DURABLE POWER OF ATTORNEY FOR HEALTH CARE. 123

FORM 24   Kansas: DURABLE POWER OF ATTORNEY FOR HEALTH CARE DECISIONS 124

FORM 25   Maine: DURABLE FINANCIAL POWER OF ATTORNEY (notices only) 126

FORM 26   Maine: ADVANCE HEALTH CARE DIRECTIVE. 127

FORM 27   Maryland: HEALTH CARE DECISION MAKING FORMS 130

FORM 28   Massachusetts: MASSACHUSETTS HEALTH CARE PROXY 134

FORM 29   Michigan: LIMITED POWER OF ATTORNEY (child care) 137

FORM 30   Minnesota: STATUTORY SHORT FORM POWER OF ATTORNEY (financial) 138

FORM 31   Minnesota: DURABLE POWER OF ATTORNEY FOR HEALTH CARE. 140

FORM 32   Mississippi: DURABLE POWER OF ATTORNEY FOR HEALTH CARE 141

FORM 33   Montana: POWER OF ATTORNEY (financial) 143

FORM 34   Nebraska: POWER OF ATTORNEY (financial). 145

FORM 35   Nebraska: POWER OF ATTORNEY FOR HEALTH CARE. 146

FORM 36   Nevada: DURABLE POWER OF ATTORNEY FOR HEALTH CARE DECISIONS. 148

FORM 37   New Hampshire: DURABLE POWER OF ATTORNEY FOR HEALTH CARE 152

FORM 38   New Mexico: STATUTORY POWER OF ATTORNEY (financial & health care) . . . 154

FORM 39   New Mexico: OPTIONAL ADVANCED HEALTH-CARE DIRECTIVE 157

FORM 40   New York: DURABLE GENERAL POWER OF ATTORNEY (financial). 160

FORM 41   New York: DURABLE GENERAL POWER OF ATTORNEY (financial - springing) . 163

FORM 42   New York: NONDURABLE GENERAL POWER OF ATTORNEY (financial) 167

FORM 43   New York: AFFIDAVIT THAT POWER OF ATTORNEY IS IN FULL FORCE 170

FORM 44   New York: HEALTH CARE PROXY 171

FORM 45   North Carolina: NORTH CAROLINA STATUTORY SHORT FORM GENERAL
           POWER OF ATTORNEY (financial) 172

FORM 46   North Carolina: HEALTH CARE POWER OF ATTORNEY 174

FORM 47   North Dakota: STATUTORY FORM DURABLE POWER OF ATTORNEY
           FOR HEALTH CARE. 177

FORM 48   Oklahoma: ADVANCE DIRECTIVE FOR HEALTH CARE (health care & living will) 182

FORM 49   Oregon: POWER OF ATTORNEY FOR HEALTH CARE 186

FORM 50   South Carolina: HEALTH CARE POWER OF ATTORNEY. 188

FORM 51   Tennessee: DURABLE POWER OF ATTORNEY FOR FINANCIAL MANAGEMENT. . . 191

FORM 52   Tennessee: DURABLE POWER OF ATTORNEY FOR HEALTH CARE 192

FORM 53   Texas: STATUTORY DURABLE POWER OF ATTORNEY (financial). 194

FORM 54   Texas: DURABLE POWER OF ATTORNEY FOR HEALTH CARE 196

FORM 55   Utah: SPECIAL POWER OF ATTORNEY (appoints agent to execute living will) . . 199

FORM 56   Vermont: DURABLE POWER OF ATTORNEY FOR HEALTH CARE. 200

FORM 57   Virginia: ADVANCE MEDICAL DIRECTIVE (health care & living will) 202

FORM 58   West Virginia: MEDICAL POWER OF ATTORNEY 204

FORM 59   Wisconsin: STATUTORY POWER OF ATTORNEY (financial) 205

FORM 60   Wisconsin: POWER OF ATTORNEY FOR HEALTH CARE 206

FORM 61   LIMITED POWER OF ATTORNEY 210

DURABLE POWER OF ATTORNEY

I,_____(name),of _____
_____ (address, including county and state)
hereby appoint _____(name), to serve as my agent ("Agent")
and to exercise the powers set forth below. If said agent is unable or unwilling to act as my agent, then I appoint
the following as my successor agent(s) in the order named:
First Successor Agent: _____ (name);
Second Successor Agent: _____ (name).
This instrument shall be effective:

❏   Immediately upon the date of execution, and shall not be affected by my subsequent disability, incapacity or incompetence except as provided by statute.

❏   Upon my disability, incapacity or incompetence except as provided by statute.

❏   Immediately upon the date of execution, and shall terminate upon my disability, incapacity or incompetence.

I hereby revoke all powers of attorney, general or limited, previously granted by me, except for powers granted by me on forms provided by financial institutions granting the right to write checks on, deposit funds to and withdraw funds from accounts to which I am a signatory or granting access to a safe deposit, and except to any powers granted by me for health care decisions.

ARTICLE I.

My Agent is authorized in my Agent's sole and absolute discretion at any time, with respect to any of my property, real (including homestead property or any other interest), personal, intangible and mixed, as follows:

(1)   To sell any property that I may own now or in the future, including but not limited to contingent and expectant interests, marital rights and any rights of survivorship incident to joint tenancy or tenancy by the entirety, upon such terms, conditions and security as my Agent shall deem appropriate and to grant options with respect to sales thereof; to make such disposition of the proceeds of such sales as my Agent shall deem appropriate;

(2)   To buy every kind of property, upon such terms and conditions as my Agent shall deem appropriate; to obtain options regarding such purchases; to arrange for appropriate disposition, use, safekeeping or insuring of any such property; to buy United States Government bonds redeemable at par in payment of the federal estate tax imposed at my death; to borrow money for the purposes described herein and to secure such borrowings in such manner as my Agent shall deem appropriate; to use any credit card held in my name to make such purchases and to sign such charge slips as may be necessary to use such credit cards; to repay from any funds belonging to me any money borrowed and to pay for any purchases made or cash advanced using credit cards issued to me;

(3)   To invest and reinvest all or any part of my property in any property or interests in property, wherever located, including without being limited to securities of all kinds, bonds, debentures, notes (secured or unsecured), stocks of corporations regardless of class, interests in limited partnerships, real estate or any interest in real estate whether or not productive at the time of investment, commodities contracts of all kinds, interests in trusts, investments trusts, whether of the open or closed fund types, and participation in common, collective or pooled trust funds or annuity contracts without being limited by any statute or rule of law concerning investments by fiduciaries; to sell (including short sales) and terminate any investments whether made by me or my Agent; to establish, utilize and terminate savings and money market accounts with financial institutions of all kinds; to establish, utilize and terminate accounts (including margin accounts) with securities brokers; to

establish, utilize and terminate managing agency accounts with corporate fiduciaries; to employ, compensate and terminate the services of financial and investment advisors and consultants;

(4)   With respect to real property (including but not limited to any real property I may hereafter acquire or receive and my personal residence) to lease, sublease, release; to eject, remove and relieve tenants or other persons from, and recover possession of by all lawful means; to accept real property as a gift or as security for a loan; to collect, sue for, receive and receipt for rents and profits and to conserve, invest or utilize any such rents, profits and receipts for the purposes described in this paragraph; to do any act of management and conservation, to pay, compromise, or to contest tax assessments and to apply for refunds in connections therewith; to employ laborers; to subdivide, develop, dedicate to public use without consideration, or dedicate easements over; to maintain, protect, repair, preserve, insure, build upon, demolish, alter or improve all or any part thereof; to obtain or vacate plats and adjust boundaries; to adjust differences in valuation on exchange or partition by giving or receiving consideration; to release or partially release real property from a lien; to sell and to buy real property; to mortgage or convey by deed of trust or otherwise encumber any real property now or hereafter owned by me, whether acquired by me or for me by my Agent;

(5)   With respect to personal property; to lease, sublease, and release; to recover possession of by all lawful means; to collect, sue for , receive and receipt for rents and profits therefrom; to maintain, protect, repair, preserve, insure, alter or improve all or any part thereof; to sell and to buy the same or other personal property; to mortgage, pledge or grant other security interests in any personal property or intangibles now or hereafter owned by me, whether acquired by me or for me by my Agent;

(6)   To exercise all rights with respect to corporate securities which I now own or may hereafter acquire, including the right to sell, grant security interests in, and to buy the same or different securities; to make such payments as my Agent deems necessary, appropriate, incidental or convenient to the owning and holding of such securities; to receive, retain, expend for my benefit, invest and reinvest or make such disposition of as my Agent shall deem appropriate all additional securities, cash or property (including the proceeds from the sales of my securities) to which I may be or become entitled by reason of my ownership of any securities; to vote at all meetings of security holders, regular or special; to lend money to any corporation in which I hold any shares and to guarantee or endorse loans made to such corporation by third parties;

(7)   To apply for, demand, arbitrate, settle, sue for, collect, receive, deposit, expend for my benefit, reinvest or make such other appropriate disposition of as my Agent deems appropriate, all cash, rights to the payment of cash, property (real, personal, intangible or mixed), debts, dues rights, accounts, legacies, bequests, devises, dividends, annuities, rights or benefits to which I am now or may in the future become entitled, regardless of the identity of the individual or public or private entity involved, including but not limited to benefits payable to or for my benefit by any governmental agency or body (such as Supplemental Social Security (SSI), Medicaid, Medicare, and Social Security Disability Insurance (SSDI), and for the purposes of receiving social security benefits, my Agent is hereby appointed my "Representative Payee"); to utilize all lawful means and methods to recover such assets or rights, qualify me for such benefits and claim such benefits on my behalf, and to compromise claims and grant discharges in regard to the matters described herein; to make such compromises, releases, settlements and discharges with respect thereto as my Agent shall deem appropriate;

(8)   To create and contribute to an employee benefit plan for my benefit; to select any payment option under any IRA or employee benefit plan in which I am a participant or to change options I have selected; to make voluntary contributions to such plans; to make "roll-overs" of plan benefits into other retirement plans; to apply for and receive payments and benefits; to waive rights given to non-employee spouses under state or federal law; to borrow money and purchase assets therefrom and sell assets thereto, if authorized by any such plans; to make and change beneficiary designations, including revocable or irrevocable designations; to consent or waive consent in connection with the designation of beneficiaries and the selection of joint and survivor annuities under any employee benefit plan;

(9)   To establish accounts of all kinds, including checking and savings, for me with financial institutions of any kind, including but not limited to banks and thrift institutions; to modify, terminate, make deposits to, write checks on, make withdrawals from, or grant security interests in, all accounts in my name or with respect

to which I am an authorized signatory, whether or not any such account was established by me or for me by my Agent; to negotiate, endorse or transfer any checks or other instruments with respect to any such accounts; to contract for any services rendered by any bank or financial institution;

(10) To contract with any institution for the maintenance of a safe-deposit box in my name; to have access to all safe-deposit boxes in my name or with respect to which I am authorized signatory, whether or not the contract for such safe-deposit box was executed by me (either alone or jointly with others) or by my Agent in my name; to add to and remove from the contents of any such safe-deposit box and to terminate any contracts for such boxes;

(11) To institute, supervise, prosecute, defend, intervene in, abandon, compromise, arbitrate, settle, dismiss, and appeal from any and all legal, equitable, judicial or administrative hearings, actions, suits, proceedings, attachments, arrests or distresses, involving me in any way, including but not limited to claims by or against me arising out of property damages or personal injuries suffered by or caused by me or under such circumstances that the loss resulting therefrom will or may be imposed on me and otherwise engage in litigation involving me, my property or any interest of mine, including any property or interest of person for which or whom I have or may have any responsibility;

(12) To borrow money from any lender for my account upon such terms and conditions as my Agent shall deem appropriate and to secure such borrowing by the granting of security interests in any property or interests in property which I may now or hereafter own; to borrow money upon any life insurance policies owned by me upon my life for any purpose and to grant a security interest in such policy to secure any such loans (including the assignment and delivery of any such policies as security); and no insurance company shall be under any obligation whatsoever to determine the need for such loan or the applications of the proceeds by my Agent;

(13) To execute a revocable trust agreement with such trustee(s) as my Agent shall select which trust shall provide that all income and principal shall be paid to me, to some person for my benefit or applied for my benefit in such amounts as I or my Agent shall request or as the trustee(s) shall determine, and that on my death any remaining income and principal shall be paid to my personal representative, and that the trust may be revoked or amended by me or my Agent at any time, provided, however, that any amendment by my Agent must be such that by law or under the provisions of this instrument such amendment could have been included in the original trust agreement; to deliver and convey any or all of my assets to the trustee(s) thereof; to add any or all of my assets to such a trust already in existence at the time of the creation of this instrument or created by me or my Agent at any time thereafter; and my Agent may be sole trustee or one of several trustees; and to execute such instruments, documents and papers to effect the transfers described herein as may be necessary, appropriate, incidental or convenient; to make such transfers absolutely in fee simple or for my lifetime only with the remainder or reversion (of the property so transferred) remaining in me so that such property will be disposed of at my death by my will or by the intestacy laws of the state in which I shall die a resident;

(14) To withdraw or receive the income or corpus of any trust over which I may have a right of receipt or withdrawal; to request and receive the income or corpus of any trust with respect to which the trustee thereof has the discretionary power to make distributions to or on my behalf, and to execute and deliver to such trustee a receipt and release or similar document for the income or corpus so received; to exercise (in whole or in part), release or let lapse any power of appointment held by me, whether general or special, or any power of amendment or revocation under any trust (including any trust with respect to which I may exercise any such power only with the consent of another person, even if my Agent is such other person), whether or not such power of appointment was created by me, subject however, to any restrictions upon such exercise imposed upon my Agent and set forth in other provisions of this instrument;

(15) To purchase, maintain, surrender, collect, or cancel (a) life insurance or annuities of any kind on my life or the life of any one in whom I have an insurable interest; (b) liability insurance protecting me and my estate against third party claims; (c) hospital insurance, medical insurance, Medicare supplement insurance, custodial care insurance, and disability income insurance for me or any of my dependents; and (d) casualty insurance insuring assets of mine against loss or damage due to fire, theft, or other commonly ensured risk; to pay

all insurance premiums, to select any options under such policies, to increase or decrease coverage under any such policy, to borrow against any such policy, to pursue all insurance claims on my behalf, to adjust insurance losses, and the foregoing powers shall apply to private and public plans, including but not limited to Medicare, Medicaid, SSI and Workers' Compensation.

(16) To represent me in all tax matters; to prepare, sign, and file federal, state, or local income, gift and other tax returns of all kinds, including, where appropriate, joint returns, claims for refunds, requests for extensions of time to file returns or pay taxes, extensions and waivers of applicable periods of limitation, protests and petitions to administrative agencies or courts, including the tax court, regarding tax matters, and any and all other tax related documents, including but not limited to consents and agreements under Section 2032A of the Internal Revenue Code or any successor section thereto and consents to split gifts, closing agreements, and any power of attorney form required by the Internal Revenue Service or any state or local taxing authority; to pay taxes due, collect and make such disposition of refunds as my Agent shall deem appropriate, post bonds, receive confidential information and contest deficiencies determined by the Internal Revenue Service or any state or local taxing authority; to exercise any elections I may have under federal, state or local tax law; to allocate any generation-skipping tax exemption to which I am entitled, and generally to represent me or obtain professional representation for me in all tax matters and proceedings of all kinds and for all periods before all officers of the Internal Revenue Service or any state or local taxing authority and in all courts; to engage, compensate and discharge attorneys, accountants and other tax and financial advisors and consultants to represent or assist me in connection with all tax matters involving or in any way related to me or any property in which I have or may have an interest or responsibility;

ARTICLE II.

My Agent is authorized in my Agent's sole and absolute discretion at any time to exercise the authority described below relating to matters involving the control and management of my person, and my health and medical care. In exercising the authority granted to my Agent herein, I first direct my Agent to try to discuss with me the specifics of any proposed decision regarding the control and management of my person or my health and medical care if I am able to communicate in any manner, however rudimentary. My Agent is further instructed that if I am unable to give an informed consent to medical treatment and my Agent cannot determine the treatment choice I would want made under the circumstances, my Agent shall give or withhold such consent for me based upon any treatment choices that I may previously have expressed on the subject while competent, whether under this instrument or otherwise. If my Agent cannot determine the treatment choice I would want made under the circumstances, then my Agent should make such choice for me based upon what my Agent believes to be in my best interests. Accordingly, my Agent is authorized as follows:

(1) To request, receive and review any information, verbal or written, regarding my personal affairs or my physical or mental health, including medical and hospital records, and to execute any releases or other documents that may be required in order to obtain such information, and to disclose or deny such information to such persons, organizations, firms or corporations as my Agent shall deem appropriate;

(2) To employ and discharge medical personnel including physicians, psychiatrists, dentists, nurses, and therapists as my Agent shall deem necessary for my physical, mental and emotional well-being, and to pay them (or cause them to be paid) reasonable compensation;

(3) To give or withhold consent to any medical procedures, tests or treatments, including surgery; to arrange for my hospitalization, convalescent care, hospice or home care; to summon paramedics or other emergency medical personnel and seek emergency treatment for me, as my Agent shall deem appropriate; and under circumstances in which my Agent determines that certain medical procedures, tests or treatments are no longer of any benefit to me or where the benefits are outweighed by the burdens imposed, to revoke, withdraw, modify or change consent to such procedures, tests and treatments, as well as hospitalization, convalescent care, hospice or home care which I or my Agent have previously allowed or consented to or which may have been implied due to emergency conditions. My Agent's decisions should be guided by taking into account (a) the provisions of this instrument, (b) any reliable evidence of preferences that I may have expressed on the subject, whether before or after the execution of this document, (c) what my agent believes I would want done in

the circumstances if I were able to express myself, and (d) any information given to my Agent by the physicians treating me as to my medical diagnosis and prognosis and the intrusiveness, pain, risks and side effects of the treatment;

(4)   To take whatever steps are necessary or advisable to enable me to remain in my personnel residence as long as it is reasonable under the circumstances. I realize that my health may deteriorate so that it becomes necessary to have round-the-clock personal or nursing care, and I authorize my Agent to make all necessary arrangements, contractual or otherwise, for home health care, or care for me at any hospital, nursing home, adult congregate living facility, hospice, or similar establishment, and I direct my Agent to obtain such care (including any such equipment that might assist in my care) as is reasonable under the circumstances. Specifically, I want to remain in my personal residence as long as it is reasonable;

(5)   To exercise my right of privacy and my right to make decisions regarding my medical treatment; to consent to and arrange for the administration of pain-relieving drugs of any kind, or other surgical or medical procedures calculated to relieve pain, including unconventional pain-relief therapies which my Agent believes may be helpful to me; even though such actions may lead to permanent damage, addiction or even hasten the moment of (but not intentionally cause) my death;

(6)   To grant, in conjunction with any instructions given under this Article, releases to hospital staff, physicians, nurses and other medical and hospital administrative personnel who act in reliance on instructions given by my Agent or who render written opinions to my Agent in connection with any matter described in this Article from all liability for damages suffered or to be suffered by me; to sign documents titled or purporting to be a "Refusal to Permit Treatment" and "Leaving Hospital Against Medical Advice" as well as any necessary waivers of or releases from liability required by any hospital or physician to implement my wishes regarding medical treatment or nontreatment;

(7)   To assist and facilitate the carrying out of my wishes as set forth in any living will or life-prolonging procedures declaration I have executed; to request, require or consent to the writing of a "No-Code" or "Do Not Resuscitate" order by any attending physician.

ARTICLE III.

(1)   In connection with the exercise of the powers herein described, my Agent is fully authorized and empowered to perform any acts and things and to execute and deliver any documents, instruments, and papers necessary, appropriate, incident or convenient to such exercise, including pursuing any legal or judicial remedies to which I would otherwise be entitled to pursue.

(2)   No person, organization, corporation or entity, who relies in good faith upon the authority of my Agent under this instrument, shall incur liability to me, my estate, my heirs or assigns, as a result of such reliance.

(3)   If any part of any provision of this instrument shall be invalid or unenforceable under applicable law, such part shall be ineffective to the extent of such invalidity only, without in any way affecting the remaining parts of such provision or the remaining provisions of this instrument.

(4)   In regard to medical decisions affecting me, I intend for this instrument to be honored in any jurisdiction where it may be presented and given the most liberal interpretation available for purposes of granting my Agent the fullest amount of discretion in making decisions on my behalf. Should any physician or health care institution fail to honor this instrument, then my Agent is authorized to terminate the services of such persons and institutions and to transfer my care to another physician or health care institution that will honor the instructions of my Agent.

(5)   If this instrument has been executed in multiple originals, each such counterpart original shall have equal force and effect. Any photocopy of this instrument shall have the same force and effect as an original.

(6) This instrument and the actions taken by my Agent properly authorized hereunder shall be binding upon my heirs, successors, assigns, and personal representatives.

(7) The powers granted to my Agent are nondelegable.

IN WITNESS WHEREOF, I have executed this Durable Power Of Attorney this _____ day of
_____, _____.

Principal:

_____
Signature of Principal
Name:_____
Address:_____
_____

Soc. Sec. No._____
_____

Witnesses:

_____
Signature of Witness
Name:_____
Address:_____
_____

_____
Signature of Witness
Name:_____
Address:_____
_____

STATE OF _____   )
COUNTY OF _____   )

On this _____ day of _____, _____, before me, personally appeared
_____, principal, and _____
and _____, witnesses, who are personally known to me or who
provided _____
_____as identification, and signed the foregoing instrument in my presence.

_____
Notary Public

My Commission expires:

ACKNOWLEDGMENT AND ACCEPTANCE BY AGENT

The undersigned accepts appointment as Agent and agrees to serve as Agent under this instrument.

_____
Signature of Agent
Name:_____
Address:_____
_____
Telephone: _____
Soc. Sec. No._____

POWER OF ATTORNEY

I,_____ (name), of
_____ (address,
including county and state), do hereby appoint _____
_____ (name, address and
relationship if any), as my true and lawful attorney in fact, to bargain for, purchase, sell, convey, transfer, mortgage, maintain, or dispose of the real property described as follows:

    1.   Said attorney in fact shall have the full power and authority to do and perform all and every act that I may legally do, and every power necessary to carry out the purposes for which this power of attorney is granted.

    2.   Said attorney in fact shall have the full power and authority to negotiate and determine any and all terms, and to execute and sign any contracts, deeds, bills of sale, all necessary closing documents, mortgages, notes, leases, and any other necessary instruments in connection with the purchase, sale, management, or maintenance of said property on my behalf.

    3.   Said attorney in fact shall have the full power and authority to receive and accept any deed, bill of sale or other instrument of conveyance in connection with the purchase of said property, and to receive and accept any funds and proceeds from the sale of said property, on my behalf; and to approve and authorize the distribution of any such funds to third parties.

    4.   Said attorney in fact shall have the full power and authority to obtain, purchase, or contract for the purchase of any goods, services, or policies of insurance, which said attorney in fact may deem necessary or advisable, to repair, manage, maintain, preserve or protect said property owned by me.

    5.   I hereby revoke all previous powers of attorney relating to said property, and hereby ratify and confirm all actions of the attorney in fact appointed in this Power of Attorney. This Power of Attorney is not to be construed as limiting or restricting the general powers granted herein, except:_____
_____.

    6.   The powers and authority granted herein shall commence immediately, and shall continue until terminated in writing, or until _____, whichever occurs first.

    DATED:_____

_____
Signature of Principal

Witness: _____   Witness:_____
Name: _____   Name: _____
Address: _____   Address:_____
          _____   _____

    On this _____ day of _____, _____, personally appeared before me _____, to me personally known or who produced _____ as identification, who executed this Power of Attorney and acknowledged the same to be his/her free act and deed.

_____
Notary Public
My Commission Expires:

Durable Power of Attorney for Health Care

1. Appointment of Agent. I, _____, appoint
_____, as my agent for health care decisions (called "Agent" in the rest of this document). If my Agent shall be unable or unwilling to make decisions pursuant to this Durable Power of Attorney for Health Care, I appoint as my alternate Agent _____.

2. Effective Date and Durability. My Agent may only act if I am unable to participate in making decisions regarding my medical treatment. My attending physician and another physician or licensed psychologist shall determine, after examining me, when I am unable to participate in making my own medical decisions. This designation is suspended during any period when I regain the ability to participate in my own medical treatment decisions. I intend this document to be a Durable Power of Attorney for Health Care and it shall survive my disability or incapacity.

3. Agent's Powers. I grant my Agent full authority to make decisions for me. In making such decisions, he or she should follow my expressed wishes, either written or oral, regarding my medical treatment. If my Agent cannot determine the choice I would want based on my written or oral statements, then he or she shall choose for me based on what he or she believes to be in my best interests. I direct that my Agent comply with the following instructions or limitations:_____
_____.

4. Life-sustaining Treatment. (CHOOSE ONLY ONE.) I understand that I do not have to choose any of the instructions regarding life-sustaining treatment listed below. If I choose one, I will place a check mark by the choice and sign below my choice. If I sign one of the choices listed below, I direct that reasonable measures be taken to keep me comfortable and to relieve pain.

[ ] CHOICE 1: Life-sustaining treatment: I grant discretion to my Agent.

I do not want life-sustaining treatment (☐ including artificial delivery of food and water   ☐ except for artificial delivery of food and water) if any of the following medical conditions exist:
   a. I am in an irreversible coma or persistent vegetative state.
   b. I am terminally ill, and life-sustaining procedures would only serve to artificially delay my death.
   c. My medical condition is such that burdens of treatment outweigh the expected benefits. In making this determination, I want my Patient Advocate to consider relief of my suffering, the expenses involved, and the quality of life, if prolonged.

I expressly authorize my Agent to make decisions to withhold or withdraw treatment which would allow me to die, and I acknowledge such decisions could or would allow my death.

Signed: _____

OR

[ ] CHOICE 2: Life-sustaining treatment: withhold treatment only if I am in a coma or persistent vegetative state.

I want life-sustaining treatment (☐ including artificial delivery of food and water ☐ except for artificial delivery of food and water) unless I am in a coma or persistent vegetative state that my physician reasonably believes to be irreversible. Once my physician has reasonably concluded the I will remain unconscious for the rest of my life, I do not want life-sustaining treatment to be provided or continued.

I expressly authorize my Agent to make decisions to withhold or withdraw treatment which would allow me to die, and I acknowledge such decisions could or would allow my death.

Signed: _____

OR

[ ] CHOICE 3: Directive for maximum treatment.

I want my life to be prolonged to the greatest extent possible consistent with sound medical practice without regard to my condition, the chances I have for recovery, or the cost of the procedures, and I direct life-sustaining treatment to be provided in order to prolong my life.

Signed: _____

5. Protection of third parties who rely on the instructions of my Agent. No person or entity that relies in good faith on the instructions of my Agent pursuant to this document, without actual notice that this power has been revoked or amended, shall incur any liability to me or to my estate. If I am unable to participate in making decisions for my care and there is no Agent to act for me, I request that the instructions I have given in this document be followed and be considered conclusive evidence of my wishes.

6. Administrative provisions.

I revoke any prior durable powers of attorney for health care that I may have executed to the extent that, and only to the extent that, they grant powers and authority within the scope of the powers granted to the Agent appointed in this document.

The document shall be governed by _____ law. However, I intend for this durable power of attorney for health care to be honored in any jurisdiction where it is presented and for such jurisdiction to refer to _____ law to interpret and determine the validity and enforceability of this document.

Photocopies of this signed power of attorney shall be treated as original counterparts.

I am providing these instructions voluntarily and have not been required to give them to obtain treatment or to have care withheld or withdrawn. I am at least eighteen years of age and of solid mind.

Dated:_____   _____
                                                Signature

WITNESS STATEMENT

I declare that the person who signed this Durable Power of Attorney for Health Care did so in my presence and appears to be of sound mind and under no duress, fraud or undue influence. I am not the husband or wife, parent, child, grandchild, brother or sister of the person who signed this document. Further, I am not his or her presumptive heir and , to the best of my knowledge, I am not a beneficiary to his or her will at the time of witnessing. I am not the Agent, the physician or an employee of the life or health insurance provider for the person signing this document. Nor am I an employee of the health care facility or home for the aged where the person signing this document resides or is being treated.

Dated:_____   _____
                                                Name:_____
                                                Address: _____
                                                         _____

Dated:_____   _____
                                                Name:_____
                                                Address: _____
                                                         _____

State of _____)
County of _____)

On this _____ day of _____, _____, before me personally appeared _____, principal, and _____ and _____, witnesses, who are personally known to me or who produced _____ as identification, and signed the foregoing instrument in my presence.

                                                _____
                                                Notary Public

                                                My Commission Expires:

LIMITED POWER OF ATTORNEY FOR CHILD CARE

I/We, _____, presently residing at
_____, as the parent(s)
of _____, hereinafter referred to as my/our child(ren),
hereby delegate to _____, hereinafter referred to as
my agent, the authority to act in my place and stead with respect to each of the following powers:

1.   To enroll or withdraw my child from any school or similar institution;

2.   To consent to any necessary medical treatment, surgery, medication, therapy, hospitalization or other such care of or for my child;

3.   To employ, retain or discharge any person who may care for, counsel, treat or in any manner assist my child.

4.   To exercise the same parental rights I may exercise with respect to the care, custody and control of my child, and the discretion to exercise the same rights in my agent's home or any other place selected by my agent in his or her discretion;

5.   To perform all other acts necessary, or incidental to the execution of the powers enumerated herein;

Any lawful act performed by my agent shall be binding upon myself, my heirs, beneficiaries, personal representatives and assigns. I reserve the right to amend or revoke this Limited Power of Attorney at any time hereafter; provided, however, any institution or other party dealing with my agent may rely upon this Limited Power of Attorney until receipt by it of a duly executed copy of my revocation thereof.

Any reproduced copy of this signed original shall be deemed to be an original counterpart of this Limited Power of Attorney. This Limited Power of Attorney shall not be affected by any legal incapacity during my lifetime, except as provided by statute.

This Limited Power of Attorney shall terminate upon a subsequent written revocation or on _____, whichever shall occur first.

Dated:_____   Dated:_____

_____   _____
Signature   Signature

State of _____)
County of _____)

On this _____ day of _____, _____, before me, personally appeared
_____, principal(s), who is/are personally known to me
or who provided _____ as identification,
and signed the foregoing instrument in my presence.

_____
Notary Public
My Commission expires:

REVOCATION OF POWER OF ATTORNEY

I, _____

_____(name and address of principal), hereby revoke

the _____, which was executed by me

on _____, which appointed _____

(name of agent) as my agent. Said agent no longer has authority to act on my behalf in any matter. This revocation is effective immediately.

Date:_____

_____

Signature of Principal

Witnesses:

_____   _____

Name:_____   Name:_____

Address:_____   Address:_____

_____   _____

State of _____)
County of _____)

On this _____ day of _____, _____, before me,

personally appeared _____, who is

personally known to me or who provided _____

_____as identification, and signed the foregoing instrument in my presence.

_____

Notary Public

My Commission expires:

ADVANCE DIRECTIVE FOR HEALTH CARE

This advance directive for health care is made this _____ day of _____ (Month, year). I, _____, being 19 years of age or older, of sound mind, hereby revoke any prior advance directive for for health care, and in lieu thereof hereby willfully and voluntarily make known my desires by my instructions to others through my living will, or by my appointment of a health care proxy, or both, that my dying shall not be artificially prolonged under the circumstances set forth below, and do hereby declare:

I. LIVING WILL

If my attending physician determines that I am no longer able to give directions to my health care providers regarding my medical treatment, I direct my attending physician and other health care providers to provide, withhold, or withdraw certain treatment from me under the circumstances I have indicated below by my initials. I understand that by initialing any of the paragraphs in this Living Will I am authorizing the withholding or withdrawal of certain treatments and this may lead to my death. I understand that I will be given treatment that is necessary for comfort or to alleviate my pain except where I specifically request otherwise.

(a) *Terminal illness or injury.* If my attending physician and another physician determine that I have an incurable terminal illness or injury which will lead to my death within six months or less:

(1) I DO want medically indicated life-sustaining treatment, even if it will not cure me and will only prolong the dying process.

_____
(Initials)

OR

I do NOT want life-sustaining treatment which would not cure me but which would only prolong the dying process.

_____
(Initials)

In addition, before life-sustaining treatment is withheld or withdrawn as directed above, I direct that my attending physician shall discuss with the following persons, if they are available, the benefits and burdens of taking such action and my stated wishes in this advance directive:

_____

_____

_____
(Initials)

(2) I understand that artificially provided nutrition and hydration (tube feeding of food and water) may be necessary to preserve my life.

(i) I DO want medically indicated artificially provided nutrition and hydration, even if it will only prolong the dying process.

_____
(Initials)

OR

(ii) I do NOT want artificially provided nutrition and hydration under the circumstances initialed below:

_____ (a) even if withholding or withdrawing causes me pain.
(Initials) (OR)

_____ (b) only if withholding it or withdrawing it, in the judgment of my
(Initials) attending physician, would not cause me undue pain.

In addition, before artificially provided nutrition and hydration are withheld or withdrawn as directed above, I direct that my attending physician shall discuss with the following persons, if they are available, the benefits and burdens of taking such action and my stated wishes in this advance directive: _____

_____

_____
(Initials)

(3)   I direct that (add other medical directives, if any) (if none, state "none"): _____

_____

_____

_____
(Initials)

(b)   *Permanent unconsciousness.* If in the judgment of any attending physician and another physician, I am in a condition of permanent unconsciousness:

(1)   I DO want medically indicated life-sustaining treatment, even if it will not cure me and will only maintain me in a condition of permanent unconsciousness.

_____
(Initials)

OR

I do NOT want life-sustaining treatment which would not cure me but which would only maintain me in a condition of permanent unconsciousness.

_____
(Initials)

In addition, before life-sustaining treatment is withheld or withdrawn as directed above, I direct that my attending physician shall discuss with the following persons, if they are available, the benefits and burdens of taking such action and my stated wishes in this advance directive:

_____

_____

_____
(Initials)

(2)   I understand that artificially provided nutrition and hydration (tube feeding of food and water) may be necessary to preserve my life.

(i)   I DO want medically indicated artificially provided nutrition and hydration, even if it will only prolong the dying process.

_____
(Initials)

OR

(ii)   I do NOT want artificially provided nutrition and hydration under the circumstances initialed below:

_____   (a)   even if withholding or withdrawing causes me pain.
(Initials)

(OR)

_____   (b)   only if withholding it or withdrawing it, in the judgment of my
(Initials)   attending physician, would not cause me undue pain.

In addition, before artificially provided nutrition and hydration are withheld or withdrawn as directed above, I direct that my attending physician shall discuss with the following persons, if they are available, the benefits and burdens of taking such action and my stated wishes in this advance directive: _____

_____

_____
(Initials)

(3) I direct that (add other medical directives, if any) (if none, state "none"):

_____

_____

_____

(Initials)

II. APPOINTMENT OF MY HEALTH CARE PROXY

I understand that my health care proxy is a person whom I may choose here to make medical treatment decisions for me as described below.

(a) I do NOT want to appoint a health care proxy.

_____

(Initials)

(b) I DO want to appoint a health care proxy. If my attending physician determines that I am no longer able to give directions to my health care providers regarding my medical treatment, I direct my attending physician and other health care providers to follow the instructions of _____, whom I appoint as my health care proxy. If my health care proxy is unable to serve, I appoint _____ as my alternate health care proxy with the same authority. My health care proxy is authorized to make whatever medical treatment decisions I could make if I were able, including decisions regarding the withholding or withdrawing of life-sustaining treatment.

(i) I specifically do (   ) do not (   ) authorize my health care proxy to make decisions regarding whether artificially provided nutrition and hydration be withheld or withdrawn.

(ii) I specifically direct my health care proxy to (add other medical directives, if any) (if none, state "none"): _____

_____

_____

(Initials)

III. CONFLICTING PROVISIONS

If the decisions made by the person I have appointed as my health care proxy disagree with the instructions in my Living Will:

_____
(Initials)

I want the instructions in my Living Will to be followed.

_____
(Initials)

I want the person I have appointed as health care proxy to make the final decision.

I understand that if I do not initial either of the above, then my health care proxy will make the final decision.

IV. DEFINITIONS

As used in this advance directive for health care, the following terms have the meaning set forth below:

(a) *Artificially provided nutrition and hydration.* A medical treatment consisting of the administration of food and water through a tube or intravenous line, where I am not required to chew or swallow voluntarily. Artificially provided nutrition and hydration does not include assisted feeding, such as spoon or bottle feeding.

(b) *Life-sustaining treatment.* Any treatment, procedure, or intervention that, in the judgment of the attending physician, when applied to me, would serve only to prolong the dying process where I have a terminal illness or injury, or would serve only to maintain me in a condition of permanent unconsciousness. These procedures shall include, but are not limited to, assisted ventilation, cardiopulmonary resuscitation, renal dialysis, surgical procedures, blood transfusions, and the administration of drugs and antibiotics. Life-sustaining treatment shall not include the administration of medication or the performance of any medical treatment where, in the opinion of the attending physician, the medication or treatment is necessary to provide comfort or to alleviate pain.

(c) *Permanent unconsciousness.* A condition that, to a reasonable degree of medical certainty:

a. Will last permanently, without improvement; and

b. In which thought, sensation, purposeful action, social interaction, and awareness of self and environment are absent; and

c. Which condition has existed for a period of time sufficient, in accordance with applicable professional standards, to make such a diagnosis; and

d. Which condition is confirmed by a physician who is qualified and experienced in making such a diagnosis.

(d) *Terminally ill or injured patient.* A patient whose death is imminent or whose condition, to a reasonable degree of medical certainty, is hopeless unless he or she is artificially supported through the use of life-sustaining procedures.

V. OTHER PROVISIONS

(a) I understand that if I have been diagnosed as pregnant and that diagnosis is known to my attending physician, directions in this advance directive for health care concerning the providing, withholding, and withdrawal of life-sustaining treatment and artificially provided nutrition and hydration shall have no force or effect during the course of my pregnancy.

(b) In the absence of my ability to give directions regarding the use of life-sustaining treatment, it is my intention that this advance directive for health care shall be honored by my family, my physician)s), and health care provider(s) as the final expression of my legal right to refuse medical or surgical treatment and accept the consequences from such refusal.

(c) I understand the full import of this declaration and I am emotionally and mentally competent to make this advance directive for health care.

(d) Nothing herein shall be construed as a directive to exclude from consultation or notification any relative of mine about my health condition or dying. Written directives by me as to whether to notify or consult with certain family members shall be respected by health care workers, attorneys in fact, or surrogates.

(e) I understand that I may revoke this directive at any time.

Signed _____

City, County and State of Residence:

_____

Date: _____

The declarant has been personally known to me and I believe him or her to be of sound mind. I did not sign the declarant's signature above for or at the direction of the declarant and I am not appointed as the health care proxy therein. I am not related to the declarant by blood, adoption, or marriage, entitled to any portion of the estate of the declarant according to the laws of intestate succession or under any will of declarant or codicil thereto, or directly financially responsible for declarant's medical care.

Witness _____   Witness _____

Date _____

I, _____, accept the proxy designation of the declarant and

I, _____ accept the alternate proxy designation of the declarant.

Signed _____   Signed _____

          (proxy)   (alternate proxy)

Date _____

ALASKA GENERAL POWER OF ATTORNEY

THE POWERS GRANTED FROM THE PRINCIPAL TO THE AGENT OR AGENTS IN THE FOLLOWING DOCUMENT ARE VERY BROAD. THEY MAY INCLUDE THE POWER TO DISPOSE, SELL, CONVEY, AND ENCUMBER YOUR REAL AND PERSONAL PROPERTY, AND THE POWER TO MAKE YOUR HEALTH CARE DECISIONS. ACCORDINGLY, THE FOLLOWING DOCUMENT SHOULD ONLY BE USED AFTER CAREFUL CONSIDERATION. IF YOU HAVE ANY QUESTIONS ABOUT THIS DOCUMENT, YOU SHOULD SEEK COMPETENT ADVICE.

YOU MAY REVOKE THIS POWER OF ATTORNEY AT ANY TIME.

Pursuant to AS 13.26.338—13.26.353, I, _____ (Name of principal), of _____ (Address of principal), do hereby appoint_____
_____(Name and address of agent or agents), my attorney(s)-in-fact to act as I have checked below in my name, place, and stead in any way which I myself could do, if I were personally present, with respect to the following matters, as each of them is defined in AS 13.26.344, to the full extent that I am permitted by law to act through an agent:

THE AGENT OR AGENTS YOU HAVE APPOINTED WILL HAVE ALL THE POWERS LISTED BELOW UNLESS YOU
DRAW A LINE THROUGH A CATEGORY; AND
INITIAL THE BOX OPPOSITE THAT CATEGORY.

(A)	real estate transactions..	( )
(B)	transactions involving tangible personal property, chattels, and goods...........	( )
(C)	bonds, shares, and commodities transactions...............................	( )
(D)	banking transactions..	( )
(E)	business operating transactions.......................................	( )
(F)	insurance transactions..	( )
(G)	estate transactions...	( )
(H)	gift transactions...	( )
(I)	claims and litigation...	( )
(J)	personal relationships and affairs....................................	( )
(K)	benefits from government programs and military service................	( )
(L)	health care services..	( )
(M)	records, reports, and statements......................................	( )
(N)	delegation..	( )
(O)	all other matters, including those specified as follows:	( )

_____
_____
_____

IF YOU HAVE APPOINTED MORE THAN ONE AGENT, CHECK ONE OF THE FOLLOWING:
( )   Each agent may exercise the powers conferred separately, without the consent of any other agent.
( )   All agents shall exercise the powers conferred jointly, with the consent of all other agents.

TO INDICATE WHEN THIS DOCUMENT SHALL BECOME EFFECTIVE, CHECK ONE OF THE FOLLOWING:
( )   This document shall become effective upon the date of my signature.
( )   This document shall become effective upon the date of my disability and shall not otherwise be affected by my disability.

IF YOU HAVE INDICATED THAT THIS DOCUMENT SHALL BECOME EFFECTIVE ON THE DATE OF YOUR SIGNATURE, CHECK ONE OF THE FOLLOWING:
( )   This document shall not be affected by my subsequent disability.
( )   This document shall be revoked by my subsequent disability.

IF YOU HAVE INDICATED THAT THIS DOCUMENT SHALL BECOME EFFECTIVE UPON THE DATE OF YOUR SIGNATURE AND WANT TO LIMIT THE TERM OF THIS DOCUMENT, COMPLETE THE FOLLOWING:

This document shall only continue in effect for _____ (   ) years from the date of my signature.

IF YOU HAVE GIVEN THE AGENT AUTHORITY REGARDING HEALTH CARE SERVICES UNDER SUBDIVISION (L), COMPLETE THE FOLLOWING:

( )   I have executed a separate declaration under AS 18.12, known as a "Living Will."

( )   I have not executed a "Living Will."

( )   I have executed a separate declaration under AS 47.30.950 — 47.30.980 regarding mental health treatment. If I have appointed an attorney-in-fact under AS 47.30.950 — 47.30.980, I authorize that attorney-in-fact and the attorney-in-fact whom I have appointed in this document to serve

    ( )jointly with consent of each other as to my mental health treatment

    ( )separately without each other's consent as to my mental health treatment.

( )   I have not executed a separate declaration under AS 47.30.950 — 47.30.980.

YOU MAY DESIGNATE AN ALTERNATE ATTORNEY-IN-FACT. ANY ALTERNATE YOU DESIGNATE WILL BE ABLE TO EXERCISE THE SAME POWERS AS THE AGENT(S) YOU NAMED AT THE BEGINNING OF THIS DOCUMENT. IF YOU WISH TO DESIGNATE AN ALTERNATE OR ALTERNATES, COMPLETE THE FOLLOWING:

If the agent(s) named at the beginning of this document is unable or unwilling to serve or continue to serve, then I appoint the following agent to serve with the same powers:

First alternate or successor attorney-in-fact:_____
_____ (Name and address of alternate).

Second alternate or successor attorney-in-fact:_____
_____ (Name and address of alternate).

YOU MAY NOMINATE A GUARDIAN OR CONSERVATOR. IF YOU WISH TO NOMINATE A GUARDIAN OR CONSERVATOR, COMPLETE THE FOLLOWING:

In the event that a court decides that it is necessary to appoint a guardian or conservator for me, I hereby nominate _____
_____(name and address of person nominated) to be considered by the court for appointment to serve as my guardian or conservator, or in any similar representative capacity.

NOTICE OF REVOCATION OF THE POWERS GRANTED IN THIS DOCUMENT

You may revoke one or more of the powers granted in this document. Unless otherwise provided in this document, you may revoke a specific power granted in this power of attorney by completing a special power of attorney that includes the specific power in this document that you want to revoke. Unless otherwise provided in this document, you may revoke all the powers granted in this power of attorney by completing a subsequent power of attorney.

NOTICE TO THIRD PARTIES

A third party who relies on the reasonable representations of an attorney-in-fact as to a matter relating to a power granted by a properly executed statutory power of attorney does not incur any liability to the principal or to the principal's heirs, assigns, or estate as a result of permitting the attorney-in-fact to exercise the authority granted by the power of attorney. A third party who fails to honor a properly executed statutory form power of attorney may be liable to the principal, the attorney-in-fact, the principal's heirs, assigns, or estate for a civil penalty, plus damages, costs, and fees associated with the failure to comply with the statutory form power of attorney. If the power of attorney is one which becomes effective upon the disability of the principal, the disability of the principal is established by an affidavit, as required by law.

IN WITNESS WHEREOF, I have hereunto signed my name this _____ day of _____, _____.

_____
Signature of Principal

Acknowledged before me at _____ on _____.

_____
Signature of Officer or Notary

Health Care Power of Attorney

1. Health Care Power of Attorney

I, _____, as principal, designate

_____ as my agent for all matters relating to my health care, including, without limitation, full power to give or refuse consent to all medical, surgical, hospital and related health care. This power of attorney is effective on my inability to make or communicate health care decisions. All of my agent's actions under this power during any period when I am unable to make or communicate health care decisions or when there is uncertainty whether I am dead or alive have the same effect on my heirs, devisees and personal representatives as if I were alive, competent and acting for myself.

If my agent is unwilling or unable to serve or continue to serve, I hereby appoint _____

_____ as my agent.

I have _____ I have not _____ completed and attached a living will for purposes of providing specific direction to my agent in situations that may occur during any period when I am unable to make or communicate health care decisions or after my death. My agent is directed to implement those choices I have initialed in the living will.

I have _____ I have not _____ completed a prehospital medical directive pursuant to § 36-3251, Arizona Revised Statutes.

This health care directive is made under § 36-3221, Arizona Revised Statutes, and continues in effect for all who may rely on it except those to whom I have given notice of its revocation.

2. Autopsy (under Arizona law an autopsy may be required)

If you wish to do so, reflect your desires below:

_____ 1. I do not consent to an autopsy.

_____ 2. I consent to an autopsy.

_____ 3. My agent may give consent to or refuse an autopsy.

3. Organ Donation (Optional)

(Under Arizona law, you may make a gift of all or part of your body to a bank or storage facility or a hospital, physician or medical or dental school for transplantation, therapy, medical or dental evaluation or research or for the advancement of medical or dental science. You may also authorize your agent to do so or a member of your family to make a gift unless you give them notice that you do not want a gift made. In the space below you may make a gift yourself or state that you do not want to make a gift. If you do not complete this section, your agent will have the authority to make a gift of a part of your body pursuant to law. Note: The donation elections you make in this health care power of attorney survive your death.)

If any of the statements below reflects your desire, initial on the line next to that statement. You do not have to initial any of the statements.

If you do not check any of the statements, your agent and your family will have the authority to make a gift of all or part of your body under Arizona law.

_____ I do not want to make an organ or tissue donation and do not want my agent or family to do so.

_____ I have already signed a written agreement or donor card regarding organ and tissue donation with the following individual or institution:_____

_____ Pursuant to Arizona law, I hereby give, effective on my death:

[   ] Any needed organ or parts.

[   ] The Following part or organs listed:

_____

_____

_____

for (check one):

[   ] Any legally authorized purpose.

[   ] Transplant or therapeutic purposes only.

4. Physician Affidavit (Optional)

(Before initialing any choices above you may wish to ask questions of you physician regarding a particular treatment alternative. If you do speak with your physician it is a good idea to ask your physician to complete this affidavit and keep a copy for his file.)

I, Dr. _____ have reviewed this guidance document and have discussed with _____ any questions regarding the probable medical consequences of the treatment choices provided above. This discussion with the principal occurred on _____ (date).

I have agreed to comply with the provisions of this directive.

_____
Signature of physician

5. Living Will (Optional)

(Some general statements concerning your health care options are outlined below. If you agree with one of the statements, you should initial that statement. **Read all of these statements carefully before you initial your selection.** You can also write your own statement concerning life-sustaining treatment and other matters relating to your health care. You may initial any combination of paragraphs 1, 2, 3 and 4, but if you initial paragraph 5 the others should not be initialed.)

_____ 1. If I have a terminal condition I **do not** want my life to be prolonged and I **do not** want life-sustaining treatment, beyond comfort care, that would serve **only** to artificially delay the moment of my death.

_____ 2. If I am in a terminal condition or an irreversible coma or a persistent vegetative state that my doctors reasonably feel to be irreversible or incurable, I **do** want the medical treatment necessary to provide care that would keep me comfortable, but I **do not** want the following:

    _____ (a) Cardiopulmonary resuscitation, for example, the use of drugs, electric shock and artificial breathing.

    _____ (b) Artificially administered food and fluids.

    _____ (c) To be taken to a hospital if at all avoidable.

_____ 3. Notwithstanding my other directions, if I am known to be pregnant, I do not want life-sustaining treatment withheld or withdrawn if it is possible that the embryo/fetus will develop to the point of live birth with the continued application of life-sustaining treatment.

_____ 4. Notwithstanding my other directions I **do** want the use of all medical care necessary to treat my condition until my doctors reasonably conclude that my condition is terminal or is irreversible and incurable or I am in a persistent vegetative state.

_____ 5. I **want** my life to be prolonged to the greatest extent possible.

Other or additional statement of desires

I have _____ I have not _____ attached additional special provisions or limitations to this document to be honored in the absence of my being able to give health care directions.

_____
Signature of Principal

Witness:_____

_____

Address:_____

_____

Witness:_____

_____

Address:_____

_____

Date:_____

Time:_____

_____
Address of Agent

_____
Telephone of Agent

(Note: This document may be notarized instead of being witnessed.)

State of Arizona   )
County of _____)

On this _____ day of _____, _____ before me, personally appeared _____ (name of principal), who is personally known to me or provided _____ as identification, and acknowledged that he or she executed it.

    [NOTARY SEAL]

_____
(signature of notary public)

Uniform Statutory Form Power of Attorney

(California Probate Code Section 4401)

NOTICE: THE POWERS GRANTED BY THIS DOCUMENT ARE BROAD AND SWEEPING. THEY ARE EXPLAINED IN THE UNIFORM STATUTORY FORM POWER OF ATTORNEY ACT (CALIFORNIA PROBATE CODE SECTIONS 4400 - 4465). IF YOU HAVE ANY QUESTIONS ABOUT THESE POWERS, OBTAIN COMPETENT LEGAL ADVICE. THIS DOCUMENT DOES NOT AUTHORIZE ANYONE TO MAKE MEDICAL AND OTHER HEALTH-CARE DECISIONS FOR YOU. YOU MAY REVOKE THIS POWER OF ATTORNEY IF YOU LATER WISH TO DO SO.

I, _____

_____ (your name and address)

appoint_____

_____(name and address of the person appointed, or of each person appointed if you want to designate more than one) as my agent (attorney-in-fact) to act for me in any lawful way with respect to the following initialed subjects:

TO GRANT ALL OF THE FOLLOWING POWERS, INITIAL THE LINE IN FRONT OF (N) AND IGNORE THE LINES IN FRONT OF THE OTHER POWERS.

TO GRANT ONE OR MORE, BUT FEWER THAN ALL, OF THE FOLLOWING POWERS, INITIAL THE LINE IN FRONT OF EACH POWER YOU ARE GRANTING.

TO WITHHOLD A POWER, DO NOT INITIAL THE LINE IN FRONT OF IT. YOU MAY, BUT NEED NOT, CROSS OUT EACH POWER WITHHELD.

_____	(A)	Real property transactions.
_____	(B)	Tangible personal property transactions.
_____	(C)	Stock and bond transactions.
_____	(D)	Commodity and option transactions.
_____	(E)	Banking and other financial institution transactions.
_____	(F)	Business operating transactions.
_____	(G)	Insurance and annuity transactions.
_____	(H)	Estate, trust, and other beneficiary transactions.
_____	(I)	Claims and litigation.
_____	(J)	Personal and family maintenance.
_____	(K)	Benefits from social security, medicare, medicaid, or other governmental programs, or civil or military service.
_____	(L)	Retirement plan transactions.
_____	(M)	Tax matters.
_____	(N)	ALL OF THE POWERS LISTED ABOVE.

YOU NEED NOT INITIAL ANY OTHER LINES IF YOU INITIAL LINE (N).

SPECIAL INSTRUCTIONS:

ON THE FOLLOWING LINES YOU MAY GIVE SPECIAL INSTRUCTIONS LIMITING OR EXTENDING THE POWERS GRANTED TO YOUR AGENT. _____

_____

_____

_____

_____

_____

_____

_____

UNLESS YOU DIRECT OTHERWISE ABOVE, THIS POWER OF ATTORNEY IS EFFECTIVE IMMEDIATELY AND WILL CONTINUE UNTIL IT IS REVOKED.

This power of attorney will continue to be effective even though I become incapacitated.

STRIKE THE PRECEDING SENTENCE IF YOU DO NOT WANT THIS POWER OF ATTORNEY TO CONTINUE IF YOU BECOME INCAPACITATED.

EXERCISE OF POWER OF ATTORNEY WHERE MORE THAN ONE AGENT DESIGNATED

If I have designated more than one agent, the agents are to act _____.
IF YOU APPOINTED MORE THAN ONE AGENT AND YOU WANT EACH AGENT TO BE ABLE TO ACT ALONE WITHOUT THE OTHER AGENT JOINING, WRITE THE WORD "SEPARATELY" IN THE BLANK SPACE ABOVE. IF YOU DO NOT INSERT ANY WORD IN THE BLANK SPACE, OR IF YOU INSERT THE WORD "JOINTLY," THEN ALL OF YOUR AGENTS MUST ACT OR SIGN TOGETHER.

I agree that any third party who receives a copy of this document may act under it. Revocation of the power of attorney is not effective as to a third party until the third party has actual knowledge of the revocation. I agree to indemnify the third party for any claims that arise against the third party because of reliance on this power of attorney.

Signed this _____ day of _____, _____.

_____
(your signature)

_____
(your social security number)

State of _____, County of _____,
BY ACCEPTING OR ACTING UNDER THE APPOINTMENT, THE AGENT ASSUMES THE FIDUCIARY AND OTHER LEGAL RESPONSIBILITIES OF AN AGENT.

CERTIFICATE OF ACKNOWLEDGMENT OF NOTARY PUBLIC

State of California   )
)
County of _____)

On this _____ day of _____, _____ before me,
_____, (name of notary public) personally appeared
_____, (name of principal) personally known to me (or proved to me on the basis of satisfactory evidence) to be the person whose name is subscribed to this instrument, and acknowledged that he/she executed it in his/her authorized capacity, and that by his/her signature on this instrument the person executed this instrument.
WITNESS my hand and official seal

_____
(signature of notary public)   (seal)

STATUTORY FORM DURABLE POWER OF ATTORNEY FOR HEALTH CARE

(California Probate Code Section 4771)

WARNING TO PERSON EXECUTING THIS DOCUMENT

THIS IS AN IMPORTANT LEGAL DOCUMENT WHICH IS AUTHORIZED BY THE KEENE HEALTH CARE AGENT ACT. BEFORE EXECUTING THIS DOCUMENT, YOU SHOULD KNOW THESE IMPORTANT FACTS:

THIS DOCUMENT GIVES THE PERSON YOU DESIGNATE AS YOUR AGENT (THE ATTORNEY-IN-FACT) THE POWER TO MAKE HEALTH CARE DECISIONS FOR YOU. YOUR AGENT MUST ACT CONSISTENT WITH YOUR DESIRES AS STATED IN THIS DOCUMENT OR OTHERWISE MADE KNOWN.

EXCEPT AS YOU OTHERWISE SPECIFY IN THIS DOCUMENT, THIS DOCUMENT GIVES YOUR AGENT THE POWER TO CONSENT TO YOUR DOCTOR NOT GIVING TREATMENT OR STOPPING TREATMENT NECESSARY TO KEEP YOU ALIVE.

NOTWITHSTANDING THIS DOCUMENT, YOU HAVE THE RIGHT TO MAKE MEDICAL AND OTHER HEALTH CARE DECISIONS FOR YOURSELF AS LONG AS YOU CAN GIVE INFORMED CONSENT WITH RESPECT TO THE PARTICULAR DECISION. IN ADDITION, NO TREATMENT MAY BE GIVEN TO YOU OVER YOUR OBJECTION AT THE TIME, AND HEALTH CARE NECESSARY TO KEEP YOU ALIVE MAY NOT BE STOPPED OR WITHHELD IF YOU OBJECT AT THE TIME.

THIS DOCUMENT GIVES YOUR AGENT AUTHORITY TO CONSENT, REFUSE TO CONSENT, OR TO WITHDRAW CONSENT TO ANY CARE, TREATMENT, SERVICE, OR PROCEDURE TO MAINTAIN, DIAGNOSE, OR TREAT A PHYSICAL OR MENTAL CONDITION. THIS POWER IS SUBJECT TO ANY STATEMENT OF YOUR DESIRES AND ANY LIMITATION THAT YOU INCLUDE IN THIS DOCUMENT. YOU MAY STATE IN THIS DOCUMENT ANY TYPES OF TREATMENT THAT YOU DO NOT DESIRE. IN ADDITION, A COURT CAN TAKE AWAY THE POWER OF YOUR AGENT TO MAKE HEALTH CARE DECISIONS FOR YOU IF YOUR AGENT (1) AUTHORIZES ANYTHING THAT IS ILLEGAL, (2) ACTS CONTRARY TO YOUR KNOWN DESIRES, OR (3) WHERE YOUR DESIRES ARE NOT KNOWN, DOES ANYTHING THAT IS CLEARLY CONTRARY TO YOUR BEST INTERESTS.

THE POWERS GIVEN BY THIS DOCUMENT WILL EXIST FOR AN INDEFINITE PERIOD OF TIME UNLESS YOU LIMIT THEIR DURATION IN THIS DOCUMENT.

YOU HAVE THE RIGHT TO REVOKE THE AUTHORITY OF YOUR AGENT BY NOTIFYING YOUR AGENT OR YOUR TREATING DOCTOR, HOSPITAL, OR OTHER HEALTH CARE PROVIDER ORALLY OR IN WRITING OF THE REVOCATION.

YOUR AGENT HAS THE RIGHT TO EXAMINE YOUR MEDICAL RECORDS AND TO CONSENT TO THEIR DISCLOSURE UNLESS YOU LIMIT THIS RIGHT IN THIS DOCUMENT.

UNLESS YOU OTHERWISE SPECIFY IN THIS DOCUMENT, THIS DOCUMENT GIVES YOUR AGENT THE POWER AFTER YOU DIE TO (1) AUTHORIZE AN AUTOPSY, (2) DONATE YOUR BODY OR PARTS THEREOF FOR TRANSPLANT OR THERAPEUTIC OR EDUCATIONAL OR SCIENTIFIC PURPOSES, AND (3) DIRECT THE DISPOSITION OF YOUR REMAINS.

THIS DOCUMENT REVOKES ANY PRIOR DURABLE POWER OF ATTORNEY FOR HEALTH CARE.

YOU SHOULD CAREFULLY READ AND FOLLOW THE WITNESSING PROCEDURE DESCRIBED AT THE END OF THIS FORM. THIS DOCUMENT WILL NOT BE VALID UNLESS YOU COMPLY WITH THE WITNESSING PROCEDURE.

IF THERE IS ANYTHING IN THIS DOCUMENT THAT YOU DO NOT UNDERSTAND, YOU SHOULD ASK A LAWYER TO EXPLAIN IT TO YOU.

YOUR AGENT MAY NEED THIS DOCUMENT IMMEDIATELY IN CASE OF AN EMERGENCY THAT REQUIRES A DECISION CONCERNING YOUR HEALTH CARE. EITHER KEEP THIS DOCUMENT WHERE IT IS IMMEDIATELY AVAILABLE TO YOUR AGENT AND ALTERNATE AGENTS OR GIVE EACH OF THEM AN EXECUTED COPY OF THIS DOCUMENT. YOU MAY ALSO WANT TO GIVE YOUR DOCTOR AN EXECUTED COPY OF THIS DOCUMENT.

DO NOT USE THIS FORM IF YOU ARE A CONSERVATEE UNDER THE LANTERMAN-PETRIS-SHORT ACT AND YOU WANT TO APPOINT A CONSERVATOR AS YOUR AGENT. YOU CAN DO THAT ONLY IF THE APPOINTMENT DOCUMENT INCLUDES A CERTIFICATE OF YOUR ATTORNEY.

1. DESIGNATION OF HEALTH CARE AGENT. I,

_____

(Insert your name and address)

do hereby designate and appoint _____

(Insert name, address, and telephone number of one individual only as your agent to make health care decisions for you. None of the following may be designated as your agent: (1) your treating health care provider, (2) a nonrelative employee of your treating health care
provider, (3) an operator of a community care facility, (4) a nonrelative employee of an operator of a community care facility, (5) an operator of a residential care facility for the elderly, or (6) a nonrelative employee of a residential care facility for the elderly.)

as my attorney in fact (agent) to make health care decisions for me as authorized in this document. For purposes
of this document, "health care decision" means consent, refusal of consent, or withdrawal of consent to any care,
treatment, service, or procedure to maintain, diagnose, or treat an individual's physical or mental condition.

2. CREATION OF DURABLE POWER OF ATTORNEY FOR HEALTH CARE. By this document I
intend to create a durable power of attorney for health care under Sections 2430 to 2443, inclusive, of the
California Civil Code. This power of attorney is authorized by the Keene Health Care Agent Act and shall be
construed in accordance with the provisions of Sections 2500 to 2506, inclusive, of the California Civil Code.
This power of attorney shall not be affected by me subsequent incapacity.

3. GENERAL STATEMENT OF AUTHORITY GRANTED. Subject to any limitations in this document, I hereby grant to my agent full power and authority to make health care decisions for me to the same
extent that I could make such decisions for myself if I had the capacity to do so. In exercising this authority,
my agent shall make health care decisions that are consistent with my desires as stated in this document or otherwise made known to my agent, including, but not limited to, my desires concerning obtaining or refusing or
withdrawing life-prolonging care, treatment, services, and procedures.

(If you want to limit the authority of your agent to make health care decisions for you, you can state the limitations in paragraph 4
("Statement of Desires, Special Provisions, and Limitations") below. You can indicate your desires by including a statement of your desires
in the same paragraph.)

4. STATEMENT OF DESIRES, SPECIAL PROVISIONS, AND LIMITATIONS.

(Your agent must make health care decisions that are consistent with your know desires. You can, but are not required to, state your desires
in the space provided below. You should consider whether you want to include a statement of your desires concerning life-prolonging care,
treatment, services, and procedures. You can also include a statement of your desires concerning other matters relating to your health care.
You can also make your desires known to your agent by discussing your desires with your agent or by some other means. If there are any
types of treatment that you do not want to be used, you should state them in the space below. If you want to limit in any other way the
authority given your agent by this document, you should state the limits in the space below. If you do not state any limits, your agent will
have broad powers to make health care decisions for you, except to the extent that there are limits provided by law.)

In exercising the authority under this durable power of attorney for health care, my agent shall act consistently with my desires as stated below and is subject to the special provisions and limitations stated below:

(a) Statement of desires concerning life-prolonging care, treatment, services, and procedures:

_____
_____
_____

(b) Additional statement of desires, special provisions, and limitations:

_____
_____
_____

(You may attach additional pages if you need more space to complete your statement. If you attach additional pages, you must date and
sign EACH of the additional pages at the same time you date and sign this document.)

5. INSPECTION AND DISCLOSURE OF INFORMATION RELATING TO MY PHYSICAL OR
MENTAL HEALTH. Subject to any limitations in this document, my agent has the power and authority to do
all of the following:

(a) Request, review, and receive any information, verbal or written, regarding my physical or mental
health, including, but not limited to, medical and hospital records.

(b) Execute on my behalf any releases or other documents that may be required in order to obtain this
information.

(c) Consent to the disclosure of this information.

(If you want to limit the authority of your agent to receive and disclose information relating to your health, you must state the limitations
in paragraph 4 ("Statement of Desires, Special Provisions, and Limitations") above.)

6. SIGNING DOCUMENTS, WAIVERS, AND RELEASES. Where necessary to implement the health care decisions that my agent is authorized by this document to make, my agent has the power and authority to execute on my behalf all of the following:

(a) Documents titled or purporting to be a "Refusal to Permit Treatment" and "Leaving Hospital Against Medical Advice."

(b) Any necessary waiver or release from liability required by a hospital or physician.

7. AUTOPSY; ANATOMICAL GIFTS; DISPOSITION OF REMAINS. Subject to any limitations in this document, my agent has the power and authority to do all of the following:

(a) Authorize an autopsy under Section 7113 of the Health and Safety Code.

(b) Make a disposition of a part or parts of my body under the Uniform Anatomical Gift Act (Chapter 3.5 (commencing with Section 7150) of Part I of Division 7 of the Health and Safety Code).

(c) Direct the disposition of my remains under Section 7100 of the Health and Safety Code.

(If you want to limit the authority of your agent to consent to an autopsy, make an anatomical gift, or direct the disposition of your remains, you must state the limitations in paragraph 4 ("Statement of Desires, Special Provisions, and Limitations") above.)

8. DURATION.

(Unless you specify otherwise in the space below, this power of attorney will exist for an indefinite period of time.)

This durable power of attorney for health care expires on _____

_____

(Fill in this space ONLY if you want to limit the duration of this power of attorney.)

9. DESIGNATION OF ALTERNATE AGENTS.

(You are not required to designate any alternate agents but you may do so. Any alternate agent you designate will be able to make the same health care decisions as the agent you designated in paragraph 1, above, in the event that agent is unable or ineligible to act as your agent. If the agent you designated is your spouse, he or she becomes ineligible to act as your agent if your marriage is dissolved.)

If the person designated as my agent in paragraph 1 is not available or becomes ineligible to act as my agent to make a health care decision for me or loses the mental capacity to make health care decisions for me, or if I revoke that person's appointment or authority to act as my agent to make health care decisions for me, then I designate and appoint the following persons to serve as my agent to make health care decisions for me as authorized in this document, such persons to serve in the order listed below:

A.   First Alternate Agent _____

_____

(Insert name, address, and telephone number of first alternate agent)

B.   Second Alternate Agent _____

_____

(Insert name, address, and telephone number of second alternate agent)

10. NOMINATION OF CONSERVATOR OF PERSON.

(A conservator of the person may be appointed for you if a court decides that one should be appointed. The conservator is responsible for your physical care, which under some circumstances includes making health care decisions for you. You are not required to nominate a conservator but you may do so. The court will appoint the person you nominate unless that would be contrary to your best interests. You may, but are not required to, nominate as your conservator the same person you named in paragraph 1 as your health care agent. You can nominate an individual as your conservator in the space below.)

If a conservator of the person is to be appointed for me, I nominate the following individual to serve as conservator of the person _____

_____

(Insert name and address of person nominated as conservator of the person)

11. PRIOR DESIGNATIONS REVOKED. I revoke any prior durable power of attorney for health care.

DATE AND SIGNATURE OF PRINCIPAL

(YOU MUST DATE AND SIGN THIS POWER OF ATTORNEY)

I sign my name to this Statutory Form Durable Power of Attorney for Health Care on _____at_____, _____.

(City)   (State)

_____

(You sign here)

(THIS POWER OF ATTORNEY WILL NOT BE VALID UNLESS IT IS SIGNED BY TWO QUALIFIED WIT-
NESSES WHO ARE PRESENT WHEN YOU SIGN OR ACKNOWLEDGE YOUR SIGNATURE. IF YOU
HAVE ATTACHED ANY ADDITIONAL PAGES TO THIS FORM, YOU MUST DATE AND SIGN EACH OF
THE ADDITIONAL PAGES AT THE SAME TIME YOU DATE AND SIGN THIS POWER OF ATTORNEY.)

STATEMENT OF WITNESSES

(This document must be witnessed by two qualified adult witnesses. None of the following may be used as a witness: (1) a person you designate as your agent or alternate agent, (2) a health care provider, (3) an employee of a health care provider, (4) the operator of a community care facility, (5) an employee of an operator of a community care facility, (6) the operator of a residential care facility for the elderly, or (7) an employee of an operator of a residential care facility for the elderly. At least one of the witnesses must make the additional declaration set out following the place where the witnesses sign.)

(READ CAREFULLY BEFORE SIGNING. You can sign as a witness only if you personally know the principal or the identity of the principal is proved to you by convincing evidence.)

(To have convincing evidence of the identity of the principal, you must be presented with and reasonably rely on any one or more of the following:

(1) An identification card or driver's license issued by the California Department of Motor Vehicles that is current or has been issued within five years.

(2) A passport issued by the Department of State of the United States that is current or has been issued within five years.

(3) Any of the following documents if the document is current or has been issued within five years and contains a photograph and description of the person named on it, is signed by the person, and bears a serial or other identifying number:

(a) A passport issued by a foreign government that has been stamped by the United States Immigration and Naturalization Service.

(b) A driver's license issued by a state other than California or by a Canadian or Mexican public agency authorized to issue driver's licenses.

(c) An identification card issued by a state other than California.

(d) An identification card issued by any branch of the armed forces of the United States.

(4) If the principal is a patient in a skilled nursing facility, a witness who is a patient advocate or ombudsman may rely upon the representations of the administrator or staff of the skilled nursing facility, or of family members, as convincing evidence of the identity of the principal if the patient advocate or ombudsman believes that the representations provide a reasonable basis for determining the identity of the principal.)

(Other kinds of proof of identity are not allowed.)

I declare under penalty of perjury under the laws of California that the person who signed or acknowledged this document is personally known to me (or proved to me on the basis of convincing evidence) to be the principal, that the principal signed or acknowledged this durable power of attorney in my presence, that the principal appears to be of sound mind and under no duress, fraud, or undue influence, that I am not the person appointed as attorney in fact by this document, and that I am not a health care provider, an employee of a health care provider, the operator of a community care facility, an employee of an operator of a community care facility, the operator of a residential care facility for the elderly, nor an employee of an operator of a residential care facility for the elderly.

Signature:_____   Residence Address:_____
Print Name:_____   _____
Date:_____   _____

Signature:_____   Residence Address:_____
Print Name:_____   _____
Date:_____   _____

(AT LEAST ONE OF THE ABOVE WITNESSES MUST ALSO SIGN THE FOLLOWING DECLARATION.)

I further declare under penalty of perjury under the laws of California that I am not related to the principal by blood, marriage, or adoption, and, to the best of my knowledge, I am not entitled to any part of the estate of the principal upon the death of the principal under a will now existing or by operation of law.

Signature:_____   Signature:_____

STATEMENT OF PATIENT ADVOCATE OR OMBUDSMAN

(If you are a patient in a skilled nursing facility, one of the witnesses must be a patient advocate or ombudsman. The following statement is required only if you are a patient in a skilled nursing facility—a health care facility that provides the following basic services: skilled nursing care and supportive care to patients whose primary need is for availability of skilled nursing care on an extended basis. The patient advocate or ombudsman must sign both parts of the "Statement of Witnesses" above AND must also sign the following statement.)

I further declare under penalty of perjury under the laws of California that I am a patient advocate or ombudsman as designated by the State Department of Aging and that I am serving as a witness as required by subdivision (e) of Section 4701 of the Probate Code.

Signature:_____

COLORADO STATUTORY POWER OF ATTORNEY FOR PROPERTY

NOTICE: UNLESS YOU LIMIT THE POWER IN THIS DOCUMENT, THIS DOCUMENT GIVES YOUR AGENT THE POWER TO ACT FOR YOU, WITHOUT YOUR CONSENT, IN ANY WAY THAT YOU COULD ACT FOR YOURSELF. THE POWERS GRANTED BY THIS DOCUMENT ARE BROAD AND SWEEPING. THEY ARE EXPLAINED IN THE "UNIFORM STATUTORY FORM POWER OF ATTORNEY ACT", PART 13 OF ARTICLE 1 OF TITLE 15, COLORADO REVISED STATUTES, AND PART 6 OF ARTICLE 14 OF TITLE 15, COLORADO REVISED STATUTES. IF YOU HAVE ANY QUESTIONS ABOUT THESE POWERS, OBTAIN COMPETENT LEGAL ADVICE. THIS DOCUMENT DOES NOT AUTHORIZE ANYONE TO MAKE MEDICAL AND OTHER HEALTH-CARE DECISIONS FOR YOU. YOU MAY REVOKE THIS POWER OF ATTORNEY IF YOU LATER WISH TO DO SO.

THE PURPOSE OF THIS POWER OF ATTORNEY IS TO GIVE THE PERSON YOU DESIGNATE (YOUR "AGENT") BROAD POWERS TO HANDLE YOUR PROPERTY AND AFFAIRS, WHICH MAY INCLUDE POWERS TO PLEDGE, SELL, OR OTHERWISE DISPOSE OF ANY REAL OR PERSONAL PROPERTY WITHOUT ADVANCE NOTICE TO YOU OR APPROVAL BY YOU. THIS FORM DOES NOT IMPOSE A DUTY ON YOUR AGENT TO EXERCISE GRANTED POWERS; BUT WHEN POWERS ARE EXERCISED, YOUR AGENT MUST USE DUE CARE TO ACT FOR YOUR BENEFIT AND IN ACCORDANCE WITH THE PROVISIONS OF THIS FORM AND MUST KEEP A RECORD OF RECEIPTS, DISBURSEMENTS, AND SIGNIFICANT ACTIONS TAKEN AS AGENT. YOU MAY NAME SUCCESSOR AGENTS UNDER THIS FORM BUT NOT CO-AGENTS. UNTIL YOU REVOKE THIS POWER OF ATTORNEY OR A COURT ACTING ON YOUR BEHALF TERMINATES IT, YOUR AGENT MAY EXERCISE THE POWERS GIVEN HERE THROUGHOUT YOUR LIFETIME, EVEN AFTER YOU MAY BECOME DISABLED, UNLESS YOU EXPRESSLY LIMIT THE DURATION OF THIS POWER IN THE MANNER PROVIDED BELOW.

YOU MAY HAVE OTHER RIGHTS OR POWERS UNDER COLORADO LAW NOT SPECIFIED IN THIS FORM.

I, _____, (insert your full name and address) appoint _____ (insert the full name and address of the person appointed) as my agent (attorney-in-fact) to act for me in any lawful way with respect to the following initialed subjects:

TO GRANT ONE OR MORE OF THE FOLLOWING POWERS, INITIAL THE LINE IN FRONT OF EACH POWER YOU ARE GRANTING. TO WITHHOLD A POWER, DO NOT INITIAL THE LINE IN FRONT OF IT. YOU MAY, BUT NEED NOT, CROSS OUT EACH POWER WITHHELD.

_____ (A) Real estate transactions (when property recorded).
_____ (B) Tangible personal property transactions.
_____ (C) Stock and bond transactions.
_____ (D) Commodity and option transactions.
_____ (E) Banking and other financial institution transactions.
_____ (F) Business operating transactions.
_____ (G) Insurance and annuity transactions.
_____ (H) Estate, trust, and other beneficiary transactions.
_____ (I) Claims and litigation.
_____ (J) Personal and family maintenance.
_____ (K) Benefits from social security, medicare, medicaid, or other governmental programs or military service.
_____ (L) Retirement plan transactions.
_____ (M) Tax matters.

UNLESS YOU DIRECT OTHERWISE ABOVE, THIS POWER OF ATTORNEY IS EFFECTIVE IMMEDIATELY AND WILL CONTINUE UNTIL IT IS REVOKED OR TERMINATED AS SPECIFIED BELOW. STRIKE THROUGH AND WRITE YOUR INITIALS TO THE LEFT OF THE FOLLOWING SENTENCE IF YOU DO NOT WANT THIS POWER OF ATTORNEY TO CONTINUE IF YOU BECOME DISABLED, INCAPACITATED, OR INCOMPETENT.
    1. (   ) This power of attorney will continue to be effective even though I become disabled, incapacitated, or incompetent.

YOU MAY INCLUDE ADDITIONS TO AND LIMITATIONS ON THE AGENT'S POWERS IN THIS POWER OF ATTORNEY IF THEY ARE SPECIFICALLY DESCRIBED BELOW.

2. The powers granted above shall not include the following powers or shall be modified or limited in the following manner (here you may include any specific limitations you deem appropriate, such as a prohibition of or conditions on the sale of particular stock or real estate or special rules regarding borrowing by the agent):

_____

_____

_____

3. In addition to the powers granted above, I grant my agent the following powers (here you may add any other delegable powers, such as the power to make gifts, exercise powers of appointment, name or change beneficiaries or joint tenants, or revoke or amend any trust specifically referred to below):

_____

_____

_____

4. SPECIAL INSTRUCTIONS.   ON THE FOLLOWING LINES YOU MAY GIVE SPECIAL INSTRUCTIONS TO YOUR AGENT:

_____

_____

_____

YOUR AGENT WILL BE ENTITLED TO REIMBURSEMENT FOR ALL REASONABLE EXPENSES INCURRED IN ACTING UNDER THIS POWER OF ATTORNEY. STRIKE THROUGH AND INITIAL THE NEXT SENTENCE IF YOU DO NOT WANT YOUR AGENT TO ALSO BE ENTITLED TO REASONABLE COMPENSATION FOR SERVICES AS AGENT.

5. (   )   My agent is entitled to reasonable compensation for services rendered as agent under this power of attorney.

THIS POWER OF ATTORNEY MAY BE AMENDED IN ANY MANNER OR REVOKED BY YOU AT ANY TIME. ABSENT AMENDMENT OR REVOCATION, THE AUTHORITY GRANTED IN THIS POWER OF ATTORNEY IS EFFECTIVE WHEN THIS POWER OF ATTORNEY IS SIGNED AND CONTINUES IN EFFECT UNTIL YOUR DEATH, UNLESS YOU MAKE A LIMITATION ON DURATION BY COMPLETING THE FOLLOWING:

6. This power of attorney terminates on _____
_____ (Insert a future date or event, such as court determination of your disability, when you want this power to terminate prior to your death).

BY RETAINING THE FOLLOWING PARAGRAPH, YOU MAY, BUT ARE NOT REQUIRED TO, NAME YOUR AGENT AS GUARDIAN OF YOUR PERSON OR CONSERVATOR OF YOUR PROPERTY, OR BOTH, IF A COURT PROCEEDING IS BEGUN TO APPOINT A GUARDIAN OR CONSERVATOR, OR BOTH, FOR YOU. THE COURT WILL APPOINT YOUR AGENT AS GUARDIAN OR CONSERVATOR, OR BOTH, IF THE COURT FINDS THAT SUCH APPOINTMENT WILL SERVE YOUR BEST INTERESTS AND WELFARE. STRIKE THROUGH AND INITIAL PARAGRAPH 7 IF YOU DO NOT WANT YOUR AGENT TO ACT AS GUARDIAN OR CONSERVATOR, OR BOTH.

7. (   )   If a guardian of my person or a conservator for my property, or both, are to be appointed, I nominate the agent acting under this power of attorney as such guardian or conservator, or both, to serve without bond or security.

IF YOU WITH TO NAME SUCCESSOR AGENTS, INSERT THE NAME AND ADDRESS OF ANY SUCCESSOR AGENT IN THE FOLLOWING PARAGRAPH:

8. If any agent named by me shall die, become incapacitated, resign, or refuse to accept the office of agent, I name the following each to act alone and successively, in the order named, as successor to such agent:

_____

_____

For purposes of this paragraph 8, a person is considered to be incapacitated if and while the person is a minor or a person adjudicated incapacitated or if the person is unable to give prompt and intelligent consideration to business matters, as certified by a licensed physician.

I agree that any third party who receives a copy of this document may act under it. Revocation of the power of attorney is not effective as to a third party until the third party learns of the revocation. I agree to indemnify the third party for any claims that arise against the third party because of reliance on this power of attorney.

Signed on _____, _____.

IF THERE IS ANYTHING ABOUT THIS FORM THAT YOU DO NOT UNDERSTAND, IT MAY BE IN YOUR BEST INTEREST TO CONSULT A COLORADO LAWYER RATHER THAN SIGN THIS FORM.

_____
(Your signature)

_____
(Your social security number)

YOU MAY, BUT ARE NOT REQUIRED TO, REQUEST YOUR AGENT AND SUCCESSOR AGENTS TO PRO-VIDE SPECIMEN SIGNATURES BELOW. IF YOU INCLUDE SPECIMEN SIGNATURES IN THIS POWER OF ATTORNEY, YOU MUST COMPLETE THE CERTIFICATION OPPOSITE THE SIGNATURES OF THE AGENTS.

NOTICE TO AGENTS: BY EXERCISING POWERS UNDER THIS DOCUMENT, THE AGENT ASSUMES THE FIDU-CIARY AND OTHER LEGAL RESPONSIBILITIES OF AN AGENT UNDER COLORADO LAW.

Specimen signatures of agent (and successors)	I certify that the signatures of my agent (and successors) are correct.
_____ Agent	_____ Principal
_____ Successor Agent	_____ Principal
_____ Successor Agent	_____ Principal

STATE OF COLORADO   )
) ss.
COUNTY OF _____)

This document was acknowledged before me on _____ (date) by_____
_____ (name of principal). (,who certifies the correctness of the sig-nature(s) of the agent(s).) My commission expires: _____

_____
Notary public

CONNECTICUT STATUTORY SHORT FORM DURABLE POWER OF ATTORNEY

Notice: The powers granted by this document are broad and sweeping. They are defined in Connecticut Statutory Short Form Power of Attorney Act, section 1-42 to 1-56, inclusive, of the general statutes, which expressly permits the use of any other or different form of power of attorney desired by the parties concerned. The grantor of any power of attorney or the attorney-in-fact may make application to a court of probate for an accounting as provided in subsection (b) of section 45a-175.

Know All Men by These Presents, which are intended to constitute a GENERAL POWER OF ATTORNEY pursuant to Connecticut Statutory Short Form Power of Attorney Act:

That I _____
_____(insert name and address of the principal)
do hereby appoint _____
_____
_____ (insert name and address of the agent, or each agents, if more than one is designated) my attorney(s)-in-fact TO ACT _____.

If more than one agent is designated and the principal wishes each agent alone to be able to exercise the power conferred, insert in the blank the word "severally". Failure to make any insertion or the insertion of the word "jointly" shall require the agents to act jointly.

First: In my name, place and stead in any way which I myself could do, if I were personally present, with respect to the following matters as each of them is defined in the Connecticut Statutory Short Form Power of Attorney Act to the extent that I am permitted by law to act through an agent:

(Strike out and initial in the opposite box any one or more of the subdivisions as to which the principal does NOT desire to give the agent authority. Such elimination of any one or more of subdivisions (A) to (L), inclusive, shall automatically constitute an elimination also of subdivision (M).

To strike out any subdivision the principal must draw a line through the test of that subdivision AND write his initial in the box opposite.

(A) real estate transactions;.. (   )
(B) chattel and goods transactions;... (   )
(C) bond, share and commodity transactions;............................... (   )
(D) banking transactions;... (   )
(E) business operating transactions;... (   )
(F) insurance transactions;.. (   )
(G) estate transactions;... (   )
(H) claims and litigation;.. (   )
(I) personal relationships and affairs;.. (   )

(J) benefits from military service;... (   )

(K) records, reports and statements;.. (   )

(L) health care decisions;... (   )

(M) all other matters;... (   ):

_____

_____

(Special provisions and limitations may be included in the statutory short form power of attorney only if they conform to the requirements of the Connecticut Statutory Short Form Power of Attorney Act.)

Second: With full and unqualified authority to delegate any or all of the foregoing powers to any person or persons whom my attorney(s)-in-fact shall select;

Third: Hereby ratifying and confirming all that said attorney(s) or substitute(s) do or cause to be done.

IN WITNESS WHEREOF I have hereunto signed my name and affixed my seal this _____ day of _____, _____.

_____ (Signature of Principal) (Seal)

On the date written above, _____ declared to us that this instrument was [his/her] durable power of attorney, and requested us to act as witnesses to it. [He/She] signed it in our presence, all of us being present at the same time. We now sign this instrument as witnesses.

_____, Witness   _____

_____, Witness   _____

ACKNOWLEDGMENT

State of _____

County of _____

The foregoing instrument was acknowledged before me this _____ by _____.

_____(Signature)

Title or Rank_____

Serial No. if any_____

ADVANCE HEALTH-CARE DIRECTIVE

EXPLANATION

You have the right to give instructions about your own health care. You also have the right to name someone else to make health-care decisions for you. This form lets you do either or both of these things. It also lets you express your wishes regarding anatomical gifts and the designation of your primary physician. If you use this form, you may complete or modify all or any part of it. You are free to use a different form.

Part 1 of this form is a power of attorney for health care. Part 1 lets you name another individual as agent to make health-care decisions for you if you become incapable of making your own decisions. You may also name an alternate agent to act for you if your first choice is not willing, able or reasonably available to make decisions for you. Unless related to you, an agent may not have a controlling interest in or be an operator or employee of a residential long-term health-care institution at which you are receiving care. If you do not have a qualifying condition (terminal illness/injury or permanent unconsciousness), your agent may make all health-care decisions for you except for decisions providing, withholding or withdrawing of a life sustaining procedure. Unless you limit the agent's authority, your agent will have the right to:

(a) Consent or refuse consent to any care, treatment, service or procedure to maintain, diagnose or otherwise affect a physical or mental condition unless it's a life-sustaining procedure or otherwise required by law.

(b) Select or discharge health-care providers and health-care institutions;

If you have a qualifying condition, your agent may make all health-care decisions for you, including, but not limited to:

(c) The decisions listed in (a) and (b).

(d) Consent or refuse consent to life sustaining procedures, such as, but not limited to, cardiopulmonary resuscitation and orders not to resuscitate.

(e) Direct the providing, withholding or withdrawal of artificial nutrition and hydration and all other forms of health care.

Part 2 of this form lets you give specific instructions about any aspect of your health care. Choices are provided for you to express your wishes regarding the provision, withholding or withdrawal of treatment to keep you alive, including the provision of artificial nutrition and hydration as well as the provision of pain relief. Space is also provided for you to add to the choices you have made or for you to write out any additional instructions for other than end of life decisions.

Part 3 of this form lets you express an intention to donate your bodily organs and tissues following your death.

Part 4 of this form lets you designate a physician to have primary responsibility for your health care.

After completing this form, sign and date the form at the end. It is required that 2 other individuals sign as witnesses. Give a copy of the signed and completed form to your physician, to any other health-care providers you may have, to any health-care institution at which you are receiving care and to any health-care agents you have named. You should talk to the person you have named as agent to make sure that the person understands your wishes and is willing to take the responsibility.

You have the right to revoke this advance health-care directive or replace this form at any time.

* * * * * * * * * * * * * * * * * * *

PART 1: POWER OF ATTORNEY FOR HEALTH CARE

(1) DESIGNATION OF AGENT: I designate the following individual as my agent to make health-care decisions for me:

_____

(name of individual you choose as agent)

(address)	(city)	(state)	(zip code)

(home phone)	(work phone)

OPTIONAL: If I revoke my agent's authority or if my agent is not willing, able or reasonably available to make a health-care decision for me, I designate as my first alternate agent:

_____
(name of individual you choose as first alternate agent)

(address)	(city)	(state)	(zip code)

(home phone)	(work phone)

OPTIONAL: If I revoke the authority of my agent and first alternate agent or if neither is willing, able or reasonably available to make a health-care decision for me, I designate as my second alternate agent:

_____
(name of individual you choose as second alternate agent)

(address)	(city)	(state)	(zip code)

(home phone)	(work phone)

(2) AGENT'S AUTHORITY: If I am not in a qualifying condition my agent is authorized to make all health-care decisions for me, except decisions about life-sustaining procedures and as I state here; and if I am in a qualifying condition, my agent is authorized to make all health-care decisions for me, except as I state here:

_____
_____
_____
(Add additional sheets if needed.)

(3) WHEN AGENT'S AUTHORITY BECOMES EFFECTIVE: My agent's authority becomes effective when my primary physician determines I lack the capacity to make my own health-care decisions. As to decisions concerning the providing, withholding and withdrawal of life-sustaining procedures my agent's authority becomes effective when my primary physician determines I lack the capacity to make my own health-care decisions and my primary physician and another physician determine that I am in a terminal condition or permanently unconscious.

(4) AGENT'S OBLIGATIONS: My agent shall make health-care decisions for me in accordance with this power of attorney for health care, any instructions I give in Part 2 of this form, and my other wishes to the extent known to my agent. To the extent my wishes are unknown, my agent shall make health-care decisions for me in accordance with what my agent determines to be in my best interest. In determining my best interest, my agent shall consider my personal values to the extent known to my agent.

(5) NOMINATION OF GUARDIAN: If a guardian of my person needs to be appointed for me by a court, (please check one):

      [   ]   I nominate the agent(s) whom I named in this form in the order designated to act as guardian.

[   ]   I nominate the following to be guardian in the order designated:

_____

_____

[   ]   I do not nominate anyone to be guardian.

PART 2. INSTRUCTIONS FOR HEALTH CARE

If you are satisfied to allow your agent to determine what is best for you in making end-of-life decisions, you need not fill out this part of the form. If you do fill out this part of the form, you may strike any wording you do not want.

(6) END-OF-LIFE DECISIONS: If I am in a qualifying condition, I direct that my health-care providers and others involved in my care provide, withhold, or withdraw treatment in accordance with the choice I have marked below:

Choice Not To Prolong Life

I do not want my life to be prolonged if: (please check all that apply)

_____   (i)   I have a terminal condition (an incurable condition caused by injury, disease, or illness which, to a reasonable degree of medical certainty, makes death imminent and from which, despite the application of life-sustaining procedures, there can be no recovery) and regarding artificial nutrition and hydration,

I make the following specific directions:	I want used	I do not want used
Artificial nutrition through a conduit	_____	_____
Hydration through a conduit	_____	_____

_____(ii)   I become permanently unconscious (a medical condition that has been diagnosed in accordance with currently accepted medical standards that has lasted at least 4 weeks and with reasonable medical certainty as total and irreversible loss of consciousness and capacity for interaction with the environment. The term includes, without limitation, a persistent vegetative state or irreversible coma) and regarding artificial nutrition and hydration,

I make the following specific directions:	I want used	I do not want used
Artificial nutrition through a conduit	_____	_____
Hydration through a conduit	_____	_____

Choice To Prolong Life

_____   I want my life to be prolonged as long as possible within the limits of generally accepted health-care standards.

RELIEF FROM PAIN: Except as I state in the following space, I direct treatment for alleviation of pain or discomfort be provided at all times, even if it hastens my death: _____

_____

_____

(7) OTHER MEDICAL INSTRUCTIONS: (If you do not agree with any of the optional choices above and wish to write you own, or if you wish to add to the instructions you have given above, you may do so here.) I direct that:

_____

_____

(Add additional sheets if necessary.)

PART 3: ANATOMICAL GIFTS AT DEATH

(OPTIONAL)

(8) I am mentally competent and 18 years or more of age.

I hereby make this anatomical gift to take effect upon my death. The marks in the appropriate squares and words filled into the blanks below indicate my desires.

I give: [   ] my body;   [   ] any needed organs or parts;

           [   ] the following organs or parts: _____

To the following person or institutions:

           [   ] the physician in attendance at my death;

           [   ] the hospital in which I die;

           [   ] the following named physician, hospital, storage bank or other medical institution:

_____

           [   ] the following individual for treatment:

_____

for the following purposes: [   ] any purpose authorized by law;   [   ] transplantation;

           [   ] therapy;   [   ] research;   [   ] medical education.

PART 4:. PRIMARY PHYSICIAN

(9) I designate the following physician as my primary physician:

_____

(name of physician)   (phone)

_____

(address)   (city)   (state)   (zip code)

OPTIONAL: If the physician I have designated above is not willing, able or reasonably available to act as my primary physician, I designate the following physician as my primary physician:

_____

(name of physician)   (phone)

_____

(address)   (city)   (state)   (zip code)

Primary Physician shall mean a physician designated by an individual or the individual's agent or guardian, to have primary responsibility for the individual's health care or, in the absence of a designation or if the designated physician is not reasonably available, a physician who undertakes the responsibility.

                  *

(10)   EFFECT OF COPY: A copy of this form has the same effect as the original.

(11)   SIGNATURE: Sign and date the form here: I understand the purposes and effect of this document.

_____   _____

(date)   (sign your name)

_____   _____

(address)   (print your name)

_____

(city)   (state)   (zip code)

(12) SIGNATURE OF WITNESSES:

Statement Of Witnesses

SIGNED AND DECLARED by the above-named declarant as and for his/her written declaration under 16 Del.C. §§ 2502 and 2503, in our presence, who in his/her presence, at his/her request, and in the presence of each other, have hereunto subscribed our names as witnesses, and state:

A. That the Declarant is mentally competent.
B. That neither of them:
   1. Is related to the declarant by blood, marriage or adoption;
   2. Is entitled to any portion of the estate of the declarant under any will of the declarant or codicil thereto then existing nor, at the time of the executing of the advance health care directive, is so entitled by operation of law then existing;
   3. Has, at the time of the execution of the advance health-care directive, a present or inchoate claim against any portion of the estate of the declarant;
   4. Has a direct financial responsibility for the declarant's medical care;
   5. Has a controlling interest in or is an operator or an employee of a residential long-term health-care institution in which the declarant is a resident; or
   6. Is under eighteen years of age.
C. That if the declarant is a resident of a sanitarium, rest home, nursing home, boarding home or related institution, one of the witnesses, _____, is at the time of the execution of the advance health-care directive, a patient advocate or ombudsman designated by the Division of Services for Aging and Adults with Physical Disabilities or the Public Guardian.

First witness	Second witness
_____	_____
(print name)	(print name)
_____	_____
(address)	(address)
_____ (state)	_____ (state)
(city)	(city)
_____	_____
(signature of witness)	(signature of witness)
_____	_____
(date)	(date)

POWER OF ATTORNEY FOR HEALTH CARE

INFORMATION ABOUT THIS DOCUMENT

THIS IS AN IMPORTANT LEGAL DOCUMENT. BEFORE SIGNING THIS DOCUMENT, IT IS VITAL FOR YOU TO KNOW AND UNDERSTAND THESE FACTS:

THIS DOCUMENT GIVES THE PERSON YOU NAME AS YOUR ATTORNEY IN FACT THE POWER TO MAKE HEALTH-CARE DECISIONS FOR YOU IF YOU CANNOT MAKE THE DECISIONS FOR YOURSELF.

AFTER YOU HAVE SIGNED THIS DOCUMENT, YOU HAVE THE RIGHT TO MAKE HEALTH-CARE DECISIONS FOR YOURSELF IF YOU ARE MENTALLY COMPETENT TO DO SO. IN ADDITION, AFTER YOU HAVE SIGNED THIS DOCUMENT, NO TREATMENT MAY BE GIVEN TO YOU OR STOPPED OVER YOUR OBJECTION IF YOU ARE MENTALLY COMPETENT TO MAKE THAT DECISION.

YOU MAY STATE IN THIS DOCUMENT ANY TYPE OF TREATMENT THAT YOU DO NOT DESIRE AND ANY THAT YOU WANT TO MAKE SURE YOU RECEIVE.

YOU HAVE THE RIGHT TO TAKE AWAY THE AUTHORITY OF YOUR ATTORNEY IN FACT, UNLESS YOU HAVE BEEN ADJUDICATED INCOMPETENT, BY NOTIFYING YOUR ATTORNEY IN FACT OR HEALTH-CARE PROVIDER EITHER ORALLY OR IN WRITING. SHOULD YOU REVOKE THE AUTHORITY OF YOUR ATTORNEY IN FACT, IT IS ADVISABLE TO REVOKE IN WRITING AND TO PLACE COPIES OF THE REVOCATION WHEREVER THIS DOCUMENT IS LOCATED.

IF THERE IS ANYTHING IN THIS DOCUMENT THAT YOU DO NOT UNDERSTAND, YOU SHOULD ASK A SOCIAL WORKER, LAWYER, OR OTHER PERSON TO EXPLAIN IT TO YOU.

* * * * *

YOU SHOULD KEEP A COPY OF THIS DOCUMENT AFTER YOU HAVE SIGNED IT. GIVE A COPY TO THE PERSON YOU NAME AS YOUR ATTORNEY IN FACT. IF YOU ARE IN A HEALTH-CARE FACILITY, A COPY OF THIS DOCUMENT SHOULD BE INCLUDED IN YOUR MEDICAL RECORD.

I, _____, hereby appoint:

_____	_____
name	home address
_____	_____
home telephone number	
_____	_____
work telephone number	

as my attorney in fact to make health-care decisions for me if I become unable to make my own health-care decisions. This gives my attorney in fact the power to grant, refuse, or withdraw consent on my behalf for any health-care service, treatment or procedure. My attorney in fact also has the authority to talk to health-care personnel, get information and sign forms necessary to carry out these decisions.

If the person named as my attorney in fact is not available or is unable to act as my attorney in fact, I appoint the following persons to serve in the order listed below:

1.

_____	_____
name	home address
_____	_____
home telephone number	
_____	_____
work telephone number	

2.

_____	_____
name	home address
_____	_____
home telephone number	
_____	_____
work telephone number	

With this document, I intend to create a power of attorney for health care, which shall take effect if I become incapable of making my own health-care decisions and shall continue during that incapacity.

My attorney in fact shall make health-care decisions as I direct below or as I make known to my attorney in fact in some other way.

(a) STATEMENT OF DIRECTIVES CONCERNING LIFE-PROLONGING CARE, TREATMENT, SERVICES, AND PROCEDURES:

_____
_____
_____

(b) SPECIAL PROVISIONS AND LIMITATIONS:

_____
_____
_____

BY MY SIGNATURE I INDICATE THAT I UNDERSTAND THE PURPOSE AND EFFECT OF THIS DOCUMENT.

I sign my name to this form on _____
(date)

at:_____ (address).

_____
(Signature)

WITNESSES

I declare that the person who signed or acknowledged this document is personally known to me, that the person signed or acknowledged this durable power of attorney for health care in my presence, and that the person appears to be of sound mind and under no duress, fraud, or undue influence. I am not the person appointed as the attorney in fact by this document, nor am I the health-care provider of the principal or an employee of the health-care provider of the principal.

First Witness

Signature:_____
Home Address:_____
Print Name:_____
Date:_____

Second Witness

Signature:_____
Home Address:_____
Print Name:_____
Date:_____

(AT LEAST 1 OF THE WITNESSES LISTED ABOVE SHALL ALSO SIGN THE FOLLOWING DECLARATION.)

I further declare that I am not related to the principal by blood, marriage or adoption, and, to the best of my knowledge, I am not entitled to any part of the estate of the principal under a currently existing will or by operation of law.

Signature:_____

Signature:_____

DESIGNATION OF HEALTH CARE SURROGATE

Name:(Last)_____(First)_____(Middle Initial)_____

In the event that I have been determined to be incapacitated to provide informed consent for medical treatment and surgical and diagnostic procedures, I wish to designate as my surrogate for health care decisions:

Name:_____

Address:_____

_____ Zip Code:_____

Phone:_____

If my surrogate is unwilling or unable to perform his duties, I wish to designate as my alternate surrogate:

Name:_____

Address:_____

_____ Zip Code:_____

Phone:_____

I fully understand that this designation will permit my designee to make health care decisions and to provide, withhold, or withdraw consent on my behalf; to apply for public benefits to defray the cost of health care; and to authorize my admission to or transfer from a health care facility.

Additional instructions (optional):_____

_____

_____

I further affirm that this designation is not being made as a condition of treatment or admission to a health care facility. I will notify and send a copy of this document to the following persons other than my surrogate, so they may know who my surrogate is.

Name(s):_____

_____

_____

Signed: _____

Date: _____

Witnesses: 1. _____

              2. _____

FINANCIAL POWER OF ATTORNEY

County of _____

State of Georgia

I, _____, (hereinafter "Principal"), a resident of
_____ County, Georgia, do hereby constitute and appoint
_____ my true and lawful attorney-in-fact (hereinafter
"Agent") for me and give such person the power(s) specified below to act in my name, place,
and stead in any way which I, myself, could do if I were personally present with respect to
the following matters:

(Directions: To give the Agent the powers described in paragraphs 1 through 13, place your initials on the blank line at the end of each paragraph. If you DO NOT want to give a power to
the Agent, strike through the paragraph or a line within the paragraph and place your initials
beside the stricken paragraph or stricken line. The powers described in any paragraph not initialed or which has been struck through will not be conveyed to the Agent. Both the Principal
and the Agent must sign their full names at the end of the last paragraph.)

1. **Bank and Credit Union Transactions:** To make, receive, sign, endorse, execute, acknowledge, deliver, and possess checks, drafts, bills of exchange, letters of credit, notes, stock certificates, withdrawal receipts and deposit instruments relating to accounts or deposits in, or
certificates of deposit of banks, savings and loans, credit unions, or other institutions or associations. _____

2. **Payment Transactions:** To pay all sums of money, at any time or times, that may hereafter be owing by me upon any account, bill of exchange, check, draft, purchase, contract,
note, or trade acceptance made, executed, endorsed, accepted, and delivered by me or for me
in my name, by my Agent. _____

3. **Real Property Transactions:** To lease, sell, mortgage, purchase, exchange, and acquire,
and to agree, bargain, and contract for the lease, sale, purchase, exchange, and acquisition of,
and to accept, take, receive, and possess any interest in real property whatsoever, on such
terms and conditions, and under such covenants, as my Agent shall deem proper; and to
maintain, repair, tear down, alter, rebuild, improve, manage, insure, move, rent, lease,, sell,
convey, subject to liens, mortgages, and security deeds, and in any way or manner deal with
all or any part of any interest in real property whatsoever, including specifically, but without
limitation, real property lying and being situate in the State of Georgia, under such terms
and conditions, and under such covenants, as my Agent shall deem proper and may for all
deferred payments accept purchase money notes payable to me and secured by mortgages or
deeds to secure debt, and may from time to time collect and cancel any of said notes, mortgages, security interests, or deeds to secure debt. _____

4. **Personal Property Transactions:** To lease, sell, mortgage, purchase, exchange, and
acquire, and to agree, bargain, and contract for the lease, sale, purchase, exchange, and acquisition of, and to accept, take, receive, and possess any personal property whatsoever, tangible
or intangible, or interest thereto, on such terms and conditions, and under such covenants, as
my Agent shall deem proper; and to maintain, repair, improve, manage, insure, rent, lease,

99

sell, convey, subject to liens or mortgages, or to take any other security interests in said property which are recognized under the Uniform Commercial Code as adopted at that time under the laws of Georgia or any applicable state, or otherwise hypothecate, and in any way or manner deal with all or any part of any real or personal property whatsoever, tangible or intangible, or any interest therein, that I own at the time of execution or may thereafter acquire, under such terms and conditions, and under such covenants, as my Agent shall deem proper. _____

5. **Stock and Bond Transactions:** To purchase, sell, exchange, surrender, assign, redeem, vote at any meeting, or otherwise transfer any and all shares of stock, bonds, or other securities in any business, association, corporation, partnership, or other legal entity, whether private or public, now or hereafter belonging to me. _____

6. **Safe Deposits:** To have free access at any time or times to any safe deposit box or vault to which I might have access. _____

7. **Borrowing:** To borrow from time to time such sums of money as my Agent may deem proper and execute promissory notes, security deeds or agreements, financing statements, or other security instruments in such form as the leader may request and renew said notes and security instruments from time to time in whole or in part. _____

8. **Business Operating Transactions:** To conduct, engage in, and otherwise transact the affairs of any and all lawful business ventures of whatever nature or kind that I may now or hereafter be involved in. _____

9. **Insurance Transactions:** To exercise or perform any act, power, duty, right, or obligation, in regard to any contract of life, accident, health, disability, liability, or other type of insurance or any combination of insurance; and to procure new or additional contracts of insurance to me to designate the beneficiary of same; provided, however, that my Agent cannot designate himself or herself as beneficiary of any such insurance contracts. _____

10. **Disputes and Proceedings:** To commence, prosecute, discontinue, or defend all actions or other legal proceedings touching my property, real or personal, or any part there or touching any matter in which I or my property, real or personal, may be in any way concerned. To defend, settle, adjust, make allowances, compound, submit to arbitration, and compromise all accounts, reckonings, claims, and demands whatsoever that now are, or hereafter shall be, pending between me and any person, firm, corporation, or other legal entity, in such manner and in all respects as my Agent shall deem proper. _____

11. **Hiring Representatives:** To hire accountants, attorneys at law, consultants, clerks, physicians, nurses, agents, servants, workmen, and others and to remove them, and to appoint others in their place, and to pay and allow the persons so employed such salaries, wages, or other remunerations, as my Agent shall deem proper. _____

12. **Tax, Social Security, and Unemployment:** To prepare, to make elections, to execute and to file all tax, social security, unemployment insurance, and informational returns required by the laws of the United States, or of any state or subdivision thereof, or of any foreign government; to prepare, to execute, and to file all other papers and instruments which the Agent

shall think to be desirable or necessary for safeguarding of me against excess or illegal taxation or against penalties imposed for claimed violation of any law or other governmental regulation; and to pay, to compromise, or to contest or to apply for refunds in connection with any taxes or assessments for which I am or may be liable. _____

13. Broad Powers: Without, in any way, limiting the foregoing, generally to do, execute, and perform any other act, deed, matter, or thing whatsoever, that should be done, executed, or performed, including but not limited to, powers conferred by Code Section 53-12-232 of the Official Code of Georgia Annotated, or that in the opinion of my Agent, should be done, executed, or performed, for my benefit or the benefit of my property, real or personal, and in my name of every nature and kind whatsoever, as fully and effectually as I could do if personally present. _____

14. Effective Date: This document will become effective upon the date of the Principal's signature unless the Principal indicates that it should become effective at a later date by completing the following, which is optional.

The powers conveyed in this document shall not become effective until the following time or upon the occurrence of the following event or contingency:

_____

_____

Note: The Principal may choose to designate one or more persons to determine conclusively that the above-specified event or contingency has occurred. Such person or persons must make a written declaration under penalty of false swearing that such event or contingency has occurred in order to make this document effective. Completion of this provision is optional.

The following person or persons are designated to determine conclusively that the above-specified event or contingency has occurred:

_____

_____

Signed: _____

Principal

_____

Agent

It is my desire and intention that this power of attorney shall not be affected by my subsequent disability, incapacity, or mental incompetence.

Any and all acts done by the Agent pursuant to the powers conveyed herein during any period of my disability or incapacity shall have the same force and effect as if I were competent and not disabled.

I may, at any time, revoke this power of attorney, but it shall be deemed to be in full force and effect as to all persons, institutions, and organizations which shall act in reliance thereon prior to the receipt of written revocation thereof signed by me and prior to receipt of actual notice of my death.

I do hereby ratify and confirm all acts whatsoever which my Agent shall do, or cause to be done, in or about the premises, by virtue of this power of attorney.

All parties dealing in good faith with my Agent may fully rely upon the power of and authority of my Agent to act for me on my behalf and in my name, and may accept and relay on agreements and other instruments entered into or executed by the agent pursuant to this power of attorney.

This instrument shall not be effective as a grant of powers to my Agent until my Agent has executed the Acceptance of Appointment appearing at the end of this instrument. This instrument shall remain effective until revocation by me or my death, whichever occurs first.

Compensation of Agent. (Directions: Initial the line following your choice.)

1. My Agent shall receive no compensation for services rendered. _____

2. My Agent shall receive reasonable compensation for services rendered. _____

3. My Agent shall receive $_____ for services rendered. _____

IN WITNESS WHEREOF, I have hereunto set my hand and seal on this _____ day of _____, _____.

_____
Principal

WITNESSES

_____   _____

_____   _____
Signature and Address   Signature and Address

Note: A notarized signature is not required unless you have initialed paragraph 3 or 4 regarding property transactions.

I, _____, a Notary Public, do hereby certify that _____ personally appeared before me this date and acknowledged the due execution of the foregoing Power of Attorney.

_____
Notary Public

State of Georgia

County of _____

ACCEPTANCE OF APPOINTMENT

I, _____ (print name), have read the foregoing Power of Attorney and am the person identified therein as Agent for _____ _____ (name of grantor of power of attorney), the Principal named therein. I hereby acknowledge the following:

I owe a duty of loyalty and good faith to the Principal, and must use the powers granted to me only for the benefit of the Principal.

I must keep the Principal's funds and other assets separate and apart from my funds and other assets and titled in the name of the Principal. I must not transfer title to any of the Principal's funds or other assets into my name alone. My name must not be added to the title of any funds or other assets of the Principal, unless I am specifically designated as Agent for the Principal in the title.

I must protect and conserve, and exercise prudence and caution in my dealings with, the Principal's funds and other assets.

I must keep a full and accurate record of my acts, receipts, and disbursements on behalf of the Principal, and be ready to account to the Principal for such acts, receipts, and disbursements at all times. I must provide an annual accounting to the Principal of my acts, receipts, and disbursements, and must furnish an accounting of such acts, receipts, and disbursements to the personal representative of the Principal's estate within 90 days after the date of death of the Principal.

I have read the compensation of Agent paragraph in the Power of Attorney and agree to abide by it.

I acknowledge my authority to act on behalf of the Principal ceases at the death of the Principal.

I hereby accept the foregoing appointment as Agent for the Principal with full knowledge of the responsibilities imposed on me, and I will faithfully carry out my duties to the best of my ability.

Dated: _____

(Signature) _____

(Address) _____

Note: A notarized signature is not required unless the Principal initialed paragraph 3 or paragraph 4 regarding property transactions.

I, _____, a Notary Public, do hereby certify that _____ personally appeared before me this date and acknowledged the due execution of the foregoing Acceptance of Appointment.

_____
Notary Public

GEORGIA STATUTORY SHORT FORM DURABLE POWER
OF ATTORNEY FOR HEALTH CARE

NOTICE: THE PURPOSE OF THIS POWER OF ATTORNEY IS TO GIVE THE PERSON YOU DESIGNATE (YOUR AGENT) BROAD POWERS TO MAKE HEALTH CARE DECISIONS FOR YOU, INCLUDING POWER TO REQUIRE, CONSENT TO, OR WITHDRAW ANY TYPE OF PERSONAL CARE OR MEDICAL TREATMENT FOR ANY PHYSICAL OR MENTAL CONDITION AND TO ADMIT YOU TO OR DISCHARGE YOU FROM ANY HOSPITAL, HOME, OR OTHER INSTITUTION; BUT NOT INCLUDING PSYCHOSURGERY, STERILIZATION, OR INVOLUNTARY HOSPITALIZATION OR TREATMENT COVERED BY TITLE 37 OF THE OFFICIAL CODE OF GEORGIA ANNOTATED. THIS FORM DOES NOT IMPOSE A DUTY ON YOUR AGENT TO EXERCISE GRANTED POWERS; BUT, WHEN A POWER IS EXERCISED, YOUR AGENT WILL HAVE TO USE DUE CARE TO ACT FOR YOUR BENEFIT AND IN ACCORDANCE WITH THIS FORM. A COURT CAN TAKE AWAY THE POWERS OF YOUR AGENT IF IT FINDS THE AGENT IS NOT ACTING PROPERLY. YOU MAY NAME COAGENTS AND SUCCESSOR AGENTS UNDER THIS FORM, BUT YOU MAY NOT NAME A HEALTH CARE PROVIDER WHO MAY BE DIRECTLY OR INDIRECTLY INVOLVED IN RENDERING HEALTH CARE TO YOU UNDER THIS POWER. UNLESS YOU EXPRESSLY LIMIT THE DURATION OF THIS POWER IN THE MANNER PROVIDED BELOW OR UNTIL YOU REVOKE THIS POWER OR A COURT ACTING ON YOUR BEHALF TERMINATES IT, YOUR AGENT MAY EXERCISE THE POWERS GIVEN IN THE POWER THROUGHOUT YOUR LIFETIME, EVEN AFTER YOU BECOME DISABLED, INCAPACITATED, OR INCOMPETENT. THE POWERS YOU GIVE YOUR AGENT, YOUR RIGHT TO REVOKE THOSE POWERS, AND THE PENALTIES FOR VIOLATING THE LAW ARE EXPLAINED MORE FULLY IN CODE SECTIONS 31-36-6, 31-36-9, AND 31-36-10 OF THE GEORGIA 'DURABLE POWER OF ATTORNEY FOR HEALTH CARE ACT' OF WHICH THIS FORM IS A PART (SEE THE BACK OF THIS FORM). THAT ACT EXPRESSLY PERMITS THE USE OF ANY DIFFERENT FORM OF POWER OF ATTORNEY YOU MAY DESIRE. IF THERE IS ANYTHING ABOUT THIS FORM THAT YOU DO NOT UNDERSTAND, YOU SHOULD ASK A LAWYER TO EXPLAIN IT TO YOU.

DURABLE POWER OF ATTORNEY made this _____ day of _____, _____.

1. I, _____

(insert name and address of principal)

hereby appoint _____

(insert name and address of agent)

as my attorney in fact (my agent) to act for me and in my name in any way I could act in person to make any and all decisions for me concerning my personal care, medical treatment, hospitalization, and health care and to require, withhold, or withdraw any type of medical treatment or procedure, even though my death may ensue. My agent shall have the same access to my medical records that I have, including the right to disclose the contents to others. My agent shall also have full power to make a disposition of any part or all of my body for medical purposes, authorize an autopsy of my body, and direct the disposition of my remains.

THE ABOVE GRANT OF POWER IS INTENDED TO BE AS BROAD AS POSSIBLE SO THAT YOUR AGENT WILL HAVE AUTHORITY TO MAKE ANY DECISION YOU COULD MAKE TO OBTAIN OR TERMINATE ANY TYPE OF HEALTH CARE, INCLUDING WITHDRAWAL OF NOURISHMENT AND FLUIDS AND OTHER LIFE-SUSTAINING OR DEATH-DELAYING MEASURES, IF YOUR AGENT BELIEVES SUCH ACTION WOULD BE CONSISTENT WITH YOUR INTENT AND DESIRES. IF YOU WISH TO LIMIT THE SCOPE OF YOUR AGENT'S POWERS OR PRESCRIBE SPECIAL RULES TO LIMIT THE POWER TO MAKE AN ANATOMICAL GIFT, AUTHORIZE AUTOPSY, OR DISPOSE OF REMAINS, YOU MAY DO SO IN THE FOLLOWING PARAGRAPHS.

2. The powers granted above shall not include the following powers or shall be subject to the following rules or limitations (here you may include any specific limitations you deem appropriate, such as your own definition of when life-sustaining or death-delaying measures should be withheld; a direction to continue nourishment and fluids or other life-sustaining or death-delaying treatment in all events; or instructions to refuse any specific types of treatment that are inconsistent with your religious beliefs or unacceptable to you for any other reason, such as blood transfusion, electroconvulsive therapy, or amputation):

_____

_____

THE SUBJECT OF LIFE-SUSTAINING OR DEATH-DELAYING TREATMENT IS OF PARTICULAR IMPORTANCE. FOR YOUR CONVENIENCE IN DEALING WITH THAT SUBJECT, SOME GENERAL STATEMENTS CONCERNING THE WITHHOLDING OR REMOVAL OF LIFE-SUSTAINING OR DEATH-DELAYING TREATMENT ARE SET FORTH BELOW. IF YOU AGREE WITH ONE OF THESE STATEMENTS, YOU MAY INITIAL THAT STATEMENT, BUT DO NOT INITIAL MORE THAN ONE:

I do not want my life to be prolonged nor do I want life-sustaining or death-delaying treatment to be provided or continued if my agent believes the burdens of the treatment outweigh the expected benefits. I want my agent to consider the relief of suffering, the expense involved, and the quality as well as the possible extension of my life in making decisions concerning life-sustaining or death-delaying treatment.   Initialed_____

I want my life to be prolonged and I want life-sustaining or death-delaying treatment to be provided or continued unless I am in a coma, including a persistent vegetative state, which my attending physician believes to be irreversible, in accordance with reasonable medical standards at the time of reference. If and when I have suffered such an irreversible coma, I want life-sustaining or death-delaying treatment to be withheld or discontinued.

Initialed_____

I want my life to be prolonged to the greatest extent possible without regard to my condition, the chances I have for recovery, or the cost of the procedures. Initialed_____

THIS POWER OF ATTORNEY MAY BE AMENDED OR REVOKED BY YOU AT ANY TIME AND IN ANY MANNER WHILE YOU ARE ABLE TO DO SO. IN THE ABSENCE OF AN AMENDMENT OR REVOCATION, THE AUTHORITY GRANTED IN THIS POWER OF ATTORNEY WILL BECOME EFFECTIVE AT THE TIME THIS POWER IS SIGNED AND WILL CONTINUE UNTIL YOUR DEATH AND WILL CONTINUE BEYOND YOUR DEATH IF ANATOMICAL GIFT, AUTOPSY, OR DISPOSITION OF REMAINS IS AUTHORIZED, UNLESS A LIMITATION ON THE BEGINNING DATE OR DURATION IS MADE BY INITIALING AND COMPLETING EITHER OR BOTH OF THE FOLLOWING:

3.   (   ) This power of attorney shall become effective on _____
_____(insert a future date or event during your lifetime, such as court determination of your disability, incapacity, or incompetency, when you want this power to first take effect).

4.   (   ) This power of attorney shall terminate on _____
_____(insert a future date or event, such as court determination of your disability, incapacity, or incompetency, when you want this power to terminate prior to your death).

IF YOU WISH TO NAME SUCCESSOR AGENTS, INSERT THE NAMES AND ADDRESSES OF SUCH SUCCESSORS IN THE FOLLOWING PARAGRAPH:

5.   If any agent named by me shall die, become legally disabled, incapacitated, or incompetent, or resign, refuse to act, or be unavailable, I name the following (each to act successively in the order named) as successors to such agent:
_____
_____

IF YOU WISH TO NAME A GUARDIAN OF YOUR PERSON IN THE EVENT A COURT DECIDES THAT ONE SHOULD BE APPOINTED, YOU MAY, BUT ARE NOT REQUIRED TO, DO SO BY INSERTING THE NAME OF SUCH GUARDIAN IN THE FOLLOWING PARAGRAPH. THE COURT WILL APPOINT THE PERSON NOMINATED BY YOU IF THE COURT FINDS THAT SUCH APPOINTMENT WILL SERVE YOUR BEST INTERESTS AND WELFARE. YOU MAY , BUT ARE NOT REQUIRED TO, NOMINATE AS YOUR GUARDIAN THE SAME PERSON NAMED IN THIS FORM AS YOUR AGENT.

6.   If a guardian of my person is to be appointed, I nominate the following to serve as such guardian:
_____

(insert name and address of nominated guardian of the person)

7.   I am fully informed as to all the contents of this form and understand the full import of this grant of powers to my agent.

Signed_____(Principal)

The principal has had an opportunity to read the above form and has signed the above form in our presence. We, the undersigned, each being over 18 years of age, witness the principal's signature at the request and in the presence of the principal, and in the presence of each other, on the day and year above set out.

Witnesses: Addresses:
_____   _____
_____   _____

Additional witness required when health care agency is signed in a hospital or skilled nursing facility.

Witness:_____   Address:_____
          Attending Physician

YOU MAY, BUT ARE NOT REQUIRED TO, REQUEST YOUR AGENT AND SUCCESSOR AGENTS TO PROVIDE SPECIMEN SIGNATURES BELOW. IF YOU INCLUDE SPECIMEN SIGNATURES IN THIS POWER OF ATTORNEY, YOU MUST COMPLETE THE CERTIFICATION OPPOSITE THE SIGNATURES OF THE AGENTS.

Specimen signatures of agent and successor(s)   I certify that the signature of my agent and successor(s) is correct.

_____   _____
          (Agent)   (Principal)

_____   _____
          (Successor agent)   (Principal)

_____   _____
          (Successor agent)   (Principal)

DURABLE POWER OF ATTORNEY FOR HEALTH CARE DECISIONS

A. Statement of Principal

Declaration made this _____ day of _____ (month, year). I, _____ _____, being of sound mind, and understanding that I have the right to request that my life be prolonged to the greatest extent possible, wilfully and voluntarily make known my desire that my attorney-in-fact ("agent") shall be authorized as set forth below and do hereby declare:

My instructions shall prevail even if they create a conflict with the desires of my relatives, hospital policies, or the principles of those providing my care.

CHECKLIST

I have considered the extent of the authority I want my agent to have with respect to health care decisions if I should develop a terminal condition or a permanent loss of the ability to communicate concerning medical treatment decisions with no reasonable chance of regaining this ability. I want my agent to request care, including medicine and procedures, for the purpose of providing comfort and pain relief. I have also considered whether my agent should have the authority to decide whether or not my life should be prolonged, and have selected one of the following provisions by putting a mark in the space provided:

(   ) My agent is authorized to decide whether my life should be prolonged through surgery, resuscitation, life sustaining medicine or procedures, and tube or other artificial feeding or provisions for fluids by a tube.

(   ) My agent is authorized to decide whether my life should be prolonged through tube or other artificial feeding or provisions for fluids by a tube.

If neither provision is selected, it shall be presumed that my agent shall have only the power to request care, including medicine and procedures, for the purpose of providing comfort and pain relief.

This durable power of attorney shall control in all circumstances. I understand that my physician may not act as my agent under this durable power of attorney.

I understand the full meaning of this durable power of attorney and I am emotionally and mentally competent to make this declaration.

Signed_____ Address_____

B. Statement of Witness

I am at least 18 years of age and
___ not related to the principal by blood, marriage, or adoption; and
___ not currently the attending physician, an employee of the attending physician, or an employee of the health care facility in which the principal is a patient.

The principal is personally known to me and I believe the principal to be of sound mind.

Witness_____ Witness_____
Address_____ Address_____

C. Statement of Agent

I am at least 18 years of age, I accept the appointment under this durable power of attorney as the attorney-in-fact ("agent") of the principal, and I am not the physician of the principal. The principal is personally known to me and I believe the principal to be of sound mind.

Agent_____ Address_____

D. Notarization

Subscribed, sworn to and acknowledged before me by _____, the principal, and subscribed and sworn to before me by _____ and _____, witnesses, this _____ day of _____, _____
(SEAL)

Signed_____

_____
(Official capacity of officer)

A Durable Power of Attorney for Health Care

1. DESIGNATION OF HEALTH CARE AGENT. I, _____
_____ (Insert your name and address)
do hereby designate and appoint_____
_____(Insert name, address, and telephone number of one individual only as your agent to make health care decisions for you. None of the following may be designated as your agent: (1) your treating health care provider, (2) a nonrelative employee of your treating health care provider, (3) an operator of a community care facility, or (4) a nonrelative employee of an operator of a community care facility), as my attorney in fact (agent) to make health care decisions for me as authorized in this document. For the purposes of this document, "health care decision" means consent, refusal of consent, or withdrawal of consent to any care, treatment, service, or procedure to maintain, diagnose, or treat an individual's physical condition.

2. CREATION OF DURABLE POWER OF ATTORNEY FOR HEALTH CARE. By this document I intend to create a durable power of attorney for health care. This power of attorney shall not be affected by my subsequent incapacity.

3. GENERAL STATEMENT OF AUTHORITY GRANTED. Subject to any limitations in this document, I hereby grant to my agent full power and authority to make health care decisions for me to the same extent that I could make such decisions for myself if I had the capacity to do so. In exercising this authority, my agent shall make health care decisions that are consistent with my desires as stated in this document or otherwise made known to my agent, including, but not limited to, my desires concerning obtaining or refusing or withdrawing life-prolonging care, treatment, services, and procedures. (If you want to limit the authority of your agent to make health care decisions for you, you can state the limitations in paragraph 4 below. You can indicate your desires by including a statement of your desires in the same paragraph.)

4. STATEMENT OF DESIRES, SPECIAL PROVISIONS, AND LIMITATIONS. (Your agent must make health care decisions that are consistent with your known desires. You can, but are not required to, state your desires in the space provided below. You should consider whether you want to include a statement of your desires concerning life-prolonging care, treatment, services, and procedures. You can also include a statement of your desires concerning other matters relating to your health care. You can also make your desires known to your agent by discussing your desires with your agent or by some other means. If there are any types of treatment that you do not want to be used, you should state them in the space below. If you want to limit in any other way the authority given your agent by this document, you should state the limits in the space below. If you do not state any limits, your agent will have broad powers to make health care decisions for you, except to the extent that there are limits provided by law.)

In exercising the authority under this durable power of attorney for health care, my agent shall act consistently with my desires as stated below and is subject to the special provisions and limitations stated in the living will. Additional statement of desires, special provisions and limitations:_____
_____

(You may attach additional pages if you need more space to complete your statement. If you attach additional pages, you must date and sign each of the additional pages at the same time you date and sign this document.)

5. INSPECTION AND DISCLOSURE OF INFORMATION RELATING TO MY PHYSICAL OR MENTAL HEALTH. Subject to any limitations in this document, my agent has the power and authority to do all of the following:

(a) Request, review, and receive any information, verbal or written, regarding my physical or mental health, including, but not limited to, medical and hospital records.

(b) Execute on my behalf any releases or other documents that may be required in order to obtain this information.

(c) Consent to the disclosure of this information.

(d) Consent to the donation of any of my organs for medical purposes. (If you want to limit the authority of your agent to receive and disclose information relating to your health, you must state the limitations in paragraph 4 ("Statement of Desires, Special Provisions, and Limitations") above.)

6. SIGNING DOCUMENTS, WAIVERS, AND RELEASES. Where necessary to implement the health care decisions that my agent is authorized by this document to make, my agent has the power and authority to execute on my behalf all of the following:

(a) Documents titled or purporting to be a "Refusal to Permit Treatment" and "Leaving Hospital Against Medical Advice."

(b) Any necessary waiver or release from liability required by a hospital or physician.

7. DESIGNATION OF ALTERNATE AGENTS.
(You are not required to designate any alternate agents but you may do so. Any alternate agent you designate will be able to make the same health care decisions as the agent you designated in paragraph 1, above, in the event that agent is unable or ineligible to act as your agent. If the agent you designated is your spouse, he or she becomes ineligible to act as your agent if your marriage is dissolved.)

If the person designated as my agent in paragraph 1 is not available or becomes ineligible to act as my agent to make a health care decision for me, or loses the mental capacity to make health care decisions for me, or if I revoke that person's appointment or authority to act as my agent to make health care decisions for me, then I designate and appoint the following persons to serve as my agent to make health care decisions for me as authorized in this document, such persons to serve in the order listed below:

A. First Alternate Agent_____
_____(Insert name, address, and telephone number of first alternate agent)
   B. Second Alternate Agent_____
_____(Insert name, address, and telephone number of second alternate agent)

8. PRIOR DESIGNATIONS REVOKED. I revoke any prior durable power of attorney for health care.

DATE AND SIGNATURE OF PRINCIPAL
(You Must Date and Sign This Power of Attorney)

I sign my name to this Statutory Form Durable Power of Attorney for Health Care on _____ (Date) at _____(City) , _____ (State)
_____(You sign here)
(This Power of Attorney will not be valid unless it is signed by two qualified witnesses who are present when you sign or acknowledge your signature. If you have attached any additional pages to this form, you must date and sign each of the additional pages at the same time you date and sign this Power of Attorney.)

STATEMENT OF WITNESSES

(This document must be witnessed by two qualified adult witnesses. None of the following may be used as a witness: (1) a person you designate as your agent or alternate agent, (2) a health care provider, (3) an employee of a health care provider, (4) the operator of a community care facility, (5) employees of an operator of a community care facility. At least one of the witnesses must make the additional declaration set out following the place where the witnesses sign.)

I declare under penalty of perjury under the laws of Idaho that the person who signed or acknowledged this document is personally known to me (proved to me on the basis of convincing evidence) to be the principal, that the principal signed or acknowledged this durable power of attorney in my presence, that the principal appears to be of sound mind and under no duress, fraud, or undue influence, that I am not the person appointed as attorney in fact by this document, and that I am not a health care provider, an employee of a health care provider, the operator of a community care facility, nor an employee of an operator of a community care facility.

Signature: _____   Signature:_____
Print name: _____   Print name:_____
Residence address: _____   Residence address:_____
_____   _____
Date:_____   Date:_____

(At least one of the above witnesses must also sign)

I further declare under penalty of perjury under the laws of Idaho that I am not related to the principal by blood, marriage, or adoption, and to the best of my knowledge, I am not entitled to any part of the estate of the principal upon the death of the principal under a will now existing or by operation of law.

Signature:_____   Signature:_____

NOTARY

(Signer of instrument may either have it witnessed as above or have his/her signature notarized as below, to legalize this instrument.)

State of Idaho
County of _____ ss.

On this _____ day of _____, _____

before me personally appeared_____
                              (full name of signer of instrument)
to me known (or proved to me on basis of satisfactory evidence) to be the person whose name is subscribed to this instrument, and acknowledged that he/she executed it. I declare under penalty of perjury that the person whose name is subscribed to this instrument appears to be of sound mind and under no duress, fraud or undue influence.

_____
(Signature of Notary)

[This page was intentionally left blank. See page 25]

ILLINOIS STATUTORY SHORT FORM POWER OF ATTORNEY FOR PROPERTY

(NOTICE: THE PURPOSE OF THIS POWER OF ATTORNEY IS TO GIVE THE PERSON YOU DESIG-NATE (YOUR "AGENT") BROAD POWERS TO HANDLE YOUR PROPERTY, WHICH MAY INCLUDE POWERS TO PLEDGE, SELL OR OTHERWISE DISPOSE OF ANY REAL OR PERSONAL PROPERTY WITHOUT ADVANCE NOTICE TO YOU OR APPROVAL BY YOU. THIS FORM DOES NOT IMPOSE A DUTY ON YOUR AGENT TO EXERCISE GRANTED POWERS; BUT WHEN POWERS ARE EXER-CISED, YOUR AGENT WILL HAVE TO USE DUE CARE TO ACT FOR YOUR BENEFIT AND IN ACCOR-DANCE WITH THIS FORM AND KEEP A RECORD OF RECEIPTS, DISBURSEMENTS AND SIGNIFI-CANT ACTION TAKEN AS AGENT. A COURT CAN TAKE AWAY THE POWERS OF YOUR AGENT IF IT FINDS THE AGENT IS NOT ACTING PROPERLY. YOU MAY NAME SUCCESSOR AGENTS UNDER THIS FORM BUT NOT CO-AGENTS. UNLESS YOU EXPRESSLY LIMIT THE DURATION OF THIS POWER IN THE MANNER PROVIDED BELOW, UNTIL YOU REVOKE THIS POWER OR A COURT ACTING ON YOUR BEHALF TERMINATES IT, YOUR AGENT MAY EXERCISE THE POWERS GIVEN HERE THROUGHOUT YOUR LIFETIME, EVEN AFTER YOU BECOME DISABLED. THE POWERS YOU GIVE YOUR AGENT ARE EXPLAINED MORE FULLY IN SECTION 3-4 OF THE ILLINOIS "STATUTORY SHORT FORM POWER OF ATTORNEY FOR PROPERTY LAW" OF WHICH THIS FORM IS A PART (SEE THE BACK OF THIS FORM). THAT LAW EXPRESSLY PERMITS THE USE OF ANY DIFFERENT FORM OF POWER OF ATTORNEY YOU MAY DESIRE. IF THERE IS ANYTHING ABOUT THIS FORM THAT YOU DO NOT UNDERSTAND, YOU SHOULD ASK A LAWYER TO EXPLAIN IT TO YOU.)

POWER OF ATTORNEY made this _____ day of _____ (month) _____ (year).

1.   I, _____
_____ (insert name and address of principal)
hereby appoint _____
_____ (insert name and address of agent) as my
attorney-in-fact (my "agent") to act for me and in my name (in any way I could act in person) with respect to the following powers, as defined in Section 3-4 of the "Statutory Short Form Power of Attorney for Property Law" (including all amendments), but subject to any limitation on or additions to the specified powers inserted in paragraph 2 or 3 below:

(YOU MUST STRIKE OUT ANY ONE OR MORE OF THE FOLLOWING CATEGORIES OF POWERS YOU DO NOT WANT YOUR AGENT TO HAVE. FAILURE TO STRIKE THE TITLE OF ANY CATEGORY WILL CAUSE THE POWERS DESCRIBED IN THAT CATEGORY TO BE GRANTED TO THE AGENT. TO STRIKE OUT A CATEGORY YOU MUST DRAW A LINE THROUGH THE TITLE OF THAT CATEGORY.)

(a)   Real estate transactions.
(b)   Financial institution transactions.
(c)   Stock and bond transactions.
(d)   Tangible personal property transactions.
(e)   Safe deposit box transactions.
(f)   Insurance and annuity transactions.
(g)   Retirement plan transactions.
(h)   Social Security, employment and military service benefits.
(i)   Tax matters.
(j)   Claims and litigation.
(k)   Commodity and option transactions.
(l)   Business operations.
(m)   Borrowing transactions.
(n)   Estate transactions.
(o)   All other property powers and transactions.

(LIMITATIONS ON AND ADDITIONS TO THE AGENT'S POWERS MAY BE INCLUDED IN THIS POWER OF ATTORNEY IF THEY ARE SPECIFICALLY DESCRIBED BELOW.)

Illinois Statutory Short Form Power of Attorney for Property Law

§3-4. Explanation of powers granted in the statutory short form power of attorney for property. This Section defines each category of powers listed in the statutory short form power of attorney for property and the effect of granting powers to an agent. When the title of any of the following categories is retained (not struck out) in a statutory property power form, the effect will be to grant the agent all of the principal's rights, powers and discretions with respect to the types of property and transactions covered by the retained category, subject to any limitations on the granted powers that appear on the face of the form. The agent will have authority to exercise each granted power for and in the name of the principal with respect to all of the principal's interests in every type of property or transaction covered by the granted power at the time of exercise, whether the principal's interests are direct or indirect, whole or fractional, legal, equitable or contractual, as a joint tenant or tenant in common or held in any other form; but the agent will not have power under any of the statutory categories (a) through (o) to make gifts of the principal's property, to exercise powers to appoint to others or to change any beneficiary whom the principal has designated to take the principal's interests at death under any will, trust, joint tenancy, beneficiary form or contractual arrangement. The agent will be under no duty to exercise granted powers or to assume control of or responsibility for the principal's property or affairs; but when granted powers are exercised, the agent will be required to use due care to act for the benefit of the principal in accordance with the terms of the statutory property power and will be liable for negligent exercise. The agent may act in person or through others reasonably employed by the agent for that purpose and will have authority to sign and deliver all instruments, negotiate and enter into all agreements and do all other acts reasonably necessary to implement the exercise of the powers granted to the agent.

(a) Real estate transactions. The agent is authorized to: buy, sell, exchange, rent and lease real estate (which term includes, without limitation, real estate subject to a land trust and all beneficial interests in and powers of direction under any land trust); collect all rent, sale proceeds and earnings from real estate; convey, assign and accept title to real estate; grant easements, create conditions and release rights of homestead with respect to real estate; create land trusts and exercise all powers under land trusts; hold, possess, maintain, repair, improve, subdivide, manage, operate and insure real estate; pay, contest, protest and compromise real estate taxes and assessments; and, in general, exercise all powers with respect to real estate which the principal could if present and under no disability.

(b) Financial institution transactions. The agent is authorized to: open, close, continue and control all accounts and deposits in any type of financial institution (which term includes, without limitation, banks, trust companies, savings and building and loan associations, credit unions and brokerage firms); deposit in and withdraw from and write checks on any financial institution account or deposit; and, in general, exercise all powers with respect to financial institution transactions which the principal could if present and under no disability.

(c) Stock and bond transactions. The agent is authorized to: buy and sell all types of securities (which term includes, without limitation, stocks, bonds, mutual funds and all other types of investment securities and financial instruments); collect, hold and safekeep all dividends, interest, earnings, proceeds of sale, distributions, shares, certificates and other evidence of ownership paid or distributed with respect to securities; exercise all voting rights with respect to securities in person or by proxy, enter into voting trusts and consent to limitations on the right to vote; and, in general, exercise all powers with respect to securities which the principal could if present and under no disability.

(d) Tangible personal property transactions. The agent is authorized to: buy and sell, lease, exchange, collect, possess and take title to all tangible personal property; move, store, ship, restore, maintain, repair, improve, manage, preserve, insure and safekeep tangible personal property; and, in general, exercise all powers with respect to tangible personal property which the principal could if present and under no disability.

(e) Safe deposit box transactions. The agent is authorized to: open, continue and have access to all safe deposit boxes; sign, renew, release or terminate any safe deposit contract; drill or surrender any safe deposit box; and, in general, exercise all powers with respect to safe deposit matters which the principal could if present and under no disability.

(f) Insurance and annuity transactions. The agent is authorized to: procure, acquire, continue, renew, terminate or otherwise deal with any type of insurance or annuity contract (which terms include, without limitation, life, accident, health, disability, automobile casualty, property or liability insurance); pay premiums or assessments on or surrender and collect all distributions, proceeds or benefits payable under any insurance or annuity contract; and, in general, exercise all powers with respect to insurance and annuity contracts which the principal could if present and under no disability.

(g) Retirement plan transactions. The agent is authorized to: contribute to, withdraw from and deposit funds in any type of retirement plan (which term includes, without limitation, any tax qualified or nonqualified pension, profit sharing, stock bonus, employee savings and other retirement plan, individual retirement account, deferred compensation plan and any other type of employee benefit plan); select and change payment options for the principal under

(continued on page 114)

2.   The powers granted above shall not include the following powers or shall be modified or limited in the following particulars (here you may include any specific limitations you deem appropriate, such as a prohibition or conditions on the sale of a particular stock or real estate or special rules on borrowing by the agent):

_____
_____
_____

3.   In addition to the powers granted above, I grant my agent the following powers (here you may add any other delegable powers including, without limitation, the power to make gifts, exercise powers of appointment, name or change beneficiaries or joint tenants or revoke or amend any trust specifically referred to below):

_____
_____
_____

(YOUR AGENT WILL HAVE AUTHORITY TO EMPLOY OTHER PERSONS AS NECESSARY TO ENABLE THE AGENT TO PROPERLY EXERCISE THE POWERS GRANTED IN THIS FORM, BUT YOUR AGENT WILL HAVE TO MAKE ALL DISCRETIONARY DECISIONS. IF YOU WANT TO GIVE YOUR AGENT THE RIGHT TO DELEGATE DISCRETIONARY DECISION-MAKING POWERS TO OTHERS, YOU SHOULD KEEP THE NEXT SENTENCE, OTHERWISE IT SHOULD BE STRUCK OUT.)

4.   My agent shall have the right by written instrument to delegate any or all of the foregoing powers involving discretionary decision-making to any person or persons whom my agent may select, but such delegation may be amended or revoked by an agent (including any successor) named by me who is acting under this power of attorney at the time of reference.

(YOUR AGENT WILL BE ENTITLED TO REIMBURSEMENT FOR ALL REASONABLE EXPENSES INCURRED IN ACTING UNDER THIS POWER OF ATTORNEY. STRIKE OUT THE NEXT SENTENCE IF YOU DO NOT WANT YOUR AGENT TO ALSO BE ENTITLED TO REASONABLE COMPENSATION FOR SERVICES AS AGENT.)

5.   My agent shall be entitled to reasonable compensation for services rendered as agent under this power of attorney.

(THIS POWER OF ATTORNEY MAY BE AMENDED OR REVOKED BY YOU AT ANY TIME AND IN ANY MANNER. ABSENT AMENDMENT OR REVOCATION, THE AUTHORITY GRANTED IN THIS POWER OF ATTORNEY WILL BECOME EFFECTIVE AT THE TIME THIS POWER IS SIGNED AND WILL CONTINUE UNTIL YOUR DEATH UNLESS A LIMITATION ON THE BEGINNING DATE OR DURATION IS MADE BY INITIALING AND COMPLETING EITHER (OR BOTH) OF THE FOLLOWING:)

6. (   ) This power of attorney shall become effective on _____
_____ (insert a future date or event during your lifetime, such as court determination of your disability, when you want this power to first take effect)

7. (   ) This power of attorney shall terminate_____
_____ (insert a future date or event, such as court determination of your disability, when you want this power to terminate prior to your death)

(IF YOU WISH TO NAME SUCCESSOR AGENTS, INSERT THE NAME(S) AND ADDRESS(ES) OF SUCH SUCCESSOR(S) IN THE FOLLOWING PARAGRAPH.)

8.   If any agent named by me shall die, become incompetent, resign or refuse to accept the office of agent, I name the following (each to act alone and successively, in the order named) as successor(s) to such agent:_____
_____

any retirement plan; make rollover contributions from any retirement plan to other retirement plans or individual retirement accounts; exercise all investment powers available under any type of self-directed retirement plan; and, in general, exercise all powers with respect to retirement plans and retirement plan account balances which the principal could if present and under no disability.

(h) Social Security, unemployment and military service benefits. The agent is authorized to: prepare, sign and file any claim or application for Social Security, unemployment or military service benefits; sue for, settle or abandon any claims to any benefit or assistance under any federal, state, local or foreign statute or regulation; control, deposit to any account, collect, receipt for, and take title to and hold all benefits under any Social Security, unemployment, military service or other state, federal, local or foreign statute or regulation; and, in general, exercise all powers with respect to Social Security, unemployment, military service and government benefits which the principal could if present and under no disability.

(i) Tax matters. The agent is authorized to: sign, verify and file all the principal's federal, state and local income, gift, estate, property and other tax returns, including joint returns and declarations of estimated tax; pay all taxes; claim, sue for and receive all tax refunds; examine and copy all the principal's tax returns and records; represent the principal before any federal, state or local revenue agency or taxing body and sign and deliver all tax powers of attorney on behalf of the principal as required to settle, pay and determine all tax liabilities; and, in general, exercise all powers with respect to tax matters which the principal could if present and under no disability.

(j) Claims and litigation. The agent is authorized to: institute, prosecute, defend, abandon, compromise, arbitrate, settle and dispose of any claim in favor of or against the principal or any property interests of the principal; collect and receipt for any claim or settlement proceeds and waive or release all rights of the principal; employ attorneys and others and enter into contingency agreements and other contracts as necessary in connections with litigation; and, in general, exercise all powers with respect to claims and litigation which the principal could if present and under no disability.

(k) Commodity and option transactions. The agent is authorized to: buy, sell, exchange, assign, convey, settle and exercise commodities futures contracts and call and put options on stocks and stock indices traded on a regulated options exchange and collect and receipt for all proceeds of any such transactions; establish or continue option accounts for the principal with any securities or futures broker; and, in general, exercise all powers with respect to commodities and options which the principal could if present and under no disability.

(l) Business operations. The agent is authorized to: organize or continue any business (which term includes, without limitation, any farming, manufacturing, service, mining, retailing or other type of business operation) in any form, whether as a proprietorship, joint venture, partnership, corporation, trust or other legal entity; operate, buy, sell, expand, contract, terminate or liquidate any business; direct, control, supervise, manage or participate in the operation of any business and engage, compensate and discharge business managers, employees, agents, attorneys, accountants and consultants; and, in general, exercise all powers with respect to business interests and operations which the principal could if present and under no disability.

(m) Borrowing transactions. The agent is authorized to: borrow money; mortgage or pledge any real estate or tangible or intangible personal property as security for such purposes; sign, renew, extend, pay and satisfy any notes or other forms of obligation; and, in general, exercise all powers with respect to secured and unsecured borrowing which the principal could if present and under no disability.

(n) Estate transactions. The agent is authorized to: accept, receipt for, exercise, release, reject, renounce, assign, disclaim, demand, sue for, claim and recover any legacy, bequest, devise, gift or other property interest or payment due or payable to or for the principal; assert any interest in and exercise any power over any trust, estate or property subject to fiduciary control; establish a revocable trust solely for the benefit of the principal that terminates at the death of the principal and is then distributed to the legal representative of the estate of the principal; and, in general, exercise all powers with respect to estates and trusts which the principal could if present and under no disability; provided, however, that the agent may not make or change a will and may not revoke or amend a trust revocable or amendable by the principal or require the trustee of any trust for the benefit of the principal to pay income or principal to the agent unless specific authority to that end is given, and specific reference to the trust is made, in the statutory property power form.

(o) All other property powers and transaction. The agent is authorized to: exercise all possible powers of the principal with respect to all possible types of property and interests in property, except to the extent the principal limits the generality of this category (o) by striking out one or more or categories (a) through (n) or by specifying other limitations in the statutory property power form.

For purposes of this paragraph 8, a person shall be considered to be incompetent if and while the person is a minor or an adjudicated incompetent or disabled person or the person is unable to give prompt and intelligent consideration to business matters, as certified by a licensed physician.

(IF YOU WISH TO NAME YOUR AGENT AS GUARDIAN OF YOUR ESTATE, IN THE EVENT A COURT DECIDES THAT ONE SHOULD BE APPOINTED, YOU MAY, BUT ARE NOT REQUIRED TO, DO SO BY RETAINING THE FOLLOWING PARAGRAPH. THE COURT WILL APPOINT YOUR AGENT IF THE COURT FINDS THAT SUCH APPOINTMENT WILL SERVE YOUR BEST INTERESTS AND WELFARE. STRIKE OUT PARAGRAPH 9 IF YOU DO NOT WANT YOUR AGENT TO ACT AS GUARDIAN.)

9.   If a guardian of my estate (my property) is to be appointed, I nominate the agent acting under this power of attorney as such guardian, to serve without bond or security.

10.   I am fully informed as to all the contents of this form and understand the full import of this grant of powers to my agent.

Signed _____
(principal)

(YOU MAY, BUT ARE NOT REQUIRED TO, REQUEST YOUR AGENT AND SUCCESSOR AGENTS TO PROVIDE SPECIMEN SIGNATURES BELOW. IF YOU INCLUDE SPECIMEN SIGNATURES IN THIS POWER OF ATTORNEY, YOU MUST COMPLETE THE CERTIFICATION OPPOSITE THE SIGNATURES OF THE AGENTS.)

Specimen signatures of agent
(and successors)

I certify that the signatures of my
agent (and successors) are correct.

_____
(agent)

_____
(principal)

_____
(successor agent)

_____
(principal)

_____
(successor agent)

_____
(principal)

(THIS POWER OF ATTORNEY WILL NOT BE EFFECTIVE UNLESS IT IS NOTARIZED, USING THE FORM BELOW.)

State of _____)
) SS.
County of _____)

The undersigned, a notary public in and for the above county and state, certifies that _____, known to me to be the same person whose name is subscribed as principal to the foregoing power of attorney, appeared before me in person and acknowledged signing and delivering the instrument as the free and voluntary act of the principal, for the uses and purposes therein set forth (and certified to the correctness of the signature(s) of the agent(s)).

Dated:_____ (SEAL)

_____
Notary Public
My commission expires_____

THE NAME AND ADDRESS OF THE PERSON PREPARING THIS FORM SHOULD BE INSERTED IF THE AGENT WILL HAVE POWER TO CONVEY ANY INTEREST IN REAL ESTATE.

This document was prepared by:_____

_____

[This page was intentionally left blank. See page 31.]

ILLINOIS STATUTORY SHORT FORM POWER OF ATTORNEY FOR HEALTH CARE

(NOTICE: THE PURPOSE OF THIS POWER OF ATTORNEY IS TO GIVE THE PERSON YOU DESIGNATE (YOUR "AGENT") BROAD POWERS TO MAKE HEALTH CARE DECISIONS FOR YOU, INCLUDING POWER TO REQUIRE, CONSENT TO OR WITHDRAW ANY TYPE OF PERSONAL CARE OR MEDICAL TREATMENT FOR ANY PHYSICAL OR MENTAL CONDITION AND TO ADMIT YOU TO OR DISCHARGE YOU FROM ANY HOSPITAL, HOME OR OTHER INSTITUTION. THIS FORM DOES NOT IMPOSE A DUTY ON YOUR AGENT TO EXERCISE GRANTED POWERS; BUT WHEN POWERS ARE EXERCISED, YOUR AGENT WILL HAVE TO USE DUE CARE TO ACT FOR YOUR BENEFIT AND IN ACCORDANCE WITH THIS FORM AND KEEP A RECORD OF RECEIPTS, DISBURSEMENTS AND SIGNIFICANT ACTIONS TAKEN AS AGENT. A COURT CAN TAKE AWAY THE POWERS OF YOUR AGENT IF IT FINDS THE AGENT IS NOT ACTING PROPERLY. YOU MAY NAME SUCCESSOR AGENTS UNDER THIS FORM BUT NOT CO-AGENTS, AND NO HEALTH CARE PROVIDER MAY BE NAMED. UNLESS YOU EXPRESSLY LIMIT THE DURATION OF THIS POWER IN THE MANNER PROVIDED BELOW, UNTIL YOU REVOKE THIS POWER OR A COURT ACTING ON YOUR BEHALF TERMINATES IT, YOUR AGENT MAY EXERCISE THE POWERS GIVEN HERE THROUGHOUT YOUR LIFETIME, EVEN AFTER YOU BECOME DISABLED. THE POWERS YOU GIVE YOUR AGENT, YOUR RIGHT TO REVOKE THOSE POWERS AND THE PENALTIES FOR VIOLATING THE LAW ARE EXPLAINED MORE FULLY IN SECTIONS 4-5, 4-6, 4-9 AND 4-10(b) OF THE ILLINOIS "POWERS OF ATTORNEY FOR HEALTH CARE LAW" OF WHICH THIS FORM IS A PART (SEE THE BACK OF THIS FORM). THAT LAW EXPRESSLY PERMITS THE USE OF ANY DIFFERENT FORM OF POWER OF ATTORNEY YOU MAY DESIRE. IF THERE IS ANYTHING ABOUT THIS FORM THAT YOU DO NOT UNDERSTAND, YOU SHOULD ASK A LAWYER TO EXPLAIN IT TO YOU.)

POWER OF ATTORNEY made this _____ day of _____

                                                          (month)   (year)

1.   I, _____

_____

(insert name and address of principal)

hereby appoint:

_____

_____

(insert name and address of agent)

as my attorney-in-fact (my "agent") to act for me and in my name (in any way I could act in person) to make any and all decisions for me concerning my personal care, medical treatment, hospitalization and health care and to require, withhold or withdraw any type of medical treatment or procedure, even though my death may ensue. My agent shall have the same access to my medical records that I have, including the right to disclose the contents to others. My agent shall also have full power to make a disposition of any part or all of my body for medical purposes, authorize an autopsy and direct the disposition of my remains.

(THE ABOVE GRANT OF POWER IS INTENDED TO BE AS BROAD AS POSSIBLE SO THAT YOUR AGENT WILL HAVE AUTHORITY TO MAKE ANY DECISION YOU COULD MAKE TO OBTAIN OR TERMINATE ANY TYPE OF HEALTH CARE, INCLUDING WITHDRAWAL OF FOOD AND WATER AND OTHER LIFE-SUSTAINING MEASURES, IF YOUR AGENT BELIEVES SUCH ACTION WOULD BE CONSISTENT WITH YOUR INTENT AND DESIRES. IF YOU WISH TO LIMIT THE SCOPE OF YOUR AGENT'S POWERS OR PRESCRIBE SPECIAL RULES OR LIMIT THE POWER TO MAKE AN ANATOMICAL GIFT, AUTHORIZE AUTOPSY OR DISPOSE OF REMAINS, YOU MAY DO SO IN THE FOLLOWING PARAGRAPHS.)

2.   The powers granted above shall not include the following powers or shall be subject to the following rules or limitations (here you may include any specific limitations you deem appropriate, such as: your own definition of when life-sustaining measures should be withheld; a direction to continue food and fluids or life-sustaining treatment in all events; or instructions to refuse any specific types of treatment that are inconsistent with your religious beliefs or unacceptable to you for any other reason, such as blood transfusion, electro-convulsive therapy, amputation, psychosurgery, voluntary admission to a mental institution, etc.): _____

_____

(THE SUBJECT OF LIFE-SUSTAINING TREATMENT IS OF PARTICULAR IMPORTANCE. FOR YOUR CONVENIENCE IN DEALING WITH THAT SUBJECT, SOME GENERAL STATEMENTS CONCERNING THE WITHHOLDING OR REMOVAL OF LIFE-SUSTAINING TREATMENT ARE SET FORTH BELOW. IF YOU AGREE WITH ONE OF THESE STATEMENTS, YOU MAY INITIAL THAT STATEMENT; BUT DO NOT INITIAL MORE THAN ONE):

I do not want my life to be prolonged nor do I want life-sustaining treatment to be provided or continued if my agent believes the burdens of the treatment outweigh the expected benefits. I want my agent to consider the relief of suffering, the expense involved and the quality as well as the possible extension of my life in making decisions concerning life sustaining treatment.

Initialed _____

§ 4-5. Limitations on health care agencies. Neither the attending physician nor any other health care provider may act as agent under a health care agency; however, a person who is not administering health care to the patient may act as health care agent for the patient even though the person is a physician or otherwise licensed, certified, authorized, or permitted by law to administer health care in the ordinary course of business or the practice of a profession.

§4-6. Revocation and amendment of health care agencies.

(a) Every health care agency may be revoked by the principal at any time, without regard to the principal's mental or physical condition, by any of the following methods:

1. By being obliterated, burnt, torn or otherwise destroyed or defaced in a manner indicating intention to revoke;

2. By a written revocation of the agency signed and dated by the principal or person acting at the direction of the principal; or

3. By an oral or any other expression of the intent to revoke th agency in the presence of a witness 18 years of age or older who signs and dates a writing confirming that such expression of intent was made.

(b) Every health care agency may be amended at any time by a written amendment signed and dated by the principal or person acting at the direction of the principal.

(c) Any person, other than the agent, to whom a revocation or amendment is communicated or delivered shall make all reasonable efforts to inform the agent of that fact as promptly as possible.

§4-9. Penalties. All persons shall be subject to the following sanctions in relation to health care agencies, in addition to all other sanctions applicable under any other law or rule of professional conduct:

(a) Any person shall be civilly liable who, without the principal's consent, wilfully conceals, cancels or alters a health care agency or any amendment of revocation of the agency or who falsifies or forges a health care agency, amendment or revocation.

(b) A person who falsifies or forges a health care agency or wilfully conceals or withholds personal knowledge of an amendment or revocation of a health care agency with the intent to cause a withholding or withdrawal of life-sustaining or death-delaying procedures contrary to the intent of the principal and thereby, because of such act, directly causes life-sustaining or death-delaying procedures to be withheld or withdrawn and death to the patient to be hastened shall be subject to prosecution for involuntary manslaughter.

(c) Any person who requires or prevents execution of a health care agency as a condition of insuring or providing any type of health care services to the patient shall be civilly liable and guilty of a Class A misdemeanor.

§ 4-10(b). The statutory short form power of attorney for health care (the "statutory health care power") authorizes the agent to make any and all health care decisions on behalf of the principal which the principal could make if present and under no disability, subject to any limitations on the granted powers that appear on the face of the form, to be exercised in such manner as the agent deems consistent with the intent and desires of the principal. The agent will be under no duty to exercise granted powers or to assume control of or responsibility

(continued on page 120)

I want my life to be prolonged and I want life-sustaining treatment to be provided or continued unless I am in a coma which my attending physician believes to be irreversible, in accordance with reasonable medical standards at the time of reference. If and when I have suffered irreversible coma, I want life-sustaining treatment to be withheld or discontinued.

Initialed _____

I want my life to be prolonged to the greatest extent possible without regard to my condition, the chances I have for recovery or the cost of the procedures.

Initialed _____

(THIS POWER OF ATTORNEY MAY BE AMENDED OR REVOKED BY YOU IN THE MANNER PROVIDED IN SECTION 4-6 OF THE ILLINOIS "POWERS OF ATTORNEY FOR HEALTH CARE LAW" (SEE THE BACK OF THIS FORM). ABSENT AMENDMENT OR REVOCATION, THE AUTHORITY GRANTED IN THIS POWER OF ATTORNEY WILL BECOME EFFECTIVE AT THE TIME THIS POWER IS SIGNED AND WILL CONTINUE UNTIL YOUR DEATH, AND BEYOND IF ANATOMICAL GIFT, AUTOPSY OR DISPOSITION OF REMAINS IS AUTHORIZED, UNLESS A LIMITATION ON THE BEGINNING DATE OR DURATION IS MADE BY INITIALING AND COMPLETING EITHER OR BOTH OF THE FOLLOWING:)

3. (_____) This power of attorney shall become effective on _____
_____(insert a future date or event during your lifetime, such as court determination of your disability, when you want this power to first take effect)

4. (_____) This power of attorney shall terminate on_____
_____(insert a future date or event, such as court determination of your disability, when you want this power to terminate prior to your death)

(IF YOU WISH TO NAME SUCCESSOR AGENTS, INSERT THE NAMES AND ADDRESSES OF SUCH SUCCESSORS IN THE FOLLOWING PARAGRAPH.)

5. If any agent named by me shall die, become incompetent, resign, refuse to accept the office of agent or be unavailable, I name the following (each to act alone and successively, in the order named) as successors to such agent:_____
_____

For purposes of this paragraph 5, a person shall be considered to be incompetent if and while the person is a minor or an adjudicated incompetent or disabled person or the person is unable to give prompt and intelligent consideration to health care matters, as certified by a licensed physician.

(IF YOU WISH TO NAME YOUR AGENT AS GUARDIAN OF YOUR PERSON, IN THE EVENT A COURT DECIDES THAT ONE SHOULD BE APPOINTED, YOU MAY, BUT ARE NOT REQUIRED TO, DO SO BY RETAINING THE FOLLOWING PARAGRAPH. THE COURT WILL APPOINT YOUR AGENT IF THE COURT FINDS THAT SUCH APPOINTMENT WILL SERVE YOUR BEST INTERESTS AND WELFARE. STRIKE OUT PARAGRAPH 6 IF YOU DO NOT WANT YOUR AGENT TO ACT AS GUARDIAN.)

6. If a guardian of my person is to be appointed, I nominate the agent acting under this power of attorney as such guardian, to serve without bond or security. (insert name and address of nominated guardian of the person)

7. I am fully informed as to all the contents of this form and understand the full import of this grant of powers to my agent.

Signed _____
(principal)

The principal has had an opportunity to read the above form and has signed the form or acknowledged his or her signature or mark on the form in my presence.

_____   Residing at _____
(witness)   _____

(YOU MAY, BUT ARE NOT REQUIRED TO, REQUEST YOUR AGENT AND SUCCESSOR AGENTS TO PROVIDE SPECIMEN SIGNATURES BELOW. IF YOU INCLUDE SPECIMEN SIGNATURES IN THIS POWER OF ATTORNEY YOU MUST COMPLETE THE CERTIFICATION OPPOSITE THE SIGNATURES OF THE AGENTS.)

Specimen signatures of agent (and successors).   I certify that the signatures of my agent (and successors) are correct

_____   _____
(agent)   (principal)

_____   _____
(successor agent)   (principal)

_____   _____
(successor agent)   (principal)

for the principal's health care; but when granted powers are exercised, the agent will be required to use due care to act for the benefit of the principal in accordance with the terms of the statutory health care power and will be liable for negligent exercise. The agent may act in person or through others reasonably employed by the agent for that purpose but may not delegate authority to make health care decisions. The agent may sign and deliver all instruments, negotiate and enter into all agreements and do all other acts reasonably necessary to implement the exercise of the powers granted to the agent. Without limiting the generality of the foregoing, the statutory health care power shall include the following powers, subject to any limitations appearing on the face of the form:

(1) The agent is authorized to give consent to and authorize or refuse, or to withhold or withdraw consent to, any and all types of medical care, treatment or procedures relating to the physical or mental health of the principal, including any medication program, surgical procedures, life-sustaining treatment or provision of food and fluids for the principal.

(2) The agent is authorized to admit the principal to or discharge the principal from any and all types of hospitals, institutions, homes, residential or nursing facilities, treatment centers and other health care institutions providing personal care or treatment for any type of physical or mental condition. The agent shall have the same right to visit the principal in the hospital or other institution as is granted to a spouse or adult child of the principal, any rule of the institution to the contrary notwithstanding.

(3) The agent is authorized to contract for any and all types of health care services and facilities in the name of and on behalf of the principal and to bind the principal to pay for all such services and facilities, and to have an exercise those powers over the principal's property as are authorized under the statutory property power, to the extent the agent deems necessary to pay health care costs; and the agent shall not be personally liable for any services or care contracted for on behalf of the principal.

(4) At the principal's expense and subject to reasonable rules of the health care provider to prevent disruption of the principal's health care, the agent shall have the same right th principal has to examine and copy and consent to disclosure of all the principal's medical records that the agent deems relevant to the exercise of the agent's powers, whether the records relate to mental health or any other medical condition and whether they are in the possession of or maintained by any physician, psychiatrist, psychologist, therapist, hospital, nursing home or other health care provider.

(5) The agent is authorized: to direct that an autopsy be made pursuant to Section 2 of "An Act in relation to autopsy of dead bodies," approved August 13, 1965, including all amendments; to make a disposition of any part or all of the principal's body pursuant to the Uniform Anatomical Gift Act, as now or hereafter amended; and to direct the disposition of the principal's remains.

POWER OF ATTORNEY

I, _____

_____(insert your name and address)

appoint _____

_____ (insert the name and address
of the person appointed) as my agent (attorney-in-fact) to act for me in any lawful way with
respect to the following initialed subjects, as each subject is defined and described in the
Annotated Indiana Code, which is incorporated by reference herein:

TO GRANT ONE OR MORE OF THE FOLLOWING POWERS, INITIAL THE LINE
IN FRONT OF EACH POWER YOU ARE GRANTING. TO WITHHOLD A POWER, DO
NOT INITIAL THE LINE IN FRONT OF IT. YOU MAY, BUT NEED NOT, CROSS OUT
EACH POWER WITHHELD. THE ANNOTATED INDIANA CODE SECTIONS NOTED
ARE INCORPORATED BY REFERENCE.

INITIALS

_____	a.	ALL POWERS (b THROUGH r) LISTED BELOW.
_____	b	Real property transactions. (Ann. Ind. Code § 30-5-5-2)
_____	c.	Tangible personal property transactions. (Ann. Ind. Code § 30-5-5-3)
_____	d.	Bond, share and commodity transactions. (Ann. Ind. Code § 30-5-5-4)
_____	e.	Banking transactions. (Ann. Ind. Code § 30-5-5-5)
_____	f.	Business operating transactions. (Ann. Ind. Code § 30-5-5-6)
_____	g.	Insurance transactions. (Ann. Ind. Code § 30-5-5-7)
_____	h.	Beneficiary transactions. (Ann. Ind. Code § 30-5-5-8)
_____	i.	Gift transactions. (Ann. Ind. Code § 30-5-5-9)
_____	j.	Fiduciary transactions. (Ann. Ind. Code § 30-5-5-10)
_____	k.	Claims and litigation. (Ann. Ind. Code § 30-5-5-11)
_____	l.	Family maintenance. (Ann. Ind. Code § 30-5-5-12)
_____	m.	Benefits from military service. (Ann. Ind. Code § 30-5-5-13)
_____	n.	Records, reports, and statements. (Ann. Ind. Code § 30-5-5-14)
_____	o.	Estate transactions. (Ann. Ind. Code § 30-5-5-15)
_____	p.	Health care powers. (Ann. Ind. Code §30-5-5-16)
_____	q.	Delegation of authority. (Ann. Ind. Code §30-5-5-18)
_____	r.	General authority as to all other matters. (Ann. Ind. Code §30-5-5-19)

If you checked "Health care powers," and wish your agent to be able to withdraw or withhold health care as described below, check the following box:

❑ I authorize my health care representative to make decisions in my best interest concerning withdrawal or withholding of health care (pursuant to Ann. Ind. Code
§§30-5-5-17, 16-36-1, and 16-36-4). If at any time based on my previously
expressed preferences and the diagnosis and prognosis my health care representative is satisfied that certain health care is not or would not be beneficial or that such
health care is or would be excessively burdensome, then my health care

representative may express my will that such health care be withheld or withdrawn and may consent on my behalf that any or all health care be discontinued or not instituted, even if death may result.

My health care representative must try to discuss this decision with me. However, if I am unable to communicate, my health care representative may make such a decision for me, after consultation with my physician or physicians and other relevant health care givers. To the extent appropriate, my health care representative may also discuss this decision with my family and others to the extent they are available.

CHECK ONE OF THE FOLLOWING BOXES:

❏ This power of attorney shall terminate upon my disability, incapacity or incompetence.

❏ This power of attorney is effective immediately, and shall not be affected by my disability, incapacity or incompetence.

❏ This power of attorney will become effective upon my disability, incapacity or incompetence.

Signed this _____ day of _____, _____.

_____   _____
(Your signature)   (Your social security number)

State of _____
(County) of _____

On this _____ day of _____, _____, before me, personally appeared _____ (name of principal), who is personally known to me or provided _____ as identification, and acknowledged that he or she executed it.

_____
Notary Public

DURABLE POWER OF ATTORNEY FOR HEALTH CARE

I hereby designate _____ as my attorney in fact (my agent) and give to my agent the power to make health care decisions for me. this power exists only when I am unable, in the judgment of my attending physician, to make those health care decisions. The attorney in fact must act consistently with my desires as stated in this document or otherwise made known.

Except as otherwise specified in this document, this document gives my agent the power, where otherwise consistent with the law to this state, to consent to my physician not giving health care or stopping health care which is necessary to keep me alive.

This document gives my agent power to make health care decisions on my behalf, including to consent, to refuse to consent, or to withdraw consent to the provision of any care, treatment, service, or procedure to maintain, diagnose, or treat a physical or mental condition. This power is subject to any statement of my desires and any limitations included in this document.

My agent has the right to examine my medical records and to consent to disclosure of such records.

The powers granted by this document are subject to the following instructions and limitations (if none, type in "none"): _____
_____
_____

In the event my designated agent is unable or unwilling to serve, I designate the following alternative attorneys in fact (agents), to serve in the order stated below:

First Alternative Agent: _____

Second Alternative Agent: _____

Signature: _____

123

Durable Power of Attorney for Health Care Decisions

I, _____, designate and appoint:

Name _____
Address: _____
_____
Telephone Number: _____

to be my agent for health care decisions and pursuant to the language stated below, on my behalf to:

(1) Consent, refuse consent, or withdraw consent to any care, treatment, service or procedure to maintain, diagnose or treat a physical or mental condition, and to make decisions about organ donation, autopsy and disposition of the body;

(2) make all necessary arrangements at any hospital, psychiatric hospital or psychiatric treatment facility, hospice, nursing home or similar institution; to employ or discharge health care personnel to include physicians, psychiatrists, psychologists, dentists, nurses, therapists or any other person who is licensed, certified or otherwise authorized or permitted by the laws of this state to administer health care as the agent shall deem necessary for my physical, mental; and emotional well being; and

(3) request, receive and review any information, verbal or written, regarding my personal affairs or physical or mental health including medical and hospital records and to execute any releases of other documents that may be required in order to obtain such information.

In exercising the grant of authority set forth above my agent for health care decisions shall:

_____
_____
_____

(Here may be inserted any special instructions or statement of the principal's desires to be followed by the agent in exercising the authority granted).

Limitations of Authority

(1) The powers of the agent herein shall be limited to the extent set out in writing in this durable power of attorney for health care decisions, and shall not include the power to revoke or invalidate any previously existing declaration made in accordance with the natural death act.

(2) The agent shall be prohibited from authorizing consent for the following items:

_____
_____

(3) This durable power of attorney for health care decisions shall be subject to the additional following limitations:

_____
_____

EFFECTIVE TIME

This power of attorney for health care decisions shall become effective (check one):
- ❏ immediately and shall not be affected by my subsequent disability or incapacity.
- ❏ upon the occurrence of my disability or incapacity.

REVOCATION

Any durable power of attorney for health care decisions I have previously made is hereby revoked.

This durable power of attorney for health care decisions shall be revoked (check one):
- ❏ by an instrument in writing executed, witnessed or acknowledged in the same manner as required herein.
- ❏ _____

(set out another manner of revocation, if desired.)

EXECUTION

Executed this _____, at _____, Kansas.

_____
Principal

This document must be: (1) Witnessed by two individuals of lawful age who are not the agent, not related to the principal by blood, marriage or adoption, not entitled to any portion of the principal's estate and not financially responsible for principal's health care; OR (2) acknowledged by a notary public.

_____   _____
Witness   Witness

_____   _____
Address   Address

(OR)

STATE OF _____)
                                                                    SS.
COUNTY OF _____)

This instrument was acknowledged before me on _____,
by _____.

_____
Signature of notary public

(Seal, if any)

125

DURABLE FINANCIAL POWER OF ATTORNEY

Notice to the Principal: As the "Principal," you are using this Durable Power of Attorney to grant power to another person (called the "Agent") to make decisions about you money and property and to use it on your behalf. The powers granted to the Agent are broad and sweeping. Your Agent will have the power to sell or otherwise dispose of your property and spend your money without advance notice to you or approval by you. Under this document, your Agent will continue to have these powers after you become incapacitated and you may also choose to authorize your Agent to use these powers before you become incapacitated. the powers that you give your Agent are explained more fully in the Maine Revised Statutes, title 18-A, sections 5-501 to 5-508 and in Maine case law. You have the right to revoke or take back this Durable Power of Attorney at any time as long as you are of sound mine. If there is anything about this form that you do not understand, you should ask a lawyer to explain it to you.

Notice to the Agent: As the "Agent" or "Attorney-in-fact," you are given power under this Durable Power of Attorney to make decisions about the money and property belonging to the Principal and to spend it on that person's behalf. This Durable Power of Attorney is only valid if the Principal is of sound mind when the Principal signs it. As the Agent, you are under a duty (called a "fiduciary duty") to observe the standards observed by a prudent person dealing with the property of another. The duty is explained more fully in the Maine Revised Statutes, Title 18-A, section 5-501 to 5-508 and 7-302 and in Maine case law. As the Agent, you are not entitled to use the money for your own benefit or to make gifts to yourself or others unless the Durable Power of Attorney specifically gives you the authority of do so. As the Agent, your authority under this form will end when the Principal dies and you will not have the authority to administer the estate unless you are named in the Principal's will. If you violate your fiduciary duty under this Durable Power of Attorney, you may be liable for damages and may be subject to criminal prosecution. If there is anything about this form or your duties under it that you do not understand, you should ask a lawyer to explain it to you.

ADVANCE HEALTH-CARE DIRECTIVE

Explanation

You have the right to give instructions about your own health care. You also have the right to name someone else to make health-care decisions for you. This form lets you do either or both of these things. It also lets you express your wishes regarding donation of organs and the designation of your primary physician. If you use this form, you may complete or modify all or any part of it. You are free to use a different form.

Part 1 of this form is a power of attorney for health care. Part 1 lets you name another individual as agent to make health-care decisions for you if you become incapable of making your own decisions or if you want someone else to make those decisions for you now even though you are still capable. You may also name an alternate agent to act for you if your first choice is not willing, able or reasonably available to make decisions for you. Unless related to you, your agent may not be an owner, operator or employee of a residential long-term health-care institution at which you are receiving care.

Unless the form you sign limits the authority of your agent, your agent may make all health-care decisions for you. This form has a place for you to limit the authority of your agent. You need not limit the authority of your agent if you wish to rely on your agent for all health-care decisions that may have to be made. If you choose not to limit the authority of your agent, your agent will have the right to:

(a) Consent or refuse consent to any care, treatment, service or procedure to maintain, diagnose or otherwise affect a physical or mental condition;

(b) Select or discharge health-care providers and institutions.

(c) Approve or disapprove diagnostic tests, surgical procedures, programs of medication and orders not to resuscitate; and

(d) Direct the provision, withholding or withdrawal of artificial nutrition and hydration and all other forms of health care, including life-sustaining treatment.

Part 2 of this form lets you give specific instructions about any aspect of your health care. Choices are provided for you to express your wishes regarding the provision, withholding or withdrawal of treatment to keep you alive, including the provision of artificial nutrition and hydration, as well as the provision of pain relief. Space is also provided for you to add to the choices you have made or for you to write out any additional wishes.

Part 3 of this form lets you express an intention to donate your bodily organs and tissues following your death.

Part 4 of this form lets you designate a physician to have primary responsibility for your health care.

After completing this form, sign and date the form at the end. You must have 2 other individuals sign as witnesses. Give a copy of the signed and completed form to your physician, to any other health-care providers you may have, to any health-care institution at which you are receiving care and to any health-care agents you have named. You should talk to the person you have named as agent to make sure that he or she understands your wishes and is willing to take the responsibility.

You have the right to revoke this advance health-care directive or replace this form at any time.

* * * * * * * * * * * * * * * * * * *

PART 1. POWER OF ATTORNEY FOR HEALTH CARE

(1) DESIGNATION OF AGENT: I designate the following individual as my agent to make health-care decisions for me:

_____
(name of individual you choose as agent)

_____	_____	_____	_____
(address)	(city)	(state)	(zip code)

_____	_____
(home phone)	(work phone)

OPTIONAL: If I revoke my agent's authority or if my agent is not willing, able or reasonably available to make a health-care decision for me, I designate as my first alternate agent:

_____
(name of individual you choose as first alternate agent)

_____	_____	_____	_____
(address)	(city)	(state)	(zip code)

_____	_____
(home phone)	(work phone)

OPTIONAL: If I revoke the authority of my agent and first alternate agent or if neither is willing, able or reasonably available to make a health-care decision for me, I designate as my second alternate agent:

_____
(name of individual you choose as second alternate agent)

_____
(address)   (city)   (state)   (zip code)

_____
(home phone) (work phone)

(2) AGENT'S AUTHORITY: My agent is authorized to make all health-care decisions for me, including decisions to provide, withhold or withdraw artificial nutrition and hydration and all other forms of health care to keep me alive, except as I state here:

_____
_____
_____
(Add additional sheets if needed)

(3) WHEN AGENT'S AUTHORITY BECOMES EFFECTIVE: My agent's authority becomes effective when my primary physician determines that I am unable to make my own health-care decisions unless I mark the following box. If I mark this box [   ], my agent's authority to make health-care decisions for me takes effect immediately.

(4) AGENT'S OBLIGATION: My agent shall make health-care decisions for me in accordance with this power of attorney for health care, any instructions I give in Part 2 of this form and my other wishes to the extent known to my agent. To the extent my wishes are unknown, my agent shall make health-care decisions for me in accordance with what my agent determines to be in my best interest. In determining my best interest, my agent shall consider my personal values to the extent known to my agent.

(5) NOMINATION OF GUARDIAN: If a guardian of my person needs to be appointed for me by a court, I nominate the agent designated in this form. If that agent is not willing, able or reasonably available to act as guardian, I nominate the alternate agents whom I have named, in the order designated.

PART 2. INSTRUCTIONS FOR HEALTH CARE

If you are satisfied to allow your agent to determine what is best for you in making end-of-life decisions, you need not fill out this part of the form. If you do fill out this part of the form, you may strike any wording you do not want.

(6) END-OF-LIFE DECISIONS: I direct that my health-care providers and others involved in my care provide, withhold or withdraw treatment in accordance with the choice I have marked below:

[   ] (a) Choice Not To Prolong Life: I do not want my life to be prolonged if (i) I have an incurable and irreversible condition that will result in my death within a relatively short time, (ii) I become unconscious and, to a reasonable degree of medical certainty, I will not regain consciousness, or (iii) the likely risks and burdens of treatment would outweigh the expected benefits, OR

[   ] (b) Choice To Prolong Life: I want my life to be prolonged as long as possible within the limits of generally accepted health-care standards.

(7) ARTIFICIAL NUTRITION AND HYDRATION: Artificial nutrition and hydration must be provided, withheld or withdrawn in accordance with the choice I have made in paragraph (6) unless I mark the following box. If I mark this box [   ], artificial nutrition and hydration must be provided regardless of my condition and regardless of the choice I have made in paragraph (6).

(8) RELIEF FROM PAIN: Except as I state in the following space, I direct that treatment for alleviation of pain or discomfort be provided at all times, even if it hastens my death:

_____
_____

(9) OTHER WISHES: (If you do not agree with any of the optional choices above and wish to write your own, or if you wish to add to the instructions you have given above, you may do so here.) I direct that:

_____
_____
(Add additional sheets if needed)

PART 3. DONATION OF ORGANS AT DEATH (OPTIONAL)

(10) Upon my death (mark applicable box)
    [ ] (a) I give needed organs, tissues or parts OR
    [ ] (b) I give the following organs, tissues or parts only

    _____

    [ ] (c) My gift is for the following purposes (strike any of the following you do not want)
        (i) Transplant
        (ii) Therapy
        (iii) Research
        (iv) Education

PART 4. PRIMARY PHYSICIAN (OPTIONAL)

(11) I designate the following physician as my primary physician:

_____
(name of physician)   (phone)

_____
(address)   (city)   (state)   (zip code)

OPTIONAL: If the physician I have designated above is not willing, able or reasonably available to act as my primary physician, I designate the following physician as my primary physician:

_____
(name of physician)   (phone)

_____
(address)   (city)   (state)   (zip code)

* * * * * * * * * * * * * * * * * *

(12) EFFECT OF COPY: A copy of this form has the same effect as the original.

(13) SIGNATURES: Sign and date the form here:

_____   _____
(date)   (sign your name)

_____   _____
(address)   (print your name)

_____
(city)   (state)

SIGNATURES OF WITNESSES:

       First witness   Second witness

_____   _____
(print name)   (print name)

_____   _____
(address)   (address)

_____   _____
(city)   (state)   (city)   (state)

_____   _____
(signature of witness)   (signature of witness)

_____   _____
(date)   (date)

HEALTH CARE DECISION MAKING FORMS

The following forms allow you to make some decisions about future health care issues. Form I, called a "Living Will," allows you to make decisions about life-sustaining procedures if, in the future, your death from a terminal condition is imminent despite the application of life-sustaining procedures or you are in a persistent vegetative state. Form II, called an "Advance Directive," allows you to select a health care agent, give health care instructions, or both. If you use the advance directive, you can make decisions about life-sustaining procedures in the event of terminal condition, persistent vegetative state, or end-stage condition. You can also use the advance directive to make any other health care decisions.

These forms are intended to be guides. You can use one form or both, and you may complete all or only part of the forms that you use. Different forms may also be used.

Please note: If you decide to select a health care agent that person may not be a witness to your advance directive. Also, at least one of your witnesses may not be a person who may financially benefit by reason of your death.

Form I
Living Will
(Optional Form)

If I am not able to make an informed decision regarding my health care, I direct my health care providers to follow my instructions as set forth below. (Initial those statements you wish to be included in the document and cross through those statements which do not apply.)

a. If my death from a terminal condition is imminent and even if life-sustaining procedures are used there is no reasonable expectation of my recovery—

_____ I direct that my life not be extended by life-sustaining procedures, including the administration of nutrition and hydration artificially.

_____ I direct that my life not be extended by life-sustaining procedures, except that, if I am unable to take food by mouth, I wish to receive nutrition and hydration artificially.

_____ I direct that, even in a terminal condition, I be given all available medical treatment in accordance with accepted health care standards.

_____ I direct that if I am brain dead, an anatomical gift be offered on my behalf to a patient in need of an organ or tissue transplant. If a transplant occurs, I want artificial heart/lung support devices to be continued on my behalf only until organ or tissue suitability of the patient is confirmed and organ or tissue recovery has taken place.

b. If I am in a persistent vegetative state, that is if I am not conscious and am not aware of my environment nor able to interact with others, and there is no reasonable expectation of my recovery within a medically appropriate period—

_____ I direct that my life not be extended by life-sustaining procedures, including the administration of nutrition and hydration artificially.

_____ I direct that if I am brain dead, an anatomical gift be offered on my behalf to a patient in need of an organ or tissue transplant. If a transplant occurs, I want artificial heart/lung support devices to be continued on my behalf only until organ or tissue suitability of the patient is confirmed and organ or tissue recovery has taken place.

_____ I direct that my life not be extended by life-sustaining procedures, except that, if I am unable to take food by mouth, I wish to receive nutrition and hydration artificially.

_____ I direct that I be given all available medical treatment in accordance with accepted health care standards.

c. If I am pregnant my agent shall follow these specific instructions: _____
_____
_____
_____

By signing below, I indicate that I am emotionally and mentally competent to make this living will and that I understand its purpose and effect.

_____   _____
(Date)   (Signature of Declarant)

The declarant signed or acknowledged signing this living will in my presence and based upon my personal observation the declarant appears to be a competent individual.

_____   _____
(Witness)   (Witness)
(Signature of Two Witnesses)

Form II
Advance Directive

Part A
Appointment of Health Care Agent
(Optional Form)

(Cross through if you do not want to appoint a health care agent to make health care decisions for you. If you do want to appoint an agent, cross through any items in the form that you do not want to apply.)

(1) I, _____, residing at _____
_____, appoint the following individual as my agent to make health care decisions for me_____
_____
(Full Name, Address, and Telephone Number)

Optional: If this agent is unavailable or is unable or unwilling to act as my agent, then I appoint the following person to act in this capacity _____
_____
(Full Name, Address, and Telephone Number)

(2) My agent has full power and authority to make health care decisions for me, including the power to:
  a. Request, receive, and review any information, oral or written, regarding my physical or mental health, including, but not limited to, medical and hospital records, and consent to disclosure of this information;
  b. Employ and discharge my health care providers;
  c. Authorize my admission to or discharge from (including transfer to another facility) any hospital, hospice, nursing home, adult home, or other medical care facility; and
  d. Consent to the provision, withholding, or withdrawal of health care, including, in appropriate circumstances, life-sustaining procedures.

(3) The authority of my agent is subject to the following provisions and limitations:_____
_____
_____

(4) My agent's authority becomes operative (initial the option that applies):

_____ When my attending physician and a second physician determine that I am incapable of making an informed decision regarding my health care; or

_____ When this document is signed.

(5) My agent is to make health care decisions for me based on the health care instructions I give in this document and on my wishes as otherwise known to my agent. If my wishes are unknown or unclear, my agent is to make health care decisions for me in accordance with my best interest, to be determined by my agent after considering the benefits, burdens, and risks that might result from a given treatment or course of treatment, or from the withholding or withdrawal of a treatment or course of treatment.

(6) My agent shall not be liable for the costs of care based solely on this authorization.

By signing below, I indicate that I am emotionally and mentally competent to make this appointment of a health care agent and that I understand its purpose and effect.

_____   _____
            (Date)   (Signature of Declarant)

The declarant signed or acknowledged signing this appointment of a health care agent in my presence and based upon my personal observation appears to be a competent individual.

_____   _____
            (Witness)   (Witness)
                        (Signature of Two Witnesses)

Part B
Advance Medical Directive
Health Care Instructions
(Optional Form)

(Cross through if you do not want to complete this portion of the form. If you do want to complete this portion of the form, initial those statements you want to be included in the document and cross through those statements that do not apply.)

If I am incapable of making an informed decision regarding my health care, I direct my health care providers to follow my instructions as set forth below.
(Initial all those that apply.)

(1) If my death from a terminal condition is imminent and even if life-sustaining procedures are used there is no reasonable expectation of my recovery—

_____ I direct that my life not be extended by life-sustaining procedures, including the administration of nutrition and hydration artificially.

_____ I direct that my life not be extended by life-sustaining procedures, except that, if I am unable to take food by mouth, I wish to receive nutrition and hydration artificially.

_____ I direct that if I am brain dead, an anatomical gift be offered on my behalf to a patient in need of an organ or tissue transplant. If a transplant occurs, I want artificial heart/lung support devices to be continued on my behalf only until organ or tissue suitability of the patient is confirmed and organ or tissue recovery has taken place.

(2) If I am in a persistent vegetative state, that is, if I am not conscious and am not aware of my environment or able to interact with others, and there is no reasonable expectation of my recovery —

    _____ I direct that my life not be extended by life-sustaining procedures, including the administration of nutrition and hydration artificially.

    _____ I direct that my life not be extended by life-sustaining procedures, except that, if I am unable to take food by mouth, I wish to receive nutrition and hydration artificially.

    _____ I direct that if I am brain dead, an anatomical gift be offered on my behalf to a patient in need of an organ or tissue transplant. If a transplant occurs, I want artificial heart/lung support devices to be continued on my behalf only until organ or tissue suitability of the patient is confirmed and organ or tissue recovery has taken place.

(3) If I have an end-stage condition, that is a condition caused by injury, disease, or illness, as a result of which I have suffered severe and permanent deterioration indicated by incompetency and complete physical dependency and for which, to a reasonable degree of medical certainty, treatment of the irreversible condition would be medically ineffective—

    _____ I direct that my life not be extended by life-sustaining procedures, including the administration of nutrition and hydration artificially.

    _____ I direct that my life not be extended by life-sustaining procedures, except that, if I am unable to take food by mouth, I wish to receive nutrition and hydration artificially.

    _____ I direct that if I am brain dead, an anatomical gift be offered on my behalf to a patient in need of an organ or tissue transplant. If a transplant occurs, I want artificial heart/lung support devices to be continued on my behalf only until organ or tissue suitability of the patient is confirmed and organ or tissue recovery has taken place.

(4) I direct that no matter what my condition, medication not be given to me to relieve pain and suffering, if it would shorten my remaining life.

(5) I direct that no matter what my condition, I be given all available medical treatment in accordance with accepted health care standards.

(6) If I am pregnant my agent shall follow these specific instructions: _____

_____

_____

(7) I direct (in the following space, indicate any other instructions regarding receipt or nonreceipt of any health care) _____

_____

_____

_____

By signing below, I indicate that I am emotionally and mentally competent to make this advance directive and that I understand the purpose and effect of this document.

_____   _____

          (Date)   (Signature of Declarant)

The declarant signed or acknowledged signing the foregoing advance directive in my presence and based upon personal observation appears to be a competent individual.

_____   _____

         (Witness)   (Witness)

                 (Signature of Two Witnesses)

MASSACHUSETTS HEALTH CARE PROXY

Information, Instructions, and Form

What does the Health Care Proxy Law allow?

The **Health Care Proxy** is a simple legal document that allows you to name someone you know and trust to make health care decisions for you if, for any reason and at any time, you become unable to make or communicate those decisions. It is an important document, however, because it concerns not only the choices you make about your health care, but also the relationships you have with your physician, family, and others who may be involved with your care. Read this and follow the instructions to ensure that your wishes are honored.

Under the Health Care Proxy Law (Massachusetts General Laws, Chapter 201D), any competent adult 18 years of age or over may use this form to appoint a Heath Care Agent. You (the "Principal") can appoint anyone EXCEPT the administrator, operator, or employee of a health care facility such as a hospital or nursing home where you are a patient or resident UNLESS that person is also related to you by blood, marriage, or adoption.

What can my Agent do?

Your Agent will make decisions about your health care <u>only</u> when you are, for some reason, unable to do that yourself. This means that your Agent can act for you if you are temporarily unconscious, in a coma, or have some other condition in which you cannot make or communicate health care decisions. Your Agent cannot act for you until your doctor determines, in writing, that you lack the ability to make health care decisions. Your doctor will tell you of this if there is any sign that you would understand it.

Acting with your authority, your Agent can make any health care decision that you could, if you were able. If you give your Agent full authority to act for you, he or she can consent to or refuse any medical treatment, including treatment that could keep you alive.

Your Agent will make decisions for you only after talking with your doctor or health care provider, and after fully considering all the options regarding diagnosis, prognosis, and treatment of your illness or condition. Your Agent has the legal right to get any information, including confidential medical information, necessary to make informed decisions for you.

Your Agent will make health care decisions for you according to your wishes or according to his/her assessment of your wishes, including your religious or moral beliefs. You may wish to talk first with your doctor, religious adviser, or other people before giving instructions to your Agent. It is very important that you talk with your Agent so that he or she knows what is important to you. If your Agent does not know what your wishes would be in a particular situation, your Agent will decide based on what he or she thinks would be in your best interests. After your doctor has determined that you lack the ability to make health care decisions, if you still object to any decision made by your Agent, your own decisions will be honored unless a Court determines that you lack the capacity to make health care decisions.

Your Agent's decisions will have the same authority as you would, if you were able, and will be honored over those of any other person, except for any limitation you yourself made, or except for a Court Order specifically overriding the Proxy.

How do I fill out the form?

[1] At the top of the form, print your full name and address. Print the name, address, and phone number of the person you choose as your Health Care Agent. (**Optional:** If you think your Agent might not be available at any future time, you may name a second person as an Alternate. Your Alternate will be called if your Agent is unwilling or unable to serve.)

2️⃣ Setting limits on your Agent's authority might make it difficult for your Agent to act for you in an unexpected situation. If you want your Agent to have full authority to act for you, leave the limitations space blank. If, however, you want to limit the kinds of decisions you would want your Agent or Alternate to make for you, include them in the blank.

3️⃣ **BEFORE** you sign, be sure you have two adults present who can witness you signing the document. The only people who cannot serve as witnesses are your Agent and Alternate. Then sign the document yourself. (Or, if you are physically unable, have someone else sign at your direction. The person who signs your name for you should put his/her name and address in the spaces provided.)

4️⃣ Have your witnesses fill in the date, sign their names and print their names and addresses.

5️⃣ **OPTIONAL:** On the back of the form are statements to be signed by your Agent and any Alternate. This is not required by law, but is recommended to ensure that you have talked with the person or persons who may have to make important decisions about your care and that each of them realizes the importance of the task they may have to do.

Who should have the original and copies?

After you have filled in the form, remove this information page and make at least four photocopies of the form. Keep the original yourself where it can be found easily (not in your safe deposit box). Give one copy to your doctor who will put it in your medical record. Give copies to your Agent and any Alternate. You can give additional copies to family members, your clergy and/or lawyer, and other people who may be involved in your health care decisionmaking.

How can I revoke or cancel the document?

Your Health Care Proxy is revoked when any of the following four things happen:

1. You sign another Health Care Proxy later on.
2. You legally separate from or divorce your spouse and your spouse is named in the Proxy as your Agent.
3. You notify your Agent, your doctor, or other heath care provider, orally or in writing, that you want to revoke your Health Care Proxy.
4. You do anything else that clearly shows you want to revoke the Proxy, for example, tearing up or destroying the Proxy, crossing it out, telling other people, etc.

1️⃣ I, _____, residing at
(Principal - PRINT your name)

_____,
(Street)   (City or Town)   (State)
appoint as my **Health Care Agent:** _____ of
(Name of person you choose as Agent)

_____
(Street)   (City or Town)   (State)

(OPTIONAL: If my Agent is unwilling or unable to serve, then I appoint as my **Alternate:**

_____ of
(Name of person you choose as Alternate)
_____.)
(Street)   (City or Town)   (State)

2️⃣ My Agent shall have the authority to make all health care decisions for me, including decisions about life-sustaining treatment, subject to any limitations I state below, if I am unable to make health care decisions myself. My Agent's authority becomes effective if my attending physician determines in writing that I lack the capacity to make or to communicate health care decisions. My Agent is then to have the same authority to make health care decisions as I would if I had the capacity to make them **EXCEPT** (here list the limitations, if any, you wish to place on your Agent's authority):

I direct my Agent to make health care decisions based on my Agent's assessment of my personal wishes. If my personal wishes are unknown, my Agent is to make health care decisions based on my Agent's assessment of my best interests. Photocopies of this Health Care Proxy shall have the same force and effect as the original.

3   Signed: _____

Complete only if Principal is physically unable to sign: I have signed the Principal's name above at his/her direction in the presence of the Principal and two witnesses.

_____   _____
            (Name)   (Street)

                                      _____
                                       (City/Town)   (State)

4   **WITNESS STATEMENT:** We, the undersigned, each witnessed the signing of this Health Care Proxy by the Principal or at the direction of the Principal and state that the Principal appears to be at least 18 years of age, of sound mind and under no constraint or undue influence. Neither of us is named as the Health Care Agent or Alternate in this document.
In our presence this _____ day of _____, _____.

Witness # 1 _____   Witness # 2 _____
                  (signature)   (signature)
Name (print) _____   Name (print) _____
Address: _____   Address: _____

_____   _____

5   **Statements of Health Care Agent and Alternate (OPTIONAL)**

Health Care Agent: I have been named by the Principal as the Principal's **Health Care Agent** by this Health Care Proxy. I have read this document carefully, and have personally discussed with the Principal his/her health care wishes at a time of possible incapacity. I know the Principal and accept this appointment freely. I am not an operator, administrator or employee of a hospital, clinic, nursing home, rest home, Soldiers Home or other health facility where the Principal is presently a patient or resident or had applied for admission. Or if I am a person so described, I am also related to the Principal by blood, marriage, or adoption. If called upon and to the best of my ability, I will try to carry out the Principal's wishes.

(Signature of **Health Care Agent**) _____

Alternate: I have been named by the Principal as the Principal's **Alternate** by this Health Care Proxy. I have read this document carefully, and have personally discussed with the Principal his/her health care wishes at a time of possible incapacity. I know the Principal and accept this appointment freely. I am not an operator, administrator or employee of a hospital, clinic, nursing home, rest home, Soldiers Home or other health facility where the Principal is presently a patient or resident or had applied for admission. Or if I am a person so described, I am also related to the Principal by blood, marriage, or adoption. If called upon and to the best of my ability, I will try to carry out the Principal's wishes.

(Signature of **Alternate**) _____

LIMITED POWER OF ATTORNEY

I, _____, presently residing at _____
_____, as the parent of _____,
hereinafter referred to as my child, hereby delegate to _____,
hereinafter referred to as my agent, the authority to act in my place and stead with respect to each of the following powers, and pursuant to § 405 of the Revised Probate Code of Michigan, to wit, the power:

1. To enroll or withdraw my child from any school or similar institution;

2. To consent to any necessary medical treatment, surgery, medication, therapy, hospitalization or other
such care of or for my child;

3. To employ, retain or discharge any person who may care for, counsel, treat or in any manner assist my child.

4. To exercise the same parental rights I may exercise with respect to the care, custody and control of my
child, and the discretion to exercise the same rights in my agent's home or any other place selected by my agent
in his or her discretion;

5. To perform all other acts necessary, or incidental to the execution of the powers enumerated herein;

Any lawful act performed by my agent shall be binding upon myself, my heirs, beneficiaries, personal representatives and assigns. I reserve the right to amend or revoke this Limited Power of Attorney at any time
hereafter; provided, however, any institution or other party dealing with my agent may rely upon this Limited
Power of Attorney until receipt by it of a duly executed copy of my revocation thereof.

Any reproduced copy of this signed original shall be deemed to be an original counterpart of this Limited
Power of Attorney. This Limited Power of Attorney shall not be affected by any legal incapacity during my lifetime, except as provided by statute.

This Limited Power of Attorney shall terminate, if not re-executed, six (6) months from the date which
appears below. This Limited Power of Attorney may be re-executed for a period not to exceed six (6) months
by the notarized execution of a statement referring to this Limited Power of Attorney.

_____
Signature

STATE OF MICHIGAN   )
COUNTY OF   )

On this _____ day of _____, _____, before me personally appeared
_____, to me known to be the person described in and who executed
the above Limited Power of Attorney, and who acknowledged the same to be his/her free act and deed.

_____
Notary Public
_____ County, Michigan
My Commission Expires:_____

I, _____, hereby affirm and extend the powers delegated by
the Limited Power of Attorney, originally dated _____, which document or a copy of
which document is attached hereto.

_____
Signature

STATE OF MICHIGAN   )
COUNTY OF   )

On this _____ day of _____, _____, before me personally appeared
_____, to me known to be the person described in and who executed
the above Limited Power of Attorney, and who acknowledged the same to be his/her free act and deed.

_____
Notary Public
_____ County, Michigan
My Commission Expires:_____

STATUTORY SHORT FORM POWER OF ATTORNEY
MINNESOTA STATUTES, SECTION 523.23

IMPORTANT NOTICE: The powers granted by this document are broad and sweeping. They are defined in Minnesota Statutes, section 523.24. If you have any questions about these powers, obtain competent advice. This power of attorney may be revoked by you if you wish to do so. This power of attorney is automatically terminated if it is to your spouse and proceedings are commenced for dissolution, legal separation, or annulment of your marriage. This power of attorney authorizes, but does not require, the attorney-in-fact to act for you.

PRINCIPAL (Name and Address of Person Granting the Power)

_____

_____

_____

ATTORNEY(S)-IN-FACT   SUCCESSOR ATTORNEY(S)-IN-FACT
(Name and Address)   (Optional) To act if any named attorney-in-fact
                                            dies, resigns, or is otherwise unable to serve.
                                            (Name and Address)
                                            First Successor_____

_____   _____

_____

_____   Second Successor_____

_____

_____   _____

NOTICE: If more than one attorney-in-fact is designated, make a check or "x" on the line in front of one of the following statements:

_____   Each attorney-in-fact may independently   EXPIRATION DATE (Optional)
          exercise the powers granted.
                                                         _____, _____
_____   All attorneys-in-fact must jointly exercise   Use Specific Month Day Year Only
          the powers granted.

I, (the above-named Principal) hereby appoint the above named Attorney(s)-in-Fact to act as my attorney(s)-in-fact:

FIRST: To act for me in any way that I could act with respect to the following matters, as each of them is defined in Minnesota Statutes, section 523.24:

(To grant to the attorney-in-fact any of the following powers, make a check or "x" on the line in front of each power being granted. You may, but need not, cross out each power not granted. Failure to make a check or "x" on the line in front of the power will have the effect of deleting the power unless the line in front of the power (N) is checked or x-ed.)

Check or "x"

_____   (A) real property transactions;
               I choose to limit this power to real property in _____ County, Minnesota,
               described as follows: (Use legal description. Do not use street address.)

(If more space is needed, continue on back or on an attachment.)

_____   (B) tangible personal property transactions;
_____   (C) bond, share, and commodity transactions;
_____   (D) banking transactions;
_____   (E) business operating transactions;

_____ (F) insurance transactions;
_____ (G) beneficiary transactions;
_____ (H) gift transactions;
_____ (I) fiduciary transactions;
_____ (J) claims and litigation;
_____ (K) family maintenance;
_____ (L) benefits from military service;
_____ (M) records, reports, and statements;
_____ (N) all of the powers listed in (A) through (M) above and all other matters.

SECOND: (You must indicate below whether or not this power of attorney will be effective if you become incapacitated or incompetent. Make a check or "x" on the line in front of the statement that expresses your intent.)

_____ This power of attorney shall continue to be effective if I become incapacitated or incompetent.
_____ This power of attorney shall not be effective if I become incapacitated or incompetent.

THIRD: (You must indicate below whether or not this power of attorney authorizes the attorney-in-fact to transfer your property to the attorney-in-fact. Make a check or "x" on the line in front of the statement that expresses your intent.)

_____ This power of attorney authorizes the attorney-in-fact to transfer my property to the attorney-in-fact.
_____ This power of attorney does not authorize the attorney-in-fact to transfer my property to the attorney-in-fact.

FOURTH: (You may indicate below whether or not the attorney-in-fact is required to make an accounting. Make a check or "x" on the line in front of the statement that expresses your intent.)

_____ My attorney-in-fact need not render an accounting unless I request it or the accounting is otherwise required by Minnesota Statutes, section 523.21.
_____ My attorney-in-fact must render _____
                                        (Monthly, Quarterly, Annually)

accountings to me or _____
                        (Name and Address)

during my lifetime, and a final accounting to the personal representative of my estate, if any is appointed, after my death.

In Witness Whereof I have hereunto signed my name this _____ day of _____,
_____.

_____
(Signature of Principal)

(Acknowledgment of Principal)

STATE OF MINNESOTA   )
) ss.
COUNTY OF _____)
The foregoing instrument was acknowledged before me this _____ day of _____,
_____, by _____
                  (Insert Name of Principal)

_____
(Signature of Notary Public or other Official)

This instrument was drafted by:

Specimen Signature of Attorney(s)-in-Fact
(Notarization not required)

_____   _____
_____   _____
_____   _____
                                      _____

Durable Power of Attorney for Health Care

I appoint _____ as my
agent (my attorney in fact) to make any health care decision for me when, in the judgment of my attending
physician, I am unable to make or communicate the decision myself and my agent consents to make or communicate the decision on my behalf.

My agent has the power to make any health care decision for me. This power includes the power to give
consent, to refuse consent, or to withdraw consent to any care, treatment, service, or procedure to maintain,
diagnose, or treat my physical or mental condition, including giving me food or water by artificial means. My
agent has the power, where consistent with the laws of this state, to make a health care decision to withhold
or stop health care necessary to keep me alive. It is my intention that my agent or any alternate agent has a
personal obligation to me to make health care decisions for me consistent with my expressed wishes. I understand, however, that my agent or any alternate agent has no legal duty to act.

My agent and any alternate agents have consented to act as my agent. My agent and any alternative agents
have been notified that they will be nominated as a guardian or conservator for me.

My agent must act consistently with my desires as stated in this document or as otherwise made known by
me to my agent.

My agent has the same right as I would have to receive, review, and obtain copies of my medical records
and to consent to disclosure of those records.

OPTIONAL: Designation of Alternate Agents. In the event my agent named above is unable, unwilling or
unavailable to act, I appoint the following alternate agent(s) in the order listed:

First Alternate: _____

Second Alternate: _____

OPTIONAL: Instructions and Limitations. My agent and any alternate agent shall be guided by the following
instructions and shall be limited in authority as follows:

_____
_____

DATED: _____   SIGNED: _____

STATE OF _____

COUNTY OF _____

Subscribed, sworn to, and acknowledged before me by _____
on this _____ day of _____, _____.

_____
NOTARY PUBLIC

OR

(Sign and date here in the presence of two adult witnesses, neither of whom is entitled to any part of your
estate under a will or by operation of law, and neither of whom is your proxy.)

I certify that the declarant voluntarily signed this living will in my presence and that the declarant is personally known to me. I am not named as a proxy by the living will, and to the best of my knowledge, I am not
entitled to any part of the estate of the declarant under a will or by operation of law.

Witness _____   Address _____

Witness _____   Address _____

Durable Power of Attorney for Health Care

NOTICE TO PERSON EXECUTING THIS DOCUMENT

This is an important legal document. Before executing this document, you should know these important facts:

This document gives the person you designate as the attorney in fact (your agent) the power to make health care decisions for you. This power exists only as to those health care decisions to which you are unable to give informed consent. The attorney in fact must act consistently with your desires as stated in this document or otherwise made known.

Except as you otherwise specify in this document, this document gives your agent the power to consent to your doctor not giving treatment or stopping treatment necessary to keep you alive.

Notwithstanding this document, you have the right to make medical and other health care decisions for yourself so long as you can give informed consent with respect to the particular decision. In addition, no treatment may be given to you over your objection, and health care necessary to keep you alive may not be stopped or withheld if you object at the time.

The document gives your agent authority to consent, to refuse to consent or to withdraw consent to any care, treatment, service or procedure to maintain, diagnose or treat a physical or mental condition. This power is subject to any statement of your desires and any limitations that you include in this document. You may state in this document any types of treatment that you do not desire.

In addition, a court can take away the power of your agent to make health care decisions for you if your agent (a) authorizes anything that is illegal, (b) acts contrary to your known desires, or (c) where your desires are not known, does anything that is clearly contrary to your best interests.

You have the right to revoke the authority of your agent by notifying your agent or your treating doctor, hospital or other health care provider in writing of the revocation.

Your agent has the right to examine your medical records and to consent to this disclosure unless you limit this right in this document.

Unless you otherwise specify in this document, this document gives your agent the power after you die to (a) authorize an autopsy, (b) donate your body or parts thereof for transplant or for educational, therapeutic or scientific purposes, and (c) direct the disposition of your remains.

If there is anything in this document that you do not understand, you should ask your lawyer to explain it to you.

This power of attorney will not be valid for making health care decisions unless it is either (a) signed by two (2) qualified adult witnesses who are personally known to you and who are present when you sign or acknowledge your signature or (b) acknowledged before a notary public in the state.

I, _____ (name), hereby appoint:

_____
Name

_____
Home Address

_____   _____
Work Telephone Number   Home Telephone Number

as my attorney in fact to make health care decisions for me in the event I become unable to give informed consent with respect to a given health care decision.

Subject to my special instructions below, this document gives my attorney in fact the full power to make health care decisions for me, before or after my death, to the same extent I could make decisions for myself and to the full extent permitted by law, including power to grant, refuse or withdraw consent on my behalf for any health care service, to make a disposition under the state's anatomical gift act, to authorize an autopsy, and to direct the disposition of my remains. My attorney in fact also has the authority to talk to health care personnel, get information and sign forms necessary to carry out these decisions, and also the power provided in Sections 41-41-101 through 41-41-121, Mississippi Code of 1972, as now enacted or hereafter amended, being the statutes governing the withdrawal of life-saving mechanisms.

Special instructions:_____

_____

_____

_____

If the person named as my attorney in fact is not available or is unable to act as my attorney in fact, I appoint the following person to serve in his or her place:

_____
Name

_____
Home Address

_____   _____
Work Telephone Number   Home Telephone Number

By my signature I do hereby indicate that I understand the purpose and effect of this document.

Date:_____   _____
                                                            (Signature)

STATEMENT OF WITNESSES

I declare under penalty or perjury under the laws of the State of Mississippi that the principal is personally known to me, that the principal signed or acknowledged this durable power of attorney in my presence, that the principal appears to be of sound mind and under no duress, fraud or undue influence, that I am not the person appointed as attorney in fact by this document, and that I am not a health care provider, nor an employee of a health care provider or facility.

Witness_____   Witness_____

I am not related to the principal by blood, marriage or adoption, and to the best of my knowledge, I am not entitled to any part of the estate of the principal under a will now existing or by operation of law.

                                                            Witness_____

State of _____

County of _____

On this _____ day of _____, in the year _____, before me,
_____ (insert name of notary public),
appeared _____ personally known to me (or proved to me on the basis of satisfactory evidence) to be the person whose name is subscribed to this instrument, and acknowledged that he or she executed it. I declare under the penalty of perjury that the person whose name is subscribed to this instrument appears to be of sound mind and under no duress, fraud or undue influence.

Notary Seal   _____
                                                            (Signature of Notary Public)

POWER OF ATTORNEY

NOTICE: THE POWERS GRANTED BY THIS DOCUMENT ARE BROAD AND SWEEPING. THEY ARE EXPLAINED IN THIS PART. IF YOU HAVE ANY QUESTIONS ABOUT THESE POWERS, OBTAIN COMPETENT LEGAL ADVICE. THIS DOCUMENT DOES NOT AUTHORIZE ANYONE TO MAKE MEDICAL AND OTHER HEALTH CARE DECISIONS FOR YOU. YOU MAY REVOKE THIS POWER OF ATTORNEY IF YOU LATER WISH TO DO SO.

I _____ (insert your name and address) appoint _____ _____(insert the name and address of the person appointed) as my agent (attorney-in-fact) to act for me in any lawful way with respect to the following initialed subjects:

TO GRANT ALL OF THE FOLLOWING POWERS, INITIAL THE LINE IN FRONT OF (N) AND IGNORE THE LINES IN FRONT OF THE OTHER POWERS.

TO GRANT ONE OR MORE, BUT FEWER THAN ALL, OF THE FOLLOWING POWERS, INITIAL THE LINE IN FRONT OF EACH POWER YOU ARE GRANTING.

TO WITHHOLD A POWER, DO NOT INITIAL THE LINE IN FRONT OF IT. YOU MAY, BUT NEED NOT, CROSS OUT EACH POWER WITHHELD.

INITIAL

_____ (A) real property transactions;
_____ (B) tangible personal property transactions;
_____ (C) stock and bond transactions;
_____ (D) commodity and option transactions;
_____ (E) banking and other financial institution transactions;
_____ (F) business operating transactions;
_____ (G) insurance and annuity transactions;
_____ (H) estate, trust, and other beneficiary transactions;
_____ (I) claims and litigation;
_____ (J) personal and family maintenance;
_____ (K) benefits from social security, medicare, medicaid, or other governmental programs or from military service;
_____ (L) retirement plan transactions;
_____ (M) tax matters;
_____ (N) ALL OF THE POWERS LISTED ABOVE. YOU NEED NOT INITIAL ANY OTHER LINES IF YOU INITIAL LINE (N).

SPECIAL INSTRUCTIONS:
ON THE FOLLOWING LINES, YOU MAY GIVE SPECIAL INSTRUCTIONS LIMITING
OR EXTENDING THE POWERS GRANTED TO YOUR AGENT.

_____
_____
_____
_____
_____

UNLESS YOU DIRECT OTHERWISE ABOVE, THIS POWER OF ATTORNEY IS EFFECTIVE IMMEDIATELY AND WILL CONTINUE UNTIL IT IS REVOKED.

_____   This power of attorney revokes all previous powers of attorney signed by me.

STRIKE THE PRECEDING SENTENCE IF YOU DO NOT WANT THIS POWER OF ATTORNEY TO REVOKE ALL PREVIOUS POWERS OF ATTORNEY SIGNED BY YOU.

IF YOU DO WANT THIS POWER OF ATTORNEY TO REVOKE ALL PREVIOUS POWERS OF ATTORNEY SIGNED BY YOU, YOU SHOULD READ THOSE POWERS OF ATTORNEY AND SATISFY THEIR

PROVISIONS CONCERNING REVOCATION. THIRD PARTIES WHO RECEIVED COPIES OF THOSE POWERS OF ATTORNEY SHOULD BE NOTIFIED.

_____ This power of attorney will continue to be effective if I become disabled, incapacitated, or incompetent.

STRIKE THE PRECEDING SENTENCE IF YOU DO NOT WANT THIS POWER OF ATTORNEY TO CONTINUE IF YOU BECOME DISABLED, INCAPACITATED, OR INCOMPETENT.

If it becomes necessary to appoint a conservator of my estate or guardian of my person, I nominate my agent.

STRIKE THE PRECEDING SENTENCE IF YOU DO NOT WANT TO NOMINATE YOUR AGENT AS CONSERVATOR OR GUARDIAN.

If any agent named by me dies, becomes incompetent, resigns or refuses to accept the office or agent, I name the following (each to act and successively, in the order named) as successor(s) to the agent:

1. _____
2. _____
3. _____

For purposes of this subsection, a person is considered to be incompetent if and while: (1) the person is a minor; (2) the person is an adjudicated incompetent or disabled person; (3) a conservator has been appointed to act for the person; (4) a guardian has been appointed to act for the person; or (5) the person is unable to give prompt and intelligent consideration to business matters as certified by a licensed physician.

I agree that any third party who receives a copy of this document may act under it. I may revoke this power of attorney by a written document that expressly indicates my intent to revoke. Revocation of the power of attorney is not effective as to a third party until the third party learns of the revocation. I agree to indemnify the third party for any claims that arise against the third party because of reliance on this power of attorney.

Signed this _____ day of _____, _____.

_____
(Your Signature)

_____
(Your Social Security Number)

State of _____
(County) of _____

This document was acknowledged before me on

_____
(Date) by

_____
(Name of Principal)

_____
(Signature of Notarial Officer

_____
(Title (and Rank))

[My commission expires:_____]

(Seal, if any)

BY ACCEPTING OR ACTING UNDER THE APPOINTMENT, THE AGENT ASSUMES THE FIDUCIARY AND OTHER LEGAL RESPONSIBILITIES OF AN AGENT.

POWER OF ATTORNEY

_____, a domiciliary of _____ County, Nebraska, Principal, desiring and intending to establish a Power of Attorney operative under the Nebraska Short Form Act, does hereby appoint, constitute, and designate _____, a _____ of or with an office in _____ County, Nebraska, and _____, a _____ of or with an office in _____ County, Nebraska, Agent, the lawful and true Agent and attorney in fact for Principal; and Principal does hereby further provide and stipulate in connection therewith as follows:

1. This Power of Attorney is, as marked, a
    ( ) Durable Power of Attorney and a
        ( ) Contingent Durable Power of Attorney, upon the contingency of,
            ( ) Incompetence of Principal, or
            ( ) Other Contingency:_____, or
        ( ) Present Durable Power of Attorney
    ( ) Nondurable Power of Attorney.

2. By this Power of Attorney, Principal confers upon and grants to Agent plenary power, plenary power subject to limitations, or all and each of the listed general powers as individually marked:
    ( ) Plenary Power; or
    ( ) Plenary Power Subject to Limitations, exclusive of General Powers for Domestic and Personal Concerns and for Fiduciary Relationships and
        ( ) No Other Restrictions, or
        ( ) Other Restrictions:_____; or
        ( ) General Power for Bank and Financial Transactions.
        ( ) General Power for Business Transactions.
        ( ) General Power for Chattels and Goods.
        ( ) General Power for Disputes and Litigation.
        ( ) General Power for Domestic and Personal Concerns.
        ( ) General Power for Fiduciary Relationships.
        ( ) General Power for Governmental and Other Benefits.
        ( ) General Power for Insurance Coverages and Policies.
        ( ) General Power for Proprietary Interests and Materials.
        ( ) General Power for Real Estate.
        ( ) General Power for Securities.
        ( ) General Power for Records, Reports, and Statements.

3. By this Power of Attorney, Principal makes the following additional provision or provisions:
    _____
    _____
    _____

4. This Power of Attorney revokes and supersedes all prior executed instruments of like import and remains operative until revoked.

EXECUTED AT _____, _____ County, Nebraska, on _____, _____.

_____
Principal

STATE OF NEBRASKA   )
) ss.
COUNTY OF _____)

The foregoing instrument was acknowledged before me on _____, _____, by the Principal _____.

_____
Notary Public

POWER OF ATTORNEY FOR HEALTH CARE

I appoint _____, whose address is _____ _____, and whose telephone number is _____, as my attorney in fact for health care. I appoint _____, whose address is _____ _____, and whose telephone number is _____, as my successor attorney in fact for health care. I authorize my attorney in fact appointed by this document to make health care decisions for me when I am determined to be incapable of making my own health care decisions. I have read the warning which accompanies this document and understand the consequences of executing a power of attorney for health care.

I direct that my attorney in fact comply with the following instructions or limitations:

_____

_____

_____

I direct that my attorney in fact comply with the following instructions on life-sustaining treatment: (optional) _____

_____

_____

I direct that my attorney in fact comply with the following instructions on artificially administered nutrition and hydration: (optional) _____

_____

_____

I HAVE READ THIS POWER OF ATTORNEY FOR HEALTH CARE. I UNDERSTAND THAT IT ALLOWS ANOTHER PERSON TO MAKE LIFE AND DEATH DECISIONS FOR ME IF I AM INCAPABLE OF MAKING SUCH DECISIONS. I ALSO UNDERSTAND THAT I CAN REVOKE THIS POWER OF ATTORNEY FOR HEALTH CARE AT ANY TIME BY NOTIFYING MY ATTORNEY IN FACT, MY PHYSICIAN, OR THE FACILITY IN WHICH I AM A PATIENT OR RESIDENT. I ALSO UNDERSTAND THAT I CAN REQUIRE IN THIS POWER OF ATTORNEY FOR HEALTH CARE THAT THE FACT OF MY INCAPACITY IN THE FUTURE BE CONFIRMED BY A SECOND PHYSICIAN.

_____

(Signature of person making designation/date)

DECLARATION OF WITNESSES

We declare that the principal is personally known to us, that the principal signed or acknowledged his or her signature on this power of attorney for health care in our presence, that the principal appears to be of sound mind and not under duress or undue influence, and that neither of us not the principal's attending physician is the person appointed as attorney in fact by this document.

Witnessed By:

_____   _____
(Signature of Witness/Date)   (Printed Name of Witness)

_____   _____
(Signature of Witness/Date)   (Printed Name of Witness)

OR

State of Nebraska,   )
) ss.
County of _____)

   On this _____ day of _____, _____, before me, _____ _____, a notary public in and for _____ County, personally came _____, personally to me known to be the identical person whose name is affixed to the above power of attorney for health care as principal, and I declare that he or she appears in sound mind and not under duress or undue influence, that he or she acknowledges the execution of the same to be his or her voluntary act and deed, and that I am not the attorney in fact or successor attorney in fact designated by this power of attorney for health care.

   Witness my hand and notarial seal at _____ in such county the day and year last above written.

Seal   _____
                                                      Signature of Notary Public

DURABLE POWER OF ATTORNEY FOR HEALTH CARE DECISIONS

WARNING TO PERSON EXECUTING THIS DOCUMENT

THIS IS AN IMPORTANT LEGAL DOCUMENT. IT CREATES A DURABLE POWER OF ATTORNEY FOR HEALTH CARE. BEFORE EXECUTING THIS DOCUMENT, YOU SHOULD KNOW THESE IMPORTANT FACTS:

1. THIS DOCUMENT GIVES THE PERSON YOU DESIGNATE AS YOUR ATTORNEY-IN-FACT THE POWER TO MAKE HEALTH CARE DECISIONS FOR YOU. THIS POWER IS SUBJECT TO ANY LIMITATIONS OR STATEMENT OF YOUR DESIRES THAT YOU INCLUDE IN THIS DOCUMENT. THE POWER TO MAKE HEALTH CARE DECISIONS FOR YOU MAY INCLUDE CONSENT, REFUSAL OF CONSENT, OR WITHDRAWAL OF CONSENT TO ANY CARE, TREATMENT, SERVICE, OR PROCEDURE TO MAINTAIN, DIAGNOSE, OR TREAT A PHYSICAL OR MENTAL CONDITION. YOU MAY STATE IN THIS DOCUMENT ANY TYPES OF TREATMENT OR PLACEMENTS THAT YOU DO NOT DESIRE.

2. THE PERSON YOU DESIGNATE IN THIS DOCUMENT HAS A DUTY TO ACT CONSISTENT WITH YOUR DESIRES AS STATED IN THIS DOCUMENT OR OTHERWISE MADE KNOWN OR, IF YOUR DESIRES ARE UNKNOWN, TO ACT IN YOUR BEST INTERESTS.

3. EXCEPT AS YOU OTHERWISE SPECIFY IN THIS DOCUMENT, THE POWER OF THE PERSON YOU DESIGNATE TO MAKE HEALTH CARE DECISIONS FOR YOU MAY INCLUDE THE POWER TO CONSENT TO YOUR DOCTOR NOT GIVING TREATMENT OR STOPPING TREATMENT WHICH WOULD KEEP YOU ALIVE.

4. UNLESS YOU SPECIFY A SHORTER PERIOD IN THIS DOCUMENT, THIS POWER WILL EXIST INDEFINITELY FROM THE DATE YOU EXECUTE THIS DOCUMENT AND, IF YOU ARE UNABLE TO MAKE HEALTH CARE DECISIONS FOR YOURSELF, THIS POWER WILL CONTINUE TO EXIST UNTIL THE TIME WHEN YOU BECOME ABLE TO MAKE HEALTH CARE DECISIONS FOR YOURSELF.

5. NOTWITHSTANDING THIS DOCUMENT, YOU HAVE THE RIGHT TO MAKE MEDICAL AND OTHER HEALTH CARE DECISIONS FOR YOURSELF SO LONG AS YOU CAN GIVE INFORMED CONSENT WITH RESPECT TO THE PARTICULAR DECISION. IN ADDITION, NO TREATMENT MAY BE GIVEN TO YOU OVER YOUR OBJECTION, AND HEALTH CARE NECESSARY TO KEEP YOU ALIVE MAY NOT BE STOPPED IF YOU OBJECT.

6. YOU HAVE THE RIGHT TO REVOKE THE APPOINTMENT OF THE PERSON DESIGNATED IN THIS DOCUMENT TO MAKE HEALTH CARE DECISIONS FOR YOU BY NOTIFYING THAT PERSON OF THE REVOCATION ORALLY OR IN WRITING.

7. YOU HAVE THE RIGHT TO REVOKE THE AUTHORITY GRANTED TO THE PERSON DESIGNATED IN THIS DOCUMENT TO MAKE HEALTH CARE DECISIONS FOR YOU BY NOTIFYING THE TREATING PHYSICIAN, HOSPITAL, OR OTHER PROVIDER OR HEALTH CARE ORALLY OR IN WRITING.

8. THE PERSON DESIGNATED IN THIS DOCUMENT TO MAKE HEALTH CARE DECISIONS FOR YOU HAS THE RIGHT TO EXAMINE YOUR MEDICAL RECORDS AND TO CONSENT TO THEIR DISCLOSURE UNLESS YOU LIMIT THIS RIGHT IN THIS DOCUMENT.

9. THIS DOCUMENT REVOKES ANY PRIOR DURABLE POWER OF ATTORNEY FOR HEALTH CARE.

10. IF THERE IS ANYTHING IN THIS DOCUMENT THAT YOU DO NOT UNDERSTAND, YOU SHOULD ASK A LAWYER TO EXPLAIN IT TO YOU.

1. DESIGNATION OF HEALTH CARE AGENT.

I, _____

(insert your name) do hereby designate and appoint:

    Name:_____

    Address:_____

    Telephone Number:_____

as my attorney-in-fact to make health care decisions for me as authorized in this document.

    (Insert the name and address of the person you wish to designate as your attorney-in-fact to make health care decisions for you. Unless the person is also your spouse, legal guardian or the person most closely related to you by blood, none of the following may be designated as your attorney-in-fact: (1) your treating provider of health care, (2) an employee of your treating provider of health care, (3) an operator of a health care facility, or (4) an employee of an operator of a health care facility.)

2. CREATION OF DURABLE POWER OF ATTORNEY FOR HEALTH CARE.

By this document I intend to create a durable power of attorney by appointing the person designated above to make health care decisions for me. This power of attorney shall not be affected by my subsequent incapacity.

3. GENERAL STATEMENT OF AUTHORITY GRANTED.

In the event that I am incapable of giving informed consent with respect to health care decisions, I hereby grant to the attorney-in-fact named above full power and authority to make health care decisions for me before, or after my death, including: consent, refusal or consent, or withdrawal of consent to any care, treatment, service, or procedure to maintain, diagnose, or treat a physical or mental condition, subject only to the limitations and special provisions, if any, set forth in paragraph 4 or 6.

4. SPECIAL PROVISIONS AND LIMITATIONS.

(Your attorney-in-fact is not permitted to any of the following: commitment to or placement in a mental health treatment facility, convulsive treatment, psychosurgery, sterilization, or abortion. If there are any other types of treatment or placement that you do not want your attorney-in-fact's authority to give consent for or other restrictions you wish to place on his or her attorney-in-fact's authority, you should list them in the space below. If you do not write any limitations, your attorney-in-fact will have the broad powers to make health care decisions on your behalf which are set forth in paragraph 3, except to the extent that there are limits provided by law.)

In exercising the authority under this durable power of attorney for health care, the authority of my attorney-in-fact is subject to the following special provisions and limitations: _____

_____

5. DURATION.

I understand that this power of attorney will exist indefinitely from the date I execute this document unless I establish a shorter time. If I am unable to make health care decisions for myself when this power of attorney expires, the authority I have granted my attorney-in-fact will continue to exist until the time when I become able to make health care decisions for myself.

(IF APPLICABLE)

I wish to have this power of attorney end on the following date:_____

6. STATEMENT OF DESIRES.

(With respect to decisions to withhold or withdraw life-sustaining treatment, your attorney-in-fact must make health care decisions that are consistent with your known desires. You can, but are not required to, indicate your desires below. If your desires are unknown, your attorney-in-fact has the duty to act in your best interests; and, under some circumstances, a judicial proceeding may be necessary so that a court can determine the health care decision that is in your best interests. If you wish to indicate your desires, you may INITIAL the statement or statements that reflect your desires and/or write your own statements in the space below.)

(If the statement reflects your desires, initial the box next to the statement.)

1. I desire that my life be prolonged to the greatest extent possible, without regard to my condition, the chances I have for recovery or long-term survival, or the cost of the procedures. [_____]

2. If I am in a coma which my doctors have reasonably concluded is irreversible, I desire that life-sustaining or prolonging treatments not be used. (Also should utilize provisions of NRS 449.535 to 449.690, inclusive, if this subparagraph is initialed.) [_____]

3. If I have an incurable or terminal condition or illness and no reasonable hope of long term recovery or survival, desire that life sustaining or prolonging treatments not be used. (Also should utilize provisions of NRS 449.535 to 449.690, inclusive, if this subparagraph is initialed.) [_____]

4. Withholding or withdrawal of artificial nutrition and hydration may result in death by starvation or dehydration. I want to receive or continue receiving artificial nutrition and hydration by way of the gastro-intestinal tract after all other treatment is withheld. [_____]

5. I do not desire treatment to be provided and/or continued if the burdens of the treatment outweigh the expected benefits. My attorney-in-fact is to consider the relief of suffering, the preservation or restoration or functioning, and the quality as well as the extent of the possible extension of my life. [_____]

(If you wish to change your answer, you may do so by drawing an "X" through the answer you do not want, and circling the answer you prefer.)

Other or Additional Statements of Desires:_____
_____
_____
_____

7. DESIGNATION OF ALTERNATIVE ATTORNEY-IN-FACT.
     (You are not required to designate any alternative attorney-in-fact but you may do so. Any alternative attorney-in-fact you designate will be able to make the same health care decisions as the attorney-in-fact designated in paragraph 1, page 2, in the event that he or she is unable or unwilling to act as your attorney-in-fact. Also, if the attorney-in-fact designated in paragraph 1 is your spouse, his or her designation as your attorney-in-fact is automatically revoked by law if your marriage is dissolved.)
     If the person designated in paragraph 1 as my attorney-in-fact is unable to make health care decisions for me, then I designate the following persons to serve as my attorney-in-fact to make health care decisions for me as authorized in this document, such persons to serve in the order listed below:

A. First Alternative Attorney-in-fact

Name:_____

Address:_____

_____

Telephone Number:_____

B. Second Alternative Attorney-in-fact

Name:_____

Address:_____

_____

Telephone Number:_____

8. PRIOR DESIGNATIONS REVOKED. I revoke any prior durable power of attorney for health care.

(YOUR POWER OF ATTORNEY WILL NOT BE VALID FOR MAKING HEALTH CARE DECISIONS UNLESS IT IS EITHER (1) SIGNED BY AT LEAST TWO QUALIFIED WITNESSES WHO ARE PERSONALLY KNOWN TO YOU AND WHO ARE PRESENT WHEN YOU SIGN OR ACKNOWLEDGE YOUR SIGNATURE OR (2) ACKNOWLEDGED BEFORE A NOTARY PUBLIC.)

CERTIFICATE OR ACKNOWLEDGMENT OF NOTARY PUBLIC

(You may use ACKNOWLEDGMENT before a notary public instead of the statement of witnesses.)

State of Nevada   )
) ss.
County of _____   )

     On this _____ day of _____, in the year _____, before me, _____(here insert name of notary public) personally appeared _____(here insert name of principal) personally known to me (or proved to me on the basis of satisfactory evidence) to be the person whose name is subscribed to this instrument, and acknowledged that he or she executed it. I declare under penalty or perjury that the person whose name is ascribed to this instrument appears to be of sound mind and under no duress, fraud, or undue influence.

NOTARY SEAL   _____
                                             (Signature of Notary Public)

STATEMENT OF WITNESSES

(You should carefully read and follow this witnessing procedure. This document will not be valid unless you comply with the witnessing procedure. If you elect to use witnesses instead of having this document notarized you must use two qualified adult witnesses. None of the following may be used as a witness: (1) a person you designate as the attorney-in-fact, (2) a provider of health care, (3) an employee of a provider of health care, (4) the operator of a health care facility, (5) an employee of an operator of a health care facility. At least one of the witnesses must make the additional declaration set out following the place where the witnesses sign.)

I declare under penalty of perjury that the principal is personally known to me, that the principal signed or acknowledged this durable power of attorney in my presence, that the principal appears to be of sound mind and under no duress, fraud, or undue influence, that I am not the person appointed as attorney-in-fact by this document, and that I am not a provider of health care, an employee of a provider of health care, the operator of a community care facility, nor an employee of an operator of a health care facility.

Signature:_____   Signature:_____

Print Name:_____   Print Name:_____

Residence Address:_____   Residence Address:_____

_____   _____

Date:_____   Date:_____

(AT LEAST ONE OF THE ABOVE WITNESSES MUST ALSO SIGN THE FOLLOWING DECLARA-TION.)

I declare under penalty of perjury that I am not related to the principal by blood, marriage, or adoption, and to the best of my knowledge I am not entitled to any part of the estate of the principal upon the death or the principal under a will now existing or by operation of law.

Signature:_____

Print Name:_____

Residence Address:_____

_____

Date:_____

COPIES: You should retain an executed copy of this document and give one to your attorney-in-fact. The power of attorney should be available so a copy may be given to your providers of health care.

DURABLE POWER OF ATTORNEY FOR HEALTH CARE

INFORMATION CONCERNING THE DURABLE
POWER OF ATTORNEY FOR HEALTH CARE

THIS IS AN IMPORTANT LEGAL DOCUMENT. BEFORE SIGNING THIS DOCUMENT YOU SHOULD KNOW THESE IMPORTANT FACTS:

Except to the extent you state otherwise, this document gives the person you name as your agent the authority to make any and all health care decisions for you when you are no longer capable of making them yourself. "Health care" means any treatment, service or procedure to maintain, diagnose or treat your physical or mental condition. Your agent, therefore, can have the poser to make a broad range of health care decisions for you. Your agent may consent, refuse to consent, or withdraw consent to medical treatment and may make decisions about withdrawing or withholding life-sustaining treatment. Your agent cannot consent or direct any of the following: commitment to a state institution, sterilization, or termination of treatment if you are pregnant and if the withdrawal of that treatment is deemed likely to terminate the pregnancy unless the failure to withhold the treatment will be physically harmful to you or prolong severe pain which cannot be alleviated by medication.

You may state in this document any treatment you do not desire, except as stated above, or treatment you want to be sure you receive. Your agent's authority will begin when your doctor certifies that you lack the capacity to make health care decisions. If for moral or religious reasons you do not wish to be treated by a doctor or examined by a doctor for the certification that you lack capacity, you must say so in the document and name a person to be able to certify your lack of capacity. That person may not be your agent or alternate agent or any person ineligible to be your agent. You may attach additional pages if you need more space to complete your statement.

If you want to give your agent authority to withhold or withdraw the artificial providing of nutrition and fluids, your document must say so. Otherwise, your agent will not be able to direct that. Under no conditions will your agent be able to direct the withholding of food and drink for you to eat and drink normally.

Your agent will be obligated to follow your instructions when making decisions on your behalf. Unless you state otherwise, your agent will have the same authority to make decisions about your health care as you would have had if made consistent with state law.

It is important that you discuss this document with your physician or other health care providers before you sign it to make sure that you understand the nature and range of decisions which may be made on your behalf. If you do not have a physician, you should talk with someone else who is knowledgeable about these issues and can answer your questions. You do not need a lawyer's assistance to complete this document, but if there is anything in this document that you do not understand, you should ask a lawyer to explain it to you.

The person you appoint as agent should be someone you know and trust and must be at least 18 years old. If you appoint your health or residential care provider (e.g. your physician, or an employee of a home health agency, hospital, nursing home, or residential care home, other than a relative), that person will have to choose between acting as your agent or as your health or residential care provider; the law does not permit a person to do both at the same time.

You should inform the person you appoint that you want him or her to be your health care agent. You should discuss this document with your agent and your physician and give each a signed copy. You should indicate on the document itself the people and institutions who will have signed copies. Your agent will not be liable for health care decisions made in good faith on your behalf.

Even after you have signed this document, you have the right to make health care decisions for yourself as long as you are able to do so, and treatment cannot be given to you or stopped over your objection. You have the right to revoke the authority granted to your agent by informing him or her or your health care provider orally or in writing.

This document may not be changed or modified. If you want to make changes in the document you must make an entirely new one.

You should consider designating an alternative agent in the event that your agent is unwilling, unable, unavailable, or ineligible to act as your agent. Any alternate agent you designate will have the same authority to make health care decisions for you.

THIS POWER OF ATTORNEY WILL NOT BE VALID UNLESS IT IS SIGNED IN THE PRESENCE OF TWO (2) OR MORE QUALIFIED WITNESSES WHO MUST BOTH BE PRESENT WHEN YOU SIGN AND ACKNOWLEDGE YOUR SIGNATURE. THE FOLLOWING PERSONS MAY NOT ACT AS WITNESSES:
—the person you have designated as your agent;
—your spouse;
—your lawful heirs or beneficiaries named in your will or a deed;
ONLY ONE OF THE TWO WITNESSES MAY BE YOUR HEALTH OR RESIDENTIAL CARE PROVIDER OR ONE OF THEIR EMPLOYEES.

I, _____, hereby appoint _____ of _____ as my agent to make any and all health care decisions for me, except to the extent I state otherwise in this document or as prohibited by law. This durable power of attorney for health care shall take effect in the event I become unable to make my own health care decisions.

STATEMENT OF DESIRES, SPECIAL PROVISIONS, AND LIMITATIONS REGARDING HEALTH CARE DECISIONS.

For your convenience in expressing your wishes, some general statements concerning the withholding or removal of life-sustaining treatment are set forth below. (Life-sustaining treatment is defined as procedures without which a person would die, such as but not limited to the following: cardiopulmonary resuscitation, mechanical respiration, kidney dialysis or the use of other external mechanical and technological devices, drugs to maintain blood pressure, blood transfusions, and antibiotics.) There is also a section which allows you to set forth specific directions for these or other matters. If you wish you may indicate your agreement or disagreement with any of the following statements and give your agent power to act in those specific circumstances.

1. If I become permanently incompetent to make health care decisions, and if I am also suffering from a terminal illness, I authorize my agent to direct that life-sustaining treatment be discontinued. (YES) (NO) (Circle your choice and initial beneath it.)

2. Whether terminally ill or not, if I become unconscious I authorize my agent to direct that life-sustaining treatment be discontinued. (YES) (NO) (Circle your choice and initial beneath it.)

3. I realize that situations could arise in which the only way to allow me to die would be to discontinue artificial feeding (artificial nutrition and hydration). In carrying out any instructions I have given above in #1 or #2 or any instructions I may write in #4 below, I authorize my agent to direct that (circle your choice of (a) or (b) and initial beside it:

(a) artificial nutrition and hydration not to be started or, if started, be discontinued,

-or-

(b) although all other forms of life-sustaining treatment be withdrawn, artificial nutrition and hydration continue to be given to me. (If you fail to complete item 3, your agent will not have the power to direct the withdrawal of artificial nutrition and hydration.)

4. Here you may include any specific desires or limitations you deem appropriate, such as when or what life-sustaining treatment you would want used or withheld, or instructions about refusing any specific types of treatment that are inconsistent with your religious beliefs or unacceptable to you for any other reason. You may leave this question blank if you desire. _____

_____(attach additional pages as necessary)

In the event the person I appoint above is unable, unwilling or unavailable, or ineligible to act as my health care agent, I hereby appoint _____ of _____ as alternate agent.

I hereby acknowledge that I have been provided with a disclosure statement explaining the effect of this document. I have read and understand the information contained in the disclosure statement.

The original of this document will be kept at _____

_____and the following persons and institutions will have signed copies:

_____

In witness whereof, I have hereunto signed my name this _____ day of _____, _____

_____
Signature

I declare that the principal appears to be of sound mind and free from duress at the time the durable power of attorney for health care is signed and that the principal has affirmed that he or she is aware of the nature of the document and is signing it freely and voluntarily.

Witness:_____ Address:_____

Witness:_____ Address:_____

STATE OF NEW HAMPSHIRE
COUNTY OF _____

The foregoing instrument was acknowledged before me this _____ day of _____,
_____, by _____.

_____
Notary Public/Justice of the Peace
My Commission Expires:

STATUTORY POWER OF ATTORNEY

NOTICE: THIS IS AN IMPORTANT DOCUMENT. THE POWER GRANTED BY THIS DOCUMENT ARE BROAD AND SWEEPING. THEY ARE EXPLAINED IN THE UNIFORM STATUTORY FORM POWER OF ATTORNEY ACT, CHAPTER 45, ARTICLE 5, PART 6 NMSA 1978. IF YOU HAVE ANY QUESTIONS ABOUT THESE POWERS, YOU SHOULD ASK A LAWYER TO EXPLAIN THEM TO YOU. THIS FORM DOES NOT PROHIBIT THE USE OF ANY OTHER FORM. YOU MAY REVOKE THIS POWER OF ATTORNEY IF YOU LATER WISH TO DO SO.

I, _____*(Name)*

reside at _____ *(Address)*, New Mexico. I appoint

_____(Name(s) and address(es))

to serve as my attorney(s)-in-fact.

If any attorney-in-fact appointed above is unable to serve, then I appoint _____
_____ to serve as successor attorney-in-fact in place of the person who is unable to serve.

This power of attorney shall not be affected by my incapacity but will terminate upon my death unless I have revoked it prior to my death. I intend by this power of attorney to avoid a court-supervised guardianship or conservatorship.

Should my attempt be defeated, I ask that my agent be appointed as guardian or conservator of my person or estate.

STRIKE THROUGH THE SENTENCE ABOVE IF YOU DO NOT WANT TO NOMINATE YOUR AGENT AS YOUR GUARDIAN OR CONSERVATOR.

CHECK AND INITIAL THE FOLLOWING PARAGRAPH ONLY IF YOU WANT YOUR ATTORNEY(S)-IN-FACT TO BE ABLE TO ACT ALONE AND INDEPENDENTLY OF EACH OTHER WITHOUT THE SIGNATURE OF THE OTHER(S). IF YOU DO NOT CHECK AND INITIAL THE FOLLOWING PARA-GRAPH AND MORE THAN ONE PERSON IS NAMED TO ACT ON YOUR BEHALF THEN THEY MUST ACT JOINTLY.

( )   If more than one person is appointed to serve
as my attorney-in-fact then they may act
severally, alone and independently of each other.

_____
initials

My attorney(s)-in-fact shall have the power to act in my name, place and stead in any way which I myself could do with respect to the following matters to the extent permitted by law:

INITIAL IN THE BOX IN FRONT OF EACH AUTHORIZATION WHICH YOU DESIRE TO GIVE TO YOUR ATTORNEY(S)-IN-FACT. YOUR ATTORNEY(S)-IN-FACT SHALL BE AUTHORIZED TO ENGAGE ONLY IN THOSE ACTIVITIES WHICH ARE INITIALED.

(_____) 1. real estate transactions.
(_____) 2. stock and bond transactions.
(_____) 3. commodity and option transactions.
(_____) 4. tangible personal property transactions.
(_____) 5. banking and other financial institution transactions.
(_____) 6. business operating transactions.
(_____) 7. insurance and annuity transactions.
(_____) 8. estate, trust and other beneficiary transactions.
(_____) 9. claims and litigation.
(_____) 10. personal and family maintenance.
(_____) 11. benefits from social security, medicare, medicaid or other government programs or civil or military service.

(_____)	12.	retirement plan transactions.
(_____)	13.	tax matters, including any transactions with the Internal Revenue Service.
(_____)	14.	decisions regarding lifesaving and life prolonging medical treatment.
(_____)	15.	decisions relating to medical treatment, surgical treatment, nursing care, medication, hospitalization, institutionalization in a nursing home or other facility and home health care.
(_____)	16.	transfer of property or income as a gift to the principal's spouse for the purpose of qualifying the principal for governmental medical assistance.
(_____)	17.	ALL OF THE ABOVE POWERS, INCLUDING FINANCIAL AND HEALTH CARE DECISIONS. IF YOU INITIAL THE BOX IN FRONT OF LINE 17, YOU NEED NOT INITIAL ANY OTHER LINES.

SPECIAL INSTRUCTIONS:
ON THE FOLLOWING LINES YOU MAY GIVE SPECIAL INSTRUCTIONS LIMITING OR EXTENDING THE POWERS YOU HAVE GRANTED TO YOUR AGENT.

_____

_____

CHECK AND INITIAL THE FOLLOWING PARAGRAPH IF YOU INTEND FOR THIS POWER OF ATTORNEY TO BECOME EFFECTIVE ONLY IF YOU BECOME INCAPACITATED. YOUR FAILURE TO DO SO WILL MEAN THAT YOUR ATTORNEY(S)-IN-FACT ARE EMPOWERED TO ACT ON YOUR BEHALF FROM THE TIME YOU SIGN THIS DOCUMENT UNTIL YOUR DEATH UNLESS YOU REVOKE THE POWER BEFORE YOUR DEATH.

( )

_____
initials

This power of attorney shall become effective only if I become incapacitated. My attorney(s)-in-fact shall be entitled to rely on notarized statements from two qualified health care professionals, one of whom shall be a physician, as to my incapacity. By incapacity I mean that among other things, I am unable to effectively manage my personal care, property or financial affairs.

This power of attorney will not be affected by a lapse of time. I agree that any third party who receives a copy of this power of attorney my act under it.

_____
(Signature)

_____
(Optional, but preferred: Your Social Security number)

Dated: _____, _____

NOTICE: IF THIS POWER OF ATTORNEY AFFECTS REAL ESTATE, IT MUST BE RECORDED IN THE OFFICE OF THE COUNTY CLERK IN EACH COUNTY WHERE THE REAL ESTATE IS LOCATED.

ACKNOWLEDGMENT

STATE OF NEW MEXICO)
) SS.
County of _____)

The foregoing instrument was acknowledged before me on _____, _____,
by _____.
        (seal)

_____
Notary Public

My Commission Expires:

_____

BY ACCEPTING OR ACTING UNDER THE POWER OF ATTORNEY, YOUR AGENT ASSUMES THE FIDUCIARY AND OTHER LEGAL RESPONSIBILITIES OF AN AGENT ACTING ON YOUR BEHALF. and

THIS AFFIDAVIT IS FOR THE USE OF YOUR ATTORNEY(S)-IN-FACT IF EVER YOUR ATTORNEY(S)-IN-FACT ACTS ON YOUR BEHALF UNDER YOUR WRITTEN POWER OF ATTORNEY.

AFFIDAVIT AS TO POWER OF ATTORNEY BEING IN FULL FORCE

STATE OF NEW MEXICO   )

) SS.

COUNTY OF _____)

I/we _____
being duly sworn, state:

1. _____ ("Principal")
of _____ County, New Mexico, signed a written Power of Attorney on
_____, _____, appointing the undersigned as his/her attorney(s)-in-fact. (A true copy of the power of attorney is attached hereto and incorporated herein.)

2. As attorney(s)-in-fact and under and by virtue of the Power of Attorney, I/we have this date executed the following described instrument:_____
_____.

3. At the time of executing the above described instrument I/we had no actual knowledge or actual notice of revocation or termination of the Power of Attorney by death or otherwise, or notice of any facts indicating the same.

4. I/we represent that the principal is now alive; has not, at any time, revoked or repudiated the power of attorney; and the power of attorney still is in full force and effect.

5. I/we make this affidavit for the purpose of inducing _____
_____ to accept delivery of the above described instrument, as executed by me/us in my/our capacity of attorney(s)-in-fact for the Principal.

_____, Attorney-in-fact

_____, Attorney-in-fact

Sworn to before me _____ this _____
day of _____, _____.

_____
Notary Public

My commission expires:

_____.

156

OPTIONAL ADVANCE HEALTH-CARE DIRECTIVE

Explanation

You have the right to give instructions about your own health care. You also have the right to name someone else to make health-care decisions for you. This form lets you do either or both of these things. It also lets you express your wishes regarding the designation of your primary physician.

THIS FORM IS OPTIONAL. Each paragraph and word of this form is optional. If you use this form, you may strike, complete or modify all or any part of it. You are free to use a different form. You do not have to sign any form.

PART 1 of this form is a power of attorney for health care. Part 1 lets you name another individual as agent to make health-care decisions for you if you become incapable of making your own decisions or if you want someone else to make those decisions for you now even though you are still capable. You may also name an alternate agent to act for you if your first choice is not willing, able or reasonably available to make decisions for you. Unless related to you, your agent may not be an owner, operator or employee of a health-care institution at which you are receiving care.

Unless the form you sign limits the authority of your agent, your agent may make all health-care decisions for you. This form has a place for you to limit the authority of your agent. You need not limit the authority of your agent if you wish to rely on your agent for all health-care decisions that may have to be made. If you choose not to limit the authority of your agent, your agent will have the right to:

(a) consent or refuse consent to any care, treatment, service or procedure to maintain, diagnose or otherwise affect a physical or mental condition;

(b) select or discharge health-care providers and institutions;

(c) approve or disapprove diagnostic tests, surgical procedures, programs of medication and orders not to resuscitate; and

(d) direct the provision, withholding or withdrawal of artificial nutrition and hydration and all other forms of health care.

PART 2 of this form lets you give specific instructions about any aspect of your health care. Choices are provided for you to express your wishes regarding the provision, withholding or withdrawal of treatment to keep you alive, including the provision of artificial nutrition and hydration, as well as the provision of pain relief. Space is also provided for you to add to the choices you have made or for you to write out any additional wishes.

PART 3 of this form lets you designate a physician to have primary responsibility for your health care.

After completing this form, sign and date the form at the end. It is recommended but not required that you request two other individuals to sign as witnesses. Give a copy of the signed and completed form to your physician, to any other health-care providers you may have, to any health-care institution at which you are receiving care and to any health-care agents you have named. You should talk to the person you have named as agent to make sure that he or she understands your wishes and is willing to take the responsibility.

You have the right to revoke this advance health-care directive or replace this form at any time.

* * * * * * * * * * * * * * * * * * * *

PART 1. POWER OF ATTORNEY FOR HEALTH CARE

(1) DESIGNATION OF AGENT: I designate the following individual as my agent to make health-care decisions for me:

_____

(name of individual you choose as agent)

_____

(address)   (city)   (state)   (zip code)

_____

(home phone)   (work phone)

If I revoke my agent's authority or if my agent is not willing, able or reasonably available to make a health-care decision for me, I designate as my first alternate agent:

_____
(name of individual you choose as first alternate agent)

_____
(address)   (city)   (state)   (zip code)

_____
(home phone)   (work phone)

If I revoke the authority of my agent and first alternate agent or if neither is willing, able or reasonably available to make a health-care decision for me, I designate as my second alternate agent:

_____
(name of individual you choose as second alternate agent)

_____
(address)   (city)   (state)   (zip code)

_____
(home phone)   (work phone)

(2) AGENT'S AUTHORITY: My agent is authorized to obtain and review medical records, reports and information about me and to make all health-care decisions for me, including decisions to provide, withhold or withdraw artificial nutrition, hydration and all other forms of health care to keep me alive, except as I state here: _____

_____
(Add additional sheets if needed.)

(3) WHEN AGENT'S AUTHORITY BECOMES EFFECTIVE: My agent's authority becomes effective when my primary physician and one other qualified health-care professional determine that I am unable to make my own health-care decisions, unless I mark the following box. If I mark this box [ ], my agent's authority to make health-care decisions for me takes effect immediately.

(4) AGENT'S OBLIGATIONS: My agent shall make health-care decisions for me in accordance with this power of attorney for health care, any instructions I give in Part 2 of this form and my other wishes to the extent known to my agent. To the extent my wishes are unknown, my agent shall make health-care decisions for me in accordance with what my agent determines to be in my best interest. In determining my best interest, my agent shall consider my personal values to the extent known to my agent.

(5) NOMINATION OF GUARDIAN: If a guardian of my person needs to be appointed for me by a court, I nominate the agent designated in this form. If that agent is not willing, able or reasonably available to act as guardian, I nominate the alternate agents whom I have named, in the order designated.

PART 2. INSTRUCTIONS FOR HEALTH CARE

If you are satisfied to allow your agent to determine what is best for you in making end-or-life decisions, you need not fill out this part of the form. If you do fill out this part of the form, you may strike any wording you do not want.

(6) END-OF-LIFE DECISIONS: I direct that my health-care providers and others involved in my care provide, withhold or withdraw treatment in accordance with the choice I have marked below:

[ ] (a) Choice Not To Prolong Life: I do not want my life to be prolonged if (i) I have an incurable and irreversible condition that will result in my death within a relatively short time, (ii) I become unconscious and, to a reasonable degree of medical certainty, I will not regain consciousness or (iii) the likely risks and burdens of treatment would outweigh the expected benefits, OR

[ ] (b) Choice To Prolong Life: I want my life to be prolonged as long as possible within the limits of generally accepted health-care standards.

(7) ARTIFICIAL NUTRITION AND HYDRATION: If I have selected the above choice NOT to prolong life under specified conditions, I also specify that I ____ do or ____ do not want artificial nutrition and hydration provided to me.

(8) RELIEF FROM PAIN: Except as I state in the following space, I direct that treatment for easing pain or discomfort be provided at all times, even if it hastens my death: _____

_____

_____

(Add additional sheets if needed.)

(9) OTHER WISHES: (If you wish to write your own instructions, or if you wish to add to the instructions your have given above, you may do so here.) I direct that: _____

_____

_____

(Add additional sheets if needed.)

PART 3. PRIMARY PHYSICIAN

(10) I designate the following physician as my primary physician:

_____

(name of physician)   (phone)

_____

(address)   (city)   (state)   (zip code)

If the physician I have designated above is not willing, able or reasonably available to act as my primary physician, I designate the following physician as my primary physician:

_____

(name of physician)   (phone)

_____

(address)   (city)   (state)   (zip code)

* * * * * * * * * * * * * * * * * * * *

(11) EFFECT OF COPY: A copy of this form has the same effect as the original.

(12) REVOCATION: I understand that I may revoke this OPTIONAL ADVANCE HEALTH-CARE DIRECTIVE at any time, and that if I revoke it, I should promptly notify my supervising health-care provider and any health-care institution where I am receiving care and any others to whom I have given copies of this power of attorney. I understand that I may revoke the designation of an agent only by a signed writing or by personally informing the supervising health-care provider.

(13) SIGNATURES: Sign and date the form here:

_____   _____

(date)   (sign your name)

_____   _____

(address)   (print your name)

_____   _____

(city)   (state)   (your social security number)

(Optional) SIGNATURE OF WITNESSES:

               First witness   Second witness

_____   _____

(print name)   (print name)

_____   _____

(address)   (address)

_____   _____

(city)   (state)   (city)   (state)

_____   _____

(signature of witness)   (signature of witness)

_____   _____

(date)   (date)

DURABLE GENERAL POWER OF ATTORNEY
NEW YORK STATUTORY SHORT FORM

THE POWERS YOU GRANT BELOW CONTINUE TO BE EFFECTIVE
SHOULD YOU BECOME DISABLED OR INCOMPETENT

(Caution: This is an important document. It gives the person whom you designate (your "Agent") broad powers to handle your property during your lifetime, which may include powers to mortgage, sell, or otherwise dispose of any real or personal property without advance notice to you or approval by you. These powers will continue to exist even after you become disabled, or incompetent. These powers are explained more fully in New York General Obligations Law, Article 5, Title 15, Sections 5-1502A through 5-1503, which expressly permit the use of any other or different form of power of attorney.

This document does not authorize anyone to make medical or other health care decisions. You may execute a health care proxy to do this.

If there is anything about this form that you do not understand, you should ask a lawyer to explain it to you.)

This is intended to constitute a DURABLE GENERAL POWER OF ATTORNEY pursuant to Article 5, Title 15 of the New York General Obligations Law:

I,_____
(insert your name and address)
do hereby appoint:_____
_____
(If 1 person is to be appointed agent, insert the name and address of your agent above)

_____
_____
_____
(If 2 or more persons are to be appointed agents by you insert their names and addresses above)

my attorney(s)-in-fact TO ACT
(If more than one agent is designated, CHOOSE ONE of the following two choices by putting your initials in ONE of the blank spaces to the left of your choice:)

(   ) Each agent may SEPARATELY act.

(   ) All agents must act TOGETHER.

(If neither blank space is initialed, the agents will be required to act TOGETHER)

IN MY NAME, PLACE AND STEAD in any way which I myself could do, if I were personally present, with respect to the following matters as each of them as defined in Title 15 of Article 5 of the New York General Obligations Law to the extent that I am permitted by law to act through an agent.

(DIRECTIONS: Initial in the blank space to the left of your choice any one or more of the following lettered subdivisions as to which you WANT to give your agent authority.

If the blank space to the left of any particular division is NOT initialed, **NO AUTHORITY WILL BE GRANTED** for matters that are included in that subdivision. Alternatively, the letter corresponding to each power you wish to grant may be written or typed on the blank line in subdivision "(Q)", and you may then put your initials in the blank space to the left of subdivision "(Q)" in order to grant each of the powers so indicated)

(_____) (A)   real estate transactions;
(_____) (B)   chattel and goods transactions;
(_____) (C)   bond, share and commodity transactions;
(_____) (D)   banking transactions;
(_____) (E)   business operating transactions;
(_____) (F)   insurance transactions;
(_____) (G)   estate transactions;
(_____) (H)   claims and litigation
(_____) (I)   personal relationships and affairs;
(_____) (J)   benefits from military service;
(_____) (K)   records, reports and statements;
(_____) (L)   retirement benefit transactions;
(_____) (M)   making gifts to my spouse, children and more remote descendants, and parents, not to exceed in the aggregate $10,000 to each of such persons in any year;
(_____) (N)   tax matters;
(_____) (O)   all other matters;
(_____) (P)   full and unqualified authority to my attorney(s)-in-fact to delegate any or all of the foregoing powers to any person or persons whom my attorney(s)-in-fact shall select;
(_____) (Q)   each of the above matters identified by the following letters:

_____

_____

_____

(Special provisions and limitations may be included in the statutory short form durable power of attorney only if they conform to the requirements of section 5-1503 of the New York General Obligations Law.)

This durable Power of Attorney shall not be affected by my subsequent disability or incompetence.

If every agent named above is unable or unwilling to serve, I appoint_____

_____

(insert name and address of successor)

to be my agent for all purposes hereunder.

TO INDUCE ANY THIRD PARTY TO ACT HEREUNDER, I HEREBY AGREE THAT ANY THIRD PARTY RECEIVING A DULY EXECUTED COPY OR FACSIMILE OF THIS INSTRUMENT MAY ACT HEREUNDER, AND THAT REVOCATION OR TERMINATION HEREOF SHALL BE INEFFECTIVE AS TO SUCH THIRD PARTY UNLESS AND UNTIL ACTUAL NOTICE OR KNOWLEDGE OF SUCH REVOCATION OR TERMINATION SHALL HAVE BEEN RECEIVED BY SUCH THIRD PARTY, AND I FOR MYSELF AND FOR MY HEIRS, EXECUTORS, LEGAL REPRESENTATIVES AND ASSIGNS, HEREBY AGREE TO INDEMNIFY AND HOLD HARMLESS ANY SUCH THIRD PARTY FROM AND AGAINST ANY AND ALL CLAIMS THAT MAY ARISE AGAINST SUCH THIRD PARTY BY REASON OF SUCH THIRD PARTY HAVING RELIED ON THE PROVISIONS OF THIS INSTRUMENT.

THIS DURABLE GENERAL POWER OF ATTORNEY MAY BE REVOKED BY ME AT ANY TIME.

IN WITNESS WHEREOF, I have hereunto signed my name on _____, (year)

(YOU SIGN HERE)==> _____
Signature of Principal

ACKNOWLEDGEMENT

STATE OF _____ COUNTY OF _____ ss.:

On_____before me personally came_____
_____to me known, and known to me to be the individual described in, and who executed the foregoing instrument, and he acknowledged to me that he executed the same.

_____
Notary Public

My commission expires:

DURABLE GENERAL POWER OF ATTORNEY
EFFECTIVE AT A FUTURE TIME
NEW YORK STATUTORY SHORT FORM

THE POWERS YOU GRANT BELOW CONTINUE TO BE EFFECTIVE
SHOULD YOU BECOME DISABLED OR INCOMPETENT

(Caution: This is an important document. It gives the person whom you designate (your "Agent") broad powers to handle your property during your lifetime, which may include powers to mortgage, sell, or otherwise dispose of any real or personal property without advance notice to you or approval by you. These powers will continue to exist even after you become disabled, or incompetent. These powers are explained more fully in New York General Obligations Law, Article 5, Title 15, Sections 5-1502A through 5-1503, which expressly permit the use of any other or different form of power of attorney.

This document does not authorize anyone to make medical or other health care decisions. You may execute a health care proxy to do this.

If there is anything about this form that you do not understand, you should ask a lawyer to explain it to you.)

This is intended to constitute a POWER OF ATTORNEY EFFECTIVE AT A FUTURE TIME pursuant to Article 5, Title 15 of the New York General Obligations Law:

I,_____
(insert your name and address)

do hereby appoint:_____
_____
(If 1 person is to be appointed agent, insert the name and address of your agent above)

_____
_____
_____
(If 2 or more persons are to be appointed agents by you insert their names and addresses above)

my attorney(s)-in-fact TO ACT
(If more than one agent is designated, CHOOSE ONE of the following two choices by putting your initials in ONE of the blank spaces to the left of your choice:)

(   ) Each agent may SEPARATELY act.

(   ) All agents must act TOGETHER.

(If neither blank space is initialed, the agents will be required to act TOGETHER)

TO TAKE EFFECT upon the occasion of the signing of a written statement EITHER:

(INSTRUCTIONS: COMPLETE OR OMIT SECTION (I) -OR- SECTION (II) BELOW BUT NEVER COMPLETE BOTH SECTIONS (I) AND (II) BELOW. IF YOU DO NOT COMPLETE EITHER SECTION (I) OR SECTION (II) BELOW, IT SHALL BE PRESUMED THAT YOU WANT THE PROVISIONS OF SECTION (I) BELOW TO APPLY.)

(I) by a physician or physicians named herein by me at this point:

Dr._____

_____
(Insert full name(s) and address(es) of certifying Physician(s) chosen by you)

or if no physician or physicians are named hereinabove, or if the physician or physicians named hereinabove are unable to act, by my regular physician, or by a physician who has treated me within one year preceding the date of such signing, or by a licensed psychologist or psychiatrist, certifying that I am suffering from diminished capacity that would preclude me from conducting my affairs in a competent manner;

-OR-

(II) by a person or persons named herein by me at this point:_____

_____

_____
(Insert full name(s) and addresses of certifying Person(s) chosen by you)

CERTIFYING that the following specified event has occurred:_____

_____

_____

(Insert hereinabove the specified event the certification of which will cause THIS POWER OF ATTORNEY to take effect)

IN MY NAME, PLACE AND STEAD in any way which I myself could do, if I were personally present, with respect to the following matters as each of them as defined in Title 15 of Article 5 of the New York General Obligations Law to the extent that I am permitted by law to act through an agent:

(DIRECTIONS: Initial in the blank space to the left of your choice any one or more of the following lettered subdivisions as to which you WANT to give your agent authority. If the blank space to the left of any particular division is NOT initialed, NO AUTHORITY WILL BE GRANTED for matters that are included in that subdivision. Alternatively, the letter corresponding to each power you wish to grant may be written or typed on the blank line in subdivision "(Q)", and you may then put your initials in the blank space to the left of subdivision "(Q)" in order to grant each of the powers so indicated)

(_____) (A) real estate transactions;
(_____) (B) chattel and goods transactions;
(_____) (C) bond, share and commodity transactions;
(_____) (D) banking transactions;
(_____) (E) business operating transactions;
(_____) (F) insurance transactions;
(_____) (G) estate transactions;
(_____) (H) claims and litigation
(_____) (I) personal relationships and affairs;
(_____) (J) benefits from military service;
(_____) (K) records, reports and statements;
(_____) (L) retirement benefit transactions;
(_____) (M) making gifts to my spouse, children and more remote descendants, and parents, not to exceed in the aggregate $10,000 to each of such persons in any year;
(_____) (N) tax matters;
(_____) (O) all other matters;
(_____) (P) full and unqualified authority to my attorney(s)-in-fact to delegate any or all of the foregoing powers to any person or persons whom my attorney(s)-in-fact shall select;
(_____) (Q) each of the above matters identified by the following letters:

This durable Power of Attorney shall not be affected by my subsequent disability or incompetence.

(Special provisions and limitations may be included in the statutory short form durable power of attorney only if they conform to the requirements of section 5-1503 of the New York General Obligations Law.)

If every agent named above is unable or unwilling to serve, I appoint_____

_____

_____

(insert name and address of successor)

to be my agent for all purposes hereunder.

TO INDUCE ANY THIRD PARTY TO ACT HEREUNDER, I HEREBY AGREE THAT ANY THIRD PARTY RECEIVING A DULY EXECUTED COPY OR FACSIMILE OF THIS INSTRUMENT MAY ACT HEREUNDER, AND THAT REVOCATION OR TERMINATION HEREOF SHALL BE INEFFECTIVE AS TO SUCH THIRD PARTY UNLESS AND UNTIL ACTUAL NOTICE OR KNOWLEDGE OF SUCH REVOCATION OR TERMINATION SHALL HAVE BEEN RECEIVED BY SUCH THIRD PARTY, AND I FOR MYSELF AND FOR MY HEIRS, EXECUTORS, LEGAL REPRESENTATIVES AND ASSIGNS, HEREBY AGREE TO INDEMNIFY AND HOLD HARMLESS ANY SUCH THIRD PARTY FROM AND AGAINST ANY AND ALL CLAIMS THAT MAY ARISE AGAINST SUCH THIRD PARTY BY REASON OF SUCH THIRD PARTY HAVING RELIED ON THE PROVISIONS OF THIS INSTRUMENT.

THIS DURABLE GENERAL POWER OF ATTORNEY MAY BE REVOKED BY ME AT ANY TIME.

IN WITNESS WHEREOF, I have hereunto signed my name on _____, _____(year)

(YOU SIGN HERE)==> _____
                                    Signature of Principal

ACKNOWLEDGEMENT

STATE OF _____ COUNTY OF _____
ss.:

On _____before me personally came_____ _____to me known, and known to me to be the individual described in, and who executed the foregoing instrument, and he acknowledged to me that he executed the same.

                                    _____
                                    Notary Public

                                    My commission expires:

NONDURABLE GENERAL POWER OF ATTORNEY
NEW YORK STATUTORY SHORT FORM

THE POWERS YOU GRANT BELOW CEASE TO BE EFFECTIVE SHOULD YOU BECOME DISABLED OR INCOMPETENT

(CAUTION: THIS IS AN IMPORTANT DOCUMENT. IT GIVES THE PERSON WHOM YOU DESIGNATE (YOUR "AGENT") BROAD POWERS TO HANDLE YOUR PROPERTY DURING YOUR LIFETIME, WHICH MAY INCLUDE POWERS TO MORTGAGE, SELL, OR OTHERWISE DISPOSE OF ANY REAL OR PERSONAL PROPERTY WITHOUT ADVANCE NOTICE TO YOU OR APPROVAL BY YOU. THESE POWERS WILL TERMINATE IF YOU BECOME DISABLED OR INCOMPE-TENT. THESE POWERS ARE EXPLAINED MORE FULLY IN NEW YORK GENERAL OBLIGATIONS LAW, ARTICLE 5, TITLE 15, SECTIONS 5-120A THROUGH 5-1503, WHICH EXPRESSLY PERMIT THE USE OF ANY OTHER OR DIFFERENT FORM OF POWER OF ATTORNEY.

THIS DOCUMENT DOES NOT AUTHORIZE ANYONE TO MAKE MEDICAL OR OTHER HEALTH CARE DECISIONS. YOU MAY EXECUTE A HEALTH CARE PROXY TO DO THIS.

IF THERE IS ANYTHING ABOUT THIS FORM THAT YOU DO NOT UNDER-STAND, YOU SHOULD ASK A LAWYER TO EXPLAIN IT TO YOU.)

THIS is intended to constitute a NONDURABLE GENERAL POWER OF ATTOR-NEY pursuant to Article 5, Title 15 of the New York General Obligations Law:

I,_____
(insert your name and address)

do hereby appoint:_____
_____

(If 1 person is to be appointed agent, insert the name and address of your agent above)

_____
_____
_____

(If 2 or more persons are to be appointed agents by you, insert their names and addresses above)

my attorney(s)-in-fact TO ACT

(If more than one agent is designated, CHOOSE ONE of the following two choices by putting your initials in ONE of the blank spaces to the left of your choice:)

(   ) Each agent may SEPARATELY act.

(   ) All agents must act TOGETHER.

(If neither blank space is initialed, the agents will be required to act TOGETHER)

IN MY NAME, PLACE AND STEAD in any way which I myself could do, if I were personally present, with respect to the following matters as each of them as defined in Title 15 of Article 5 of the New York General Obligations Law to the extent that I am permitted by law to act through an agent:

(DIRECTIONS: Initial in the blank space to the left of your choice any one or more of the following lettered subdivisions as to which you WANT to give your agent authority.

If the blank space to the left of any particular division is NOT initialed, NO AUTHORITY WILL BE GRANTED for matters that are included in that subdivision. ALTERNATIVELY, the letter corresponding to each power you wish to grant may be written or typed on the blank line in subdivision "(Q)", and you may then put your initials in the blank space to the left of subdivision "(Q)" in order to grant each of the powers so indicated)

(_____) (A) real estate transactions;

(_____) (B) chattel and goods transactions;

(_____) (C) bond, share and commodity transactions;

(_____) (D) banking transactions;

(_____) (E) business operating transactions;

(_____) (F) insurance transactions;

(_____) (G) estate transactions;

(_____) (H) claims and litigation

(_____) (I) personal relationships and affairs;

(_____) (J) benefits from military service;

(_____) (K) records, reports and statements;

(_____) (L) retirement benefit transactions;

(_____) (M) making gifts to my spouse, children and more remote descendants, and parents, not to exceed in the aggregate $10,000 to each of such persons in any year;

(_____) (N) tax matters;

(_____) (O) all other matters;

(_____) (P) full and unqualified authority to my attorney(s)-in-fact to delegate any or all of the foregoing powers to any person or persons whom my attorney(s)-in-fact shall select;

(_____) (Q) each of the above matters identified by the following letters:

(Special provisions and limitations may be included in the statutory short form durable power of attorney only if they conform to the requirements of section 5-1503 of the New York General Obligations Law.)

If every agent named above is unable or unwilling to serve, I appoint_____

_____

_____

(insert name and address of successor)

to be my agent for all purposes hereunder.

TO INDUCE ANY THIRD PARTY TO ACT HEREUNDER, I HEREBY AGREE THAT ANY THIRD PARTY RECEIVING A DULY EXECUTED COPY OR FACSIMILE OF THIS INSTRUMENT MAY ACT HEREUNDER, AND THAT REVOCATION OR TERMINATION HEREOF SHALL BE INEFFECTIVE AS TO SUCH THIRD PARTY UNLESS AND UNTIL ACTUAL NOTICE OR KNOWLEDGE OF SUCH REVOCATION OR TERMINATION SHALL HAVE BEEN RECEIVED BY SUCH THIRD PARTY, AND I FOR MYSELF AND FOR MY HEIRS, EXECUTORS, LEGAL REPRESENTATIVES AND ASSIGNS, HEREBY AGREE TO INDEMNIFY AND HOLD HARMLESS ANY SUCH THIRD PARTY FROM AND AGAINST ANY AND ALL CLAIMS THAT MAY ARISE AGAINST SUCH THIRD PARTY BY REASON OF SUCH THIRD PARTY HAVING RELIED ON THE PROVISIONS OF THIS INSTRUMENT.

THIS NONDURABLE GENERAL POWER OF ATTORNEY MAY BE REVOKED BY ME AT ANY TIME.

IN WITNESS WHEREOF, I have hereunto signed my name on _____ , _____(year)

(YOU SIGN HERE)==>   _____
                                   (Signature of Principal)

ACKNOWLEDGEMENT

STATE OF _____   COUNTY OF _____ ss.:

On_____before me personally came_____ _____to me known, and known to me to be the individual described in, and who executed the foregoing instrument, and he acknowledged to me that he executed the same.

_____
Notary Public

My commission expires:

AFFIDAVIT THAT POWER OF ATTORNEY IS IN FULL FORCE
(Sign before a notary public)

STATE OF _____ COUNTY OF _____ ss.:

_____, being duly sworn, deposes and says:

1. The Principal within did, in writing, appoint me as the Principal's true and lawful ATTORNEY-IN-FACT in the within Power of Attorney.

2. I have no actual knowledge or actual notice of revocation or termination of the Power of Attorney by death or otherwise, or knowledge of any facts indicating the same. I further represent that the Principal is alive, has not revoked or repudiated the Power of Attorney and the Power of Attorney still is in full force and effect.

3. I make this affidavit for the purpose of inducing

to accept delivery of the following Instrument(s), as executed by me in my capacity as the ATTORNEY-IN-FACT, with full knowledge that this affidavit will be relied upon in accepting the execution and delivery of the Instrument(s) and in paying good and valuable consideration therefor:

_____

Sworn to before me on this
_____ day of _____, _____

_____
Notary Public

My commission expires:

HEALTH CARE PROXY

I _____ (name of principal) hereby appoint

_____
_____ (name, home address and telephone number of agent) as my health
care agent to make any and all health care decisions for me, except to the extent I state otherwise.

This health care proxy shall take effect in the event I become unable to make my own health care decisions.
NOTE: Although not necessary, and neither encouraged nor discouraged, you may wish to state instructions
or wishes, and limit your agent's authority. Unless your agent knows your wishes about artificial nutrition and
hydration, your agent will not have authority to decide about artificial nutrition and hydration. If you choose
to state instructions, wishes, or limits, please do so below:

_____
_____
_____
_____
_____
_____

I direct my agent to make health care decisions in accordance with my wishes and instructions as stated
above or as otherwise known to him or her. I also direct my agent to abide by any limitations on his or her
authority as stated above or as otherwise known to him or her.

In the event the person I appoint is unable, unwilling or unavailable to act as my health care agent, I hereby
appoint _____
_____(name, home address and telephone number of alternate agent) as my health care agent.

I understand that, unless I revoke it, this proxy will remain in effect indefinitely or until the date or occurrence of the condition I have stated below:

(Please complete the following if you do NOT want this health care proxy to be in effect indefinitely):

This proxy shall expire: _____
_____(Specify date or condition)

Signature:_____

Address:_____

Date:_____

I declare that the person who signed or asked another to sign this document is personally known to me and
appears to be of sound mind and acting willingly and free from duress. He or she signed (or asked another to
sign for him or her) this document in my presence and that person signed in my presence. I am not the person appointed as agent by this document.

Witness:_____

Witness:_____

Witness:_____

North Carolina Statutory Short Form of General Power of Attorney

NOTICE: THE POWERS GRANTED BY THIS DOCUMENT ARE BROAD AND SWEEPING. THEY ARE DEFINED IN CHAPTER 32A OF THE NORTH CAROLINA GENERAL STATUTES WHICH EXPRESSLY PERMITS THE USE OF ANY OTHER OR DIFFERENT FORM OF POWER OF ATTORNEY DESIRED BY THE PARTIES CONCERNED.

State of _____

County of _____

I _____, appoint _____ to be my attorney-in-fact to act in my name in any way which I myself could act for myself, with respect to the following matters as each of them is defined in Chapter 32A of the North Carolina General Statutes. (DIRECTIONS: Initial the line opposite any one or more of the subdivisions as to which the principal desires to give the attorney-in-fact authority.)

(1)   Real property transactions... _____
(2)   Personal property transactions .... _____
(3)   Bond, share, stock, securities and commodity transactions............... _____
(4)   Banking transactions.. _____
(5)   Safe deposits.. _____
(6)   Business operating transactions... _____
(7)   Insurance transactions.. _____
(8)   Estate transactions.. _____
(9)   Personal relationships and affairs... _____
(10)   Social security and unemployment.. _____
(11)   Benefits from military service... _____
(12)   Tax matters.. _____
(13)   Employment of agents.. _____
(14)   Gifts to charities, and to individuals other than the attorney-in-fact.. _____
(15)   Gifts to the named attorney-in-fact... _____

(If power of substitution and revocation is to be given, add: 'I also give to such person full power to appoint another to act as my attorney-in-fact and full power to revoke such appointment.')

_____

(If period of power of attorney is to be limited, add: "This power terminates _____, ____.")

_____

(If power of attorney is to be a durable power of attorney under the provisions of Article 2 of Chapter 32A and is to continue in effect after the incapacity or mental incompetence of the principal, add: 'This power of a attorney shall not be affected by my subsequent incapacity or mental incompetence.')

_____

_____

(If power of attorney is to take effect only after the incapacity or mental incompetence of the principal, add: 'This power of attorney shall become effective after I become incapacitated or mentally incompetent.')

_____

_____

(If power of attorney is to be effective to terminate or direct the administration of a custodial trust created under the Uniform Custodial Trust Act, add: 'In the event of my subsequent incapacity or mental incompetence, the attorney-in-fact of this power of attorney shall have the power to terminate or to direct the administration of any custodial trust of which I am the beneficiary.')

_____

_____

(If power of attorney is to be effective to determine whether a beneficiary under the Uniform Custodial Trust Act is incapacitated or ceases to be incapacitated, add: 'The attorney-in-fact of this power of attorney shall have the power to determine whether I am incapacitated or whether my incapacity has ceased for the purposes of any custodial trust of which I am the beneficiary.'

_____

_____

I waive the requirement, set out in North Carolina Gen. Stat. § 32A-11, that the attorney-in-fact files this power of attorney with the clerk of the superior court and render inventories and accounts, after my incapacity or mental incompetence, to the clerk of the superior court.

Dated _____, _____.

_____ (SEAL)
Signature

STATE OF _____ COUNTY OF _____

On this _____ day of _____, _____, personally appeared before me, the said named _____ to me known and known to be the person described in and who executed the foregoing instrument and he (or she) acknowledged that he (or she) executed the same and being duly sworn by me, made oath that the statements in the foregoing instrument are true.

My Commission Expires:_____

_____
(Signature of Notary Public)
Notary Public (Official Seal)

HEALTH CARE POWER OF ATTORNEY

(Notice: This document gives the person you designate your health care agent broad powers to make health care decisions for you, including the power to consent to your doctor not giving treatment or stopping treatment necessary to keep you alive. This power exists only as to those health care decisions for which you are unable to give informed consent.

This form does not impose a duty on your health care agent to exercise granted powers, but when a power is exercised, your health care agent will have to use due care to act in your best interests and in accordance with this document. Because the powers granted by this document are broad and sweeping, you should discuss your wishes concerning life-sustaining procedures with your health care agent.

Use of this form in the creation of a health care power of attorney is lawful and is authorized pursuant to North Carolina law. However, use of this form is an optional and nonexclusive method for creating a health care power of attorney and North Carolina law does not bar the use of any other or different form of power of attorney for health care that meets the statutory requirements.)

1. Designation of health care agent.
   I, _____, being of sound mind, hereby appoint
   Name: _____
   Home Address: _____
   Home Telephone Number: _____ Work Telephone Number: _____
   as my health care attorney-in-fact (herein referred to as my 'health care agent') to act for me and in my name (in any way I could act in person) to make health care decisions for me as authorized in this document.

   If the person named as my health care agent is not reasonably available or is unable or unwilling to act as my agent, then I appoint the following persons (each to act alone and successively, in the order named), to serve in that capacity: (Optional)
   A. Name: _____
      Home Address: _____
      Home Telephone Number: _____ Work Telephone Number: _____
   B. Name: _____
      Home Address: _____
      Home Telephone Number: _____ Work Telephone Number: _____
   Each successor health care agent designated shall be vested with the same power and duties as if originally named as my health care agent.

2. Effectiveness of appointment.
   (Notice: This health care power of attorney may be revoked by you at any time in any manner by which you are able to communicate your intent to revoke to your health care agent and your attending physician.)

   Absent revocation, the authority granted in this document shall become effective when and if the physician or physicians designated below determine that I lack sufficient understanding or capacity to make or communicate decisions relating to my health care and will continue in effect during my incapacity, until my death. This determination shall be made by the following physician or physicians (You may include here a designation of your choice, including your attending physician, or any other physician. You may also name two or more physicians, if desired, both of whom must make this determination before the authority granted to the health care agent becomes effective.):

   _____
   _____
   _____
   _____

3. General statement of authority granted.
   Except as indicated in section 4 below, I hereby grant to my health care agent named above full power and authority to make health care decisions on my behalf, including, but not limited to, the following:
   A. To request, review, and receive any information, verbal or written, regarding my physical or mental health, including, but not limited to, medical and hospital records, and to consent to the disclosure of this information.
   B. To employ or discharge my health care providers.
   C. To consent to and authorize my admission to and discharge from a hospital, nursing or convalescent home, or other institution.

174

D. To give consent for, to withdraw consent for, or to withhold consent for, X ray, anesthesia, medication, surgery, and all other diagnostic and treatment procedures ordered by or under the authorization of a licensed physician, dentist, or podiatrist. This authorization specifically includes the power to consent to measures for relief of pain.

E. To authorize the withholding or withdrawal of life-sustaining procedures when and if my physician determines that I am terminally ill, permanently in a coma, suffer severe dementia, or am in a persistent vegetative state. Life-sustaining procedures are those forms of medical care that only serve to artificially prolong the dying process and may include mechanical ventilation, dialysis, antibiotics, artificial nutrition and hydration, and other forms of medical treatment which sustain, restore or supplant vital bodily functions. Life-sustaining procedures do not include care necessary to provide comfort or alleviate pain.

I DESIRE THAT MY LIFE NOT BE PROLONGED BY LIFE-SUSTAINING PROCEDURES IF I AM TERMINALLY ILL, PERMANENTLY IN A COMA, SUFFER SEVERE DEMENTIA, OR AM IN A PERSISTENT VEGETATIVE STATE.

F. To exercise any right I may have to make a disposition of any part or all of my body for medical purposes, to donate my organs, to authorize an autopsy, and to direct the disposition of my remains

G. To take lawful actions that may be necessary to carry out these decisions, including the granting of releases of liability to medical providers.

4. Special provisions and limitations.

(Notice: The above grant of power is intended to be as broad as possible so that your health care agent will have authority to make any decisions you could make to obtain or terminate any type of health care. If you wish to limit the scope of your health care agent's powers, you may do so in this section.)

In exercising the authority to make health care decisions on my behalf, the authority of my health care agent is subject to the following special provisions and limitations (Here you may included any specific limitations you deem appropriate such as : your own definition of when life-sustaining treatment should be withheld or discontinued, or instructions to refuse any specific types of treatment that are inconsistent with your religious beliefs, or unacceptable to you for any other reason.):

_____

_____

_____

5. Guardianship provision.

If it becomes necessary for a court to appoint a guardian of my person, I nominate my health care agent acting under this document to be the guardian of my person, to serve without bond or security.

6. Reliance of third parties on health care agent.

A. No person who relies in good faith upon the authority of or any representations by my health care agent shall be liable to me, my estate, my heirs, successors, assigns, or personal representatives, for actions or omissions by my health care agent.

B. The powers conferred on my health care agent by this document may be exercised by my health care agent alone, and health care agent's signature or act under the authority granted in this document may be accepted by persons as fully authorized by me and with the same force and effect as if I were personally present, competent, and acting on my own behalf. All acts performed in good faith by my health care agent pursuant to this power of attorney are done with my consent and shall have the same validity and effect as if I were present and exercised the powers myself, and shall inure to the benefit of and bind me, my estate, my heirs, successors, assigns, and personal representatives. The authority of my health care agent pursuant to this power of attorney shall be superior to and binding upon my family, relatives, friends, and others.

7. Miscellaneous provisions.

A. I revoke any prior health care power of attorney.

B. My health care agent shall be entitled to sign, execute, deliver and acknowledge any contract or other document that may be necessary, desirable, convenient, or proper in order to exercise and carry out any of the powers described in this document and to incur reasonable costs on my behalf incident to the exercise of these powers; provided, however, that except as shall be necessary in order to exercise the powers described in this document relating to my health care, my health care agent shall not have any authority over my property or financial affairs.

C. My health care agent and my health care agent's estate, heirs, successors, and assigns are hereby released and forever discharged by me, my estate, my heirs, successors, and assigns and personal representatives from all liability and from all claims or demands of all kinds arising out of the acts or omissions of my health care agent pursuant to this document, except for willful misconduct or gross negligence.

D. No act or omission of my health care agent, or of any other person, institution, or facility acting in good faith in reliance on the authority of my health care agent pursuant to this health care power of attorney shall be considered suicide, nor the cause of my death for any civil or criminal purposes, nor shall it be considered unprofessional conduct or as lack of professional competence. Any person, institution, or facility against whom criminal or civil liability is asserted because of conduct authorized by this health care power of attorney may interpose this document as a defense.

8. Signature of principal.

By signing here, I indicate that I am mentally alert and competent, fully informed as to the contents of this document, and understand the full impost of this grant of powers to my health care agent.

_____(SEAL)   _____
Signature of Principal   Date

9. Signature of Witnesses

I hereby state that the Principal, _____, being of sound mind, signed the foregoing health care power of attorney in my presence, and that I am not related to the principal by blood or marriage, and I would not be entitled to any portion of the estate of the principal under any existing will or codicil or the principal or as an heir under the Intestate Succession Act, if the principal died on this date without a will. I also state that I am not the principal's attending physician, not an employee of the principal's attending physician, nor an employee of the health care facility in which the principal is a patient, nor an employee of a nursing home or a group care home where the principal resides. I further state that I do not have any claim against the principal.

Witness: _____   Date: _____

Witness: _____   Date: _____

STATE OF NORTH CAROLINA

COUNTY OF _____

CERTIFICATE

I, _____, a Notary Public for _____ County, North Carolina, hereby certify that _____ appeared before me and swore to me and to the witnesses in my presence that this instrument is a health care power of attorney, and that he/she willingly and voluntarily made and executed it as his/her free act and deed for the purposes expressed in it.

I further certify that _____ and _____, witnesses, appeared before me and swore that they witnessed _____ sign the attached health care power of attorney, believing him/her to be of sound mind; and also swore that at the time they witnessed the signing (i) they were not related within the third degree to him/her or his/her spouse, and (ii) they did not know nor have a reasonable expectation that they would be entitled to any portion of his/her estate upon his/her death under any will or codicil thereto then existing or under the Intestate Succession Act as it provided at that time, and (iii) they were not a physician attending him/her, nor an employee of an attending physician, nor an employee of a health facility in which he/she was a patient, nor an employee of a nursing home or any group-care home in which he/she resided, and (iv) they did not have a claim against him/her. I further certify that I am satisfied as to the genuineness and due execution of the instrument.

This the _____ day of _____, _____.

_____
Notary Public

My Commission Expires:

STATUTORY FORM DURABLE POWER OF ATTORNEY FOR HEALTH CARE

WARNING TO PERSON EXECUTING THIS DOCUMENT

This is an important legal document that is authorized by the general laws of this state. Before executing this document, you should know these important facts:

You must be at least eighteen years of age for this document to be legally valid and binding.

This document gives the person you designate as your agent (the attorney in fact) the power to make health care decisions for you. Your agent must act consistently with your desires as stated in this document or otherwise made known.

Except as you otherwise specify in this document, this document gives your agent the power to consent to your doctor not giving treatment or stopping treatment necessary to keep you alive.

Notwithstanding this document, you have the right to make medical and other health care decisions for yourself so long as you can give informed consent with respect to the particular decision.

This document gives your agent authority to request, consent to, refuse to consent to, or to withdraw consent for any care, treatment, service, or procedure to maintain, diagnose, or treat a physical or mental condition if you are unable to do so yourself. This power is subject to any statement of your desires and any limitation that you include in this document. You may state in this document any types of treatment that you do not desire. In addition, a court can take away the power of your agent to make health care decisions for you if your agent authorizes anything that is illegal; acts contrary to your known desires; or where your desires are not known, does anything that is clearly contrary to your best interest.

Unless you specify a specific period, this power will exist until you revoke it. Your agent's power and authority ceases upon your death.

You have the right to revoke the authority of your agent by notifying your agent or your treating doctor, hospital, or other health care provider orally or in writing of the revocation.

Your agent has the right to examine your medical records and to consent to their disclosure unless you limit this right in this document.

This document revokes any prior durable power of attorney for health care.

You should carefully read and follow the witnessing procedure described at the end of this form. This document will not be valid unless you comply with the witnessing procedure.

If there is anything in this document that you do not understand, you should ask a lawyer to explain it to you.

Your agent may need this document immediately in case of an emergency that requires a decision concerning your health care. Either keep this document where it is immediately available to your agent and alternate agents, if any, or give each of them an executed copy of this document. You should give your doctor an executed copy of this document.

1. DESIGNATION OF HEALTH CARE AGENT.

I, _____

_____(insert your name and address)

do hereby designate and appoint:_____

_____ (insert name, address, and telephone number of one individual only as your agent to make health care decisions for you. None of the following may be designated as your agent: your treating health care provider, a nonrelative employee of your treating health care provider, an operator of a long-term care facility, or a nonrelative employee of an operator of a long-term care facility.) as my attorney in fact (agent) to make health care decisions for me as authorized in this document. For the purposes of this document, "health care decision" means consent, refusal of consent, or withdrawal of consent to any care, treatment, service, or procedure to maintain, diagnose, or treat an individual's physical or mental condition.

2. CREATION OF DURABLE POWER OF ATTORNEY FOR HEALTH CARE. By this document I intend to create a durable power of attorney for health care.

3. GENERAL STATEMENT OF AUTHORITY GRANTED. Subject to any limitations in this document, I hereby grant to my agent full power and authority to make health care decisions for me to the same extent that I could make such decisions for myself if I had the capacity to do so. In exercising this authority, my agent shall make health care decisions that are consistent with my desires as stated in this document or otherwise made known to my agent, including my desires concerning obtaining or refusing or withdrawing life-prolonging care, treatment, services, and procedures. (If you want to limit the authority of your agent to make health care decisions for you, you can state the limitations in paragraph 4 below. You can indicate your desires by including a statement of your desires in the same paragraph.)

4. STATEMENT OF DESIRES, SPECIAL PROVISIONS, AND LIMITATIONS. (Your agent must make health care decisions that are consistent with your known desires. You can, but are not required to, state your desires in the space provided below. You should consider whether you want to include a statement of your desires concerning life-prolonging care, treatment, services, and procedures. You can also include a statement of your desires concerning other matters relating to your health care. You can also make your desires known to your agent by discussing your desires with your agent or by some other means. If there are any types of treatment that you do not want to be used, you should state them in the space below. If you want to limit in any other way the authority given your agent by this document, you should state the limits in the space below. If you do not state any limits, your agent will have broad powers to make health care decisions for you, except to the extent that there are limits provided by law.)

In exercising the authority under this durable power of attorney for health care, my agent shall act consistently with my desires as stated below and is subject to the special provisions and limitations stated below:

a. Statement of desires concerning life-prolonging care, treatment, services, and procedures: :

_____

_____

b. Additional statement of desires, special provisions, and limitations regarding
health care decisions:

_____

_____

(You may attach additional pages if you need more space to complete your statement. If you attach additional pages, you must date and sign EACH of the additional pages at the same time you date and sign this document.) If you wish to
make a gift of any bodily organ you may do so pursuant to North Dakota Century
Code chapter 23-06.2, the Uniform Anatomical Gift Act.

5. INSPECTION AND DISCLOSURE OF INFORMATION RELATING TO MY
PHYSICAL OR MENTAL HEALTH. Subject to any limitations in this document, my
agent has the power and authority to do all of the following:
   a. Request, review, and receive any information, verbal or written regarding my
   physical or mental health, including medical and hospital records.
   b. Execute on my behalf any releases or other documents that may be required in
   order to obtain this information.
   c. Consent to the disclosure of this information.
   (If you want to limit the authority of your agent to receive and disclose information relating to your health, you must state the limitations in paragraph 4 above.)

6. SIGNING DOCUMENTS, WAIVERS, AND RELEASES. Where necessary to implement the health care decisions that my agent is authorized by this document to make,
my agent has the power and authority to execute on my behalf all of the following:
   a. Documents titled or purporting to be a "Refusal to Permit Treatment" and "Leaving
      Hospital Against Medical Advice".
   b. Any necessary waiver or release from liability required by a hospital or physician.

7. DURATION. (Unless you specify a shorter period in the space below, this power of
attorney will exist until it is revoked.) This durable power of attorney for health care
expires on _____
(Fill in this space ONLY if you want the authority of your agent to end on a specific
date.)

8. DESIGNATION OF ALTERNATE AGENTS. (You are not required to designate any
alternate agents but you may do so. Any alternate agent you designate will be able to
make the same health care decisions as the agent you designated in paragraph 1,
above, in the event that agent is unable or ineligible to act as your agent. If the agent
you designated is your spouse, he or she becomes ineligible to act as your agent if your
marriage is dissolved. Your agent may withdraw whether or not you are capable of
designating another agent.)

If the person designated as my agent in paragraph 1 is not available or becomes ineligible to act as my agent to make a health care decision for me or loses the mental capacity to make health care decisions for me, or if I revoke that person's appointment or authority to act as my agent to make health care decisions for me, then I designate and appoint the following persons to serve as my agent to make health care decisions for me as authorized in this document, such persons to serve in the order listed below:

a. First Alternate Agent:_____
_____
(Insert name, address, and telephone number of first alternate agent.)

b. Second Alternate Agent:_____
_____
(Insert name, address, and telephone number of second alternate agent.)

9. PRIOR DESIGNATIONS REVOKED. I revoke any prior durable power of attorney for health care.

DATE AND SIGNATURE OF PRINCIPAL
(YOU MUST DATE AND SIGN THIS
POWER OF ATTORNEY)

I sign my name to this Statutory Form Durable Power of Attorney For Health Care on
_____ at _____.
      (date)   (city)   (state)

_____
(you sign here)

(THIS POWER OF ATTORNEY WILL NOT BE VALID UNLESS IT IS SIGNED BY TWO QUALIFIED WITNESSES WHO ARE PRESENT WHEN YOU SIGN OR ACKNOWLEDGE YOUR SIGNATURE. IF YOU HAVE ATTACHED ANY ADDITIONAL PAGES TO THIS FORM, YOU MUST DATE AND SIGN EACH OF THE ADDITIONAL PAGES AT THE SAME TIME YOU DATE AND SIGN THIS POWER OF ATTORNEY.)

STATEMENT OF WITNESSES

This document must be witnessed by two qualified adult witnesses. None of the following may be used as a witness:

1. A person you designate as your agent or alternate agent;
2. A health care provider;
3. An employee of a health care provider;
4. The operator of a long-term care facility;
5. An employee of an operator of a long-term care facility;
6. Your spouse
7. A person related to you by blood or adoption

8. A person entitled to inherit any part of your estate upon your death; or

9. A person who has, at the time of executing this document, any claim against your estate.

I declare under penalty of perjury that the person who signed or acknowledged this document is personally known to me to be the principal, that the principal signed or acknowledged this durable power of attorney in my presence, that the principal appears to be of sound mind and under no duress, fraud, or undue influence, that I am not the person appointed as attorney in fact by this document, and that I am not a health care provider; an employee of a health care provider; the operator of a long-term care facility; an employee of an operator of a long-term care facility; the principal's spouse; a person related to the principal by blood or adoption; a person entitled to inherit any part of the principal's estate upon death; nor a person who has, at the time of executing this document, any claim against the principal's estate.

Signature:_____

Residence Address:_____

Print Name:_____

Date:_____

Signature:_____

Residence Address:_____

Print Name:_____

Date:_____

10. ACCEPTANCE OF APPOINTMENT OF POWER OF ATTORNEY. I accept this appointment and agree to serve as agent for health care decisions. I understand I have a duty to act consistently with the desires of the principal as expressed in this appointment. I understand that this document gives me authority over health care decisions for the principal only if the principal becomes incapable. I understand that I must act in good faith in exercising my authority under this power of attorney. I understand that the principal may revoke this power of attorney at any time in any manner.

If I choose to withdraw during the time the principal is competent, I must notify the principal of my decision. If I choose to withdraw when the principal is incapable of making the principal's health care decisions, I must notify the principal physician.

_____
(Signature of agent/date)

_____
(Signature of alternate agent/date)

ADVANCE DIRECTIVE FOR HEALTH CARE

I,_____, being of sound mind and eighteen (18) years of age
or older, willfully and voluntarily make known my desire, by my instructions to others through my living will,
or by my appointment of a health care proxy, or both, that my life shall not be artificially prolonged under the
circumstances set forth below. I thus do hereby declare:

I. Living Will

a. If my attending physician and another physician determine that I am no longer able to make decisions
    regarding my medical treatment, I direct my attending physician and other health care providers, pursuant
    to the Oklahoma Rights of the Terminally Ill or Persistently Unconscious Act, to withhold or withdraw
    treatment from me under the circumstances I have indicated below by my signature. I understand that I
    will be given treatment that is necessary for my comfort or to alleviate my pain.

b. If I have a terminal condition:

    (1) I direct that life-sustaining treatment shall be withheld or withdrawn if such treatment would only pro-
        long my process of dying, and if my attending physician and another physician determine that I have
        an incurable and irreversible condition that even with the administration of life-sustaining treatment
        will cause my death within six (6) months.

        _____(signature)

    (2) I understand that the subject of the artificial administration of nutrition and hydration (food and water)
        that will only prolong the process of dying from an incurable and irreversible condition is of particular
        importance. I understand that if I do not sign this paragraph, artificially administered nutrition and
        hydration will be administered to me. I further understand that if I sign this paragraph, I am authoriz-
        ing the withholding or withdrawal of artificially administered nutrition (food) and hydration (water).

        _____(signature)

    (3) I direct that (add other medical directives, if any)_____
        _____
        _____

        _____ (signature)

c. If I am persistently unconscious:

    (1) I direct that life-sustaining treatment be withheld or withdrawn if such treatment will only serve to
        maintain me in an irreversible condition, as determined by my attending physician and another physi-
        cian, in which thought and awareness of self and environment are absent.

        _____(signature)

    (2) I understand that the subject of the artificial administration of nutrition and hydration (food and
        water) for individuals who have become persistently unconscious is of particular importance. I under-
        stand that if I do not sign this paragraph, artificially administered nutrition and hydration will be
        administered to me. I further understand that if I sign this paragraph, I am authorizing the withhold-
        ing or withdrawal of artificially administered nutrition (food) and hydration (water).

        _____(signature)

    (3) I direct that (add other medical directives, if any)_____
        _____
        _____

        _____(signature)

II. My Appointment of My Health Care Proxy

a. If my attending physician and another physician determine that I am no longer able to make decisions regarding my medical treatment, I direct my attending physician and other health care providers pursuant to the Oklahoma Rights of the Terminally Ill or Persistently Unconscious Act to follow the instructions of _____, whom I appoint as my health care proxy. If my health care proxy is unable or unwilling to serve, I appoint _____ _____as my alternate health care proxy with the same authority. My health care proxy is authorized to make whatever medical treatment decisions I could make if I were able, except that decisions regarding life-sustaining treatment can be made by my health care proxy or alternate health care proxy only as I indicate in the following sections.

b. If I have a terminal condition:

   (1) I authorize my health care proxy to direct that life-sustaining treatment be withheld or withdrawn if such treatment would only prolong my process of dying and if my attending physician and another physician determine that I have an incurable and irreversible condition that even with the administration of life- sustaining treatment will cause my death within six (6) months.

   _____(signature)

   (2) I understand that the subject of the artificial administration of nutrition and hydration (food and water) is of particular importance. I understand that if I do not sign this paragraph, artificially administered nutrition (food) or hydration (water) will be administered to me. I further understand that if I sign this paragraph, I am authorizing the withholding or withdrawal of artificially administered nutrition and hydration.

   _____(signature)

   (3) I authorize my health care proxy to (add other medical directives, if any)_____
   _____
   _____

   _____(signature)

c. If I am persistently unconscious:

   (1) I authorize my health care proxy to direct that life-sustaining treatment be withheld or withdrawn if such treatment will only serve to maintain me in an irreversible condition, as determined by my attending physician and another physician, in which thought and awareness of self and environment are absent.

   _____(signature)

   (2) I understand that the subject of the artificial administration of nutrition and hydration (food and water) is of particular importance. I understand that if I do not sign this paragraph, artificially administered nutrition (food) and hydration (water) will be administered to me. I further understand that if I sign this paragraph, I am authorizing the withholding and withdrawal of artificially administered nutrition and hydration.

   _____ (signature)

   (3) I authorize my health care proxy to (add other medical directives, if any)_____
   _____
   _____

   _____(signature)

III. Anatomical Gifts

I direct that at the time of my death my entire body or designated body organs or body parts be donated for purposes of transplantation, therapy, advancement or medical or dental science or research or education pursuant to the provisions of the Uniform Anatomical Gift Act. Death means either irreversible cessation of circulatory and respiratory functions or irreversible cessation of all functions of the entire brain, including the brain stem. I specifically donate:

[   ] My entire body; or
[   ] The following body organs or parts:

( ) lungs,	( ) liver,	( ) pancreas,	( ) heart,	( ) kidneys,
( ) brain,	( ) skin,	( ) bones/marrow,	( ) bloods/fluids,	( ) tissue,
( ) arteries,	( ) eyes/cornea/lens,	( ) glands,	( ) other: _____	

_____(signature)

IV. Conflicting Provisions

I understand that if I have completed both a living will and have appointed a health care proxy, and if there is a conflict between my health care proxy's decision and my living will, my living will shall take precedence unless I indicate otherwise. _____

_____(signature)

V. General Provisions

a. I understand that if I have been diagnosed as pregnant and that diagnosis is known to my attending physician, this advance directive shall have no force or effect during the course of my pregnancy.

b. In the absence of my ability to give directions regarding the use of life-sustaining procedures, it is my intention that this advance directive shall be honored by my family and physicians as the final expression of my legal right to refuse medical or surgical treatment including, but not limited to, the administration of any life-sustaining procedures, and I accept the consequences of such refusal.

c. This advance directive shall be in effect until it is revoked.

d. I understand that I may revoke this advance directive at any time.

e. I understand and agree that if I have any prior directives, and, if I sign this advance directive, my prior directives are revoked.

f. I understand the full importance of this advance directive and I am emotionally and mentally competent to make this advance directive.

Signed this _____ day of _____ , _____.

_____
(Signature)

_____
City, County and State of Residence

The principal is personally known to me and I believe the principal to be of sound mind. I am eighteen (18) years of age or older. I am not related to the principal by blood or marriage, or related to the attorney-in-fact by blood or marriage. The principal has declared to me that this instrument is his power of attorney granting to the named attorney-in-fact the power and authority specified herein, and that he has willingly made and executed it as his free and voluntary act for the purposes herein expressed.

_____
(Signature of Witness)

_____

_____
(Address)

_____
(Signature of Witness)

_____

_____
(Address)

STATE OF OKLAHOMA   )
) SS.

COUNTY OF _____)

Before me, the undersigned authority, on the _____ day of _____, _____, personally appeared _____ (principal), _____ (witness), and _____ (witness), whose names are subscribed to the foregoing instrument in their respective capacities, and all of said persons being by me duly sworn, the principal declared to me and to the said witnesses in my presence that the instrument is his or her power of attorney, and that the principal has willingly and voluntarily made and executed it as the free act and deed of the principal for the purposes therein expressed, and the witnesses declared to me that they were each eighteen (18) years of age or over, and that neither of them is related to the principal by blood or marriage, or related to the attorney-in-fact by blood or marriage.

_____
Notary Public

My Commission Expires:

_____

POWER OF ATTORNEY FOR HEALTH CARE

I appoint _____, whose address is _____ _____, and whose telephone number is _____, as my attorney-in-fact for health care decisions. I appoint _____, whose address is _____ _____, and whose telephone number is _____, as my alternative attorney-in-fact for health care decisions. I authorize my attorney-in-fact appointed by this document to make health care decisions for me when I am incapable of making my own health care decisions. I have read the warning below and understand the consequences of appointing a power of attorney for health care.

I direct that my attorney-in-fact comply with the following instructions or limitations:

_____
_____

In addition, I direct that my attorney-in-fact have authority to make decisions regarding the following:

_____ Withholding or withdrawal of life-sustaining procedures with the understanding that death may result.

_____ Withholding or withdrawal of artificially administered hydration or nutrition or both with the understanding that dehydration, malnutrition and death may result.

_____
(Signature of person making appointment/Date)

DECLARATION OF WITNESS

We declare that the principal is personally known to us, that the principal signed or acknowledged the principal's signature on this power of attorney for health care in our presence, that the principal appears to be of sound mind and not under duress, fraud or undue influence, that neither of us is the person appointed as attorney-in-fact by this document or the principal's attending physician.

Witnessed By:

_____   _____
(Signature of Witness/Date)   (Printed Name of Witness)

_____   _____
(Signature of Witness/Date)   (Printed Name of Witness)

ACCEPTANCE OF APPOINTMENT OF POWER OF ATTORNEY

I accept this appointment and agree to serve as attorney-in-fact for health care decisions. I understand I have a duty to act consistently with the desires of the principal as expressed in this appointment. I understand that this document gives me authority over health care decisions for the principal only if the principal becomes incapable. I understand that I must act in good faith in exercising my authority under this power of attorney. I understand that the principal may revoke this power of attorney at any time in any manner, and that I have a duty to inform the principal's attending physician promptly upon any revocation.

_____
(Signature of Attorney-in-fact/Date)

_____
(Printed name)

_____
(Signature of Alternate Attorney-in-fact/Date)

WARNING TO PERSON APPOINTING A POWER OF ATTORNEY FOR HEALTH CARE

This is an import legal document. It creates a power of attorney for health care. Before signing this document, you should know these important facts:

This document gives the person you designate as your attorney-in-fact the power to make health care decisions for you, subject to any limitations, specifications or statement of your desires that you include in this document.

For this document to be effective, your attorney-in-fact must accept the appointment in writing.

The person you designate in this document has a duty to act consistently with your desires as stated in this document or otherwise made known or, if your desires are unknown, to act in a manner consistent with what the person in good faith believes to be in your best interest. The person you designate in this document does, however, have the right to withdraw from this duty at any time.

This power will continue in effect for a period of seven years unless you become unable to participate in health care decisions for yourself during that period. If this occurs, the power will continue in effect until you are able to participate in those decisions again.

You have the right to revoke the appointment of the person you designated in this document at any time by notifying that person or your health care provider of the revocation orally or in writing.

Despite this document, you have the right to make medical and other health care decisions for yourself as long as you are able to participate knowledgeably in those decisions.

If there is anything in this document that you do not understand, you should ask a lawyer to explain it to you. This power of attorney will not be valid for making health care decisions unless it is signed by two qualified witnesses who are personally known to you and who are present when you sign or acknowledge your signature.

HEALTH CARE POWER OF ATTORNEY
(SOUTH CAROLINA STATUTORY FORM)
INFORMATION ABOUT THIS DOCUMENT

THIS IS AN IMPORTANT LEGAL DOCUMENT. BEFORE SIGNING THIS DOCUMENT, YOU SHOULD KNOW THESE IMPORTANT FACTS:

1. THIS DOCUMENT GIVES THE PERSON YOU NAME AS YOUR AGENT THE POWER TO MAKE HEALTH CARE DECISIONS FOR YOU IF YOU CANNOT MAKE THE DECISION FOR YOURSELF. THIS POWER INCLUDES THE POWER TO MAKE DECISIONS ABOUT LIFE-SUSTAINING TREATMENT. UNLESS YOU STATE OTHERWISE, YOUR AGENT WILL HAVE THE SAME AUTHORITY TO MAKE DECISIONS ABOUT YOUR HEALTH CARE AS YOU WOULD HAVE.

2. THIS POWER IS SUBJECT TO ANY LIMITATIONS OR STATEMENTS OF YOUR DESIRES THAT YOU INCLUDE IN THIS DOCUMENT. YOU MAY STATE IN THIS DOCUMENT ANY TREATMENT YOU DO NOT DESIRE OR TREATMENT YOU WANT TO BE SURE YOU RECEIVE. YOUR AGENT WILL BE OBLIGATED TO FOLLOW YOUR INSTRUCTIONS WHEN MAKING DECISIONS ON YOUR BEHALF. YOU MAY ATTACH ADDITIONAL PAGES IF YOU NEED MORE SPACE TO COMPLETE THE STATEMENT.

3. AFTER YOU HAVE SIGNED THIS DOCUMENT, YOU HAVE THE RIGHT TO MAKE HEALTH CARE DECISIONS FOR YOURSELF IF YOU ARE MENTALLY COMPETENT TO DO SO. AFTER YOU HAVE SIGNED THIS DOCUMENT, NO TREATMENT MAY BE GIVEN TO YOU OR STOPPED OVER YOUR OBJECTION IF YOU ARE MENTALLY COMPETENT TO MAKE THAT DECISION.

4. YOU HAVE THE RIGHT TO REVOKE THIS DOCUMENT, AND TERMINATE YOUR AGENT'S AUTHORITY, BY INFORMING EITHER YOUR AGENT OR YOUR HEALTH CARE PROVIDER ORALLY OR IN WRITING.

5. IF THERE IS ANYTHING IN THIS DOCUMENT THAT YOU DO NOT UNDERSTAND, YOU SHOULD ASK A SOCIAL WORKER, LAWYER, OR OTHER PERSON TO EXPLAIN IT TO YOU.

6. THIS POWER OF ATTORNEY WILL NOT BE VALID UNLESS TWO PERSONS SIGN AS WITNESSES. EACH OF THESE PERSONS MUST EITHER WITNESS YOUR SIGNING OF THE POWER OF ATTORNEY OR WITNESS YOUR ACKNOWLEDGMENT THAT THE SIGNATURE ON THE POWER OF ATTORNEY IS YOURS.

THE FOLLOWING PERSONS MAY NOT ACT AS WITNESSES:

A. YOUR SPOUSE; YOUR CHILDREN, GRANDCHILDREN, AND OTHER LINEAL DESCENDANTS; YOUR PARENTS, GRANDPARENTS, AND OTHER LINEAL ANCESTORS; YOUR SIBLINGS AND THEIR LINEAL DESCENDANTS; OR A SPOUSE OF ANY OF THESE PERSONS.

B. A PERSON WHO IS DIRECTLY FINANCIALLY RESPONSIBLE FOR YOUR MEDICAL CARE.

C. A PERSON WHO IS NAMED IN YOUR WILL, OR, IF YOU HAVE NO WILL, WHO WOULD INHERIT YOUR PROPERTY BY INTESTATE SUCCESSION.

D. A BENEFICIARY OF A LIFE INSURANCE POLICY ON YOUR LIFE.

E. THE PERSONS NAMED IN THE HEALTH CARE POWER OF ATTORNEY AS YOUR AGENT OR SUCCESSOR AGENT.

F. YOUR PHYSICIAN OR AN EMPLOYEE OF YOUR PHYSICIAN.

G. ANY PERSON WHO WOULD HAVE A CLAIM AGAINST ANY PORTION OF YOUR ESTATE (PERSONS TO WHOM YOU OWE MONEY).

IF YOU ARE A PATIENT IN A HEALTH FACILITY, NO MORE THAN ONE WITNESS MAY BE AN EMPLOYEE OF THAT FACILITY.

7. YOUR AGENT MUST BE A PERSON WHO IS 18 YEARS OLD OR OLDER AND OF SOUND MIND. IT MAY NOT BE YOUR DOCTOR OR ANY OTHER HEALTH CARE PROVIDER THAT IS NOW PROVIDING YOU WITH TREATMENT; OR AN EMPLOYEE OF YOUR DOCTOR OR PROVIDER; OR A SPOUSE OF THE DOCTOR, PROVIDER, OR EMPLOYEE; UNLESS THE PERSON IS A RELATIVE OF YOURS.

8. YOU SHOULD INFORM THE PERSON THAT YOU WANT HIM OR HER TO BE YOUR HEALTH CARE AGENT. YOU SHOULD DISCUSS THIS DOCUMENT WITH YOUR AGENT AND YOUR PHYSICIAN AND GIVE EACH A SIGNED COPY. IF YOU ARE IN A HEALTH CARE FACILITY OR A NURSING CARE FACILITY, A COPY OF THIS DOCUMENT SHOULD BE INCLUDED IN YOUR MEDICAL RECORD.

1. DESIGNATION OF HEALTH CARE AGENT

I,_____, hereby appoint:
   (Principal)

_____ (Agent)

_____ (Address)

Home Telephone:_____ Work Telephone:_____ as my agent to make health care decisions for me as authorized in this document.

2. <u>EFFECTIVE DATE AND DURABILITY.</u> By this document I intend to create a durable power of attorney effective upon, and only during, any period of mental incompetence.

3. <u>AGENT'S POWERS.</u> I grant to my agent full authority to make decisions for me regarding my health care. In exercising this authority, my agent shall follow my desires as stated in this document or otherwise expressed by me or known to my agent. In making any decision, my agent shall attempt to discuss the proposed decision with me to determine my desires if I am able to communicate in any way. If my agent cannot determine the choice I would want made, then my agent shall make a choice for me based upon what my agent believes to be in my best interests. My agent's authority to interpret my desires is intended to be as broad as possible, except for any limitations I may state below.

Accordingly, unless specifically limited by Section E, below, my agent is authorized as follows:

A. To consent, refuse, or withdraw consent to any and all types of medical care, treatment, surgical procedures, diagnostic procedures, medication, and the use of mechanical or other procedures that affect any bodily function, including, but not limited to, artificial respiration, nutritional support and hydration, and cardiopulmonary resuscitation;

B. To authorize, or refuse to authorize, any medication or procedure intended to relieve pain, even though such use may lead to physical damage, addiction, or hasten the moment of, but not intentionally cause, my death;

C. To authorize my admission to or discharge, even against medical advice, from any hospital, nursing care facility, or similar facility or service;

D. To take any other action necessary to making, documenting, and assuring implementation of decisions concerning my health care, including, but not limited to, granting any waiver or release from liability required by any hospital, physician, nursing care provider, or other health care provider; signing any documents relating to refusals of treatment or the leaving of a facility against medical advice, and pursuing any legal action in my name, and at the expense of my estate to force compliance with my wishes as determined by my agent, or to seek actual or punitive damages for the failure to comply.

E. The powers granted above do not include the following powers or are subject to the following rules or limitations:

_____

_____

4. <u>ORGAN DONATION</u> (INITIAL ONLY ONE)
My agent may_____; may not_____ consent to the donation of all or any of my tissue or organs for purposes of transplantation.

5. <u>EFFECT ON DECLARATION OF A DESIRE FOR A NATURAL DEATH (LIVING WILL).</u>
I understand that if I have a valid Declaration of a Desire for a Natural Death, the instructions contained in the Declaration will be given effect in any situation to which they are applicable. My agent will have authority to make decisions concerning my health care only in situations to which the Declaration does not apply.

6. <u>STATEMENT OF DESIRES AND SPECIAL PROVISIONS.</u> With respect to any Life-Sustaining Treatment, I direct the following: (INITIAL ONLY ONE OF THE FOLLOWING 4 PARAGRAPHS)

(1) _____GRANT OF DISCRETION TO AGENT. I do not want my life to be prolonged nor do I want life-sustaining treatment to be provided or continued if my agent believes the burdens of the treatment outweigh the expected benefits. I want my agent to consider the relief of suffering, my personal beliefs, the expense involved and the quality as well as the possible extension of my life in making decisions concerning life-sustaining treatment.
OR
(2) _____DIRECTIVE TO WITHHOLD OR WITHDRAW TREATMENT. I do not want my life to be prolonged and I do not want life-sustaining treatment:
    a. if I have a condition that is incurable or irreversible and, without the administration of life-sustaining procedures, expected to result in death within a relatively short period of time; or
    b. if I am in a state of permanent unconsciousness.
OR
(3) _____DIRECTIVE FOR MAXIMUM TREATMENT. I want my life to be prolonged to the greatest extent possible, within the standards of accepted medical practice, without regard to my condition, the chances I have for recovery, or the cost of the procedures.
OR
(4) _____DIRECTIVE IN MY OWN WORDS: _____

_____

_____

7. STATEMENT OF DESIRES REGARDING TUBE FEEDING

With respect to Nutrition and Hydration provided by means of a nasogastric tube or tube into the stomach, intestines, or veins, I wish to make clear that (INITIAL ONLY ONE)

_____ I do not want to receive these forms of artificial nutrition and hydration, and they may be withheld or withdrawn under the conditions given above.;   OR

_____ I do want to receive these forms of artificial nutrition and hydration.

IF YOU DO NOT INITIAL EITHER OF THE ABOVE STATEMENTS, YOUR AGENT WILL NOT HAVE AUTHORITY TO DIRECT THAT NUTRITION AND HYDRATION NECESSARY FOR COMFORT CARE OR ALLEVIATION OF PAIN BE WITHDRAWN.

8. SUCCESSORS

If an agent named by me dies, becomes legally disabled, resigns, refuses to act, becomes unavailable, or if an agent who is my spouse is divorced or separated from me, I name the following as successors to my agent, each to act alone and successively, in the order named.

A. First Alternate Agent:
     Name: _____
     Address:_____
     Telephone:_____

B. Second Alternate Agent:
     Name: _____
     Address: _____
     Telephone: _____

9. ADMINISTRATIVE PROVISIONS

A. I revoke any prior Health Care Power of Attorney and any provisions relating to health care of any other prior power of attorney.

B. This power of attorney is intended to be valid in any jurisdiction in which it is presented.

10. UNAVAILABILITY OF AGENT

If at any relevant time the Agent or Successor Agents named herein are unable or unwilling to make decisions concerning my health care, and those decision are to be made by a guardian, by the Probate Court, or by a surrogate pursuant to the Adult Health Care Consent Act, it is my intention that the guardian, Probate Court, or surrogate make those decisions in accordance with my directions as stated in this document.

BY SIGNING HERE I INDICATE THAT I UNDERSTAND THE CONTENT OF THIS DOCUMENT AND THE EFFECT OF THIS GRANT OF POWERS TO MY AGENT.

I sign my name to this Health Care Power of Attorney on this _____ day of _____, _____.
My current home address is:

_____

Signature:_____

Name:_____

WITNESS STATEMENT

I declare, on the basis of information and belief, that the person who signed or acknowledged this document (the principal) is personally known to me, that he/she signed or acknowledged this Health Care Power of Attorney in my presence, and that he/she appears to be of sound mind and under no duress, fraud, or undue influence. I am not related to the principal by blood, marriage, or adoption, either as a spouse, a lineal ancestor, descendant of the parents of the principal, or spouse of any of them. I am not directly financially responsible for the principal's medical care. I am not entitled to any portion of the principal's estate upon his decease, whether under any will or as an heir by intestate succession, nor am I the beneficiary of an insurance policy on the principal's life, nor do I have a claim against the principal's estate as of this time. I am not the principal's attending physician, nor an employee of the attending physician. No more than one witness is an employee of a health facility in which the principal is a patient. I am not appointed as Health Care Agent or Successor Health Care Agent by this document.

Witness No. 1
     Date: _____
     Signature: _____
     Print Name: _____
     Residence Address:_____
     _____
     Telephone: _____

Witness No. 2
     Date: _____
     Signature: _____
     Print Name: _____
     Residence Address: _____
     _____
     Telephone: _____

POWER OF ATTORNEY

I, _____
_____(insert your name and address)
appoint _____
_____ (insert the name and address of the person appointed) as my attorney-in-fact (agent) to act for me in any lawful way with respect to the powers set forth, defined, and described in the Tennessee Code Annotated, Section 34-6-109, which is incorporated by reference herein; subject to any special instructions or limitations contained in paragraph 2 below. If my agent designated above shall be unable or unwilling to serve, I appoint

_____
_____ (insert name and address of alternate agent) as my alternate agent.

1. **Effective Date** (CHECK ONE OF THE FOLLOWING BOXES):

   ❑ This power of attorney shall become effective immediately, and (check one):

   ❑ shall not be affected by subsequent disability or incapacity of the principal.

   ❑ shall terminate upon the subsequent disability or incapacity of the principal.

   ❑ This power of attorney shall become effective upon the disability or incapacity of the principal.

2. **Special Instructions and Limitations** (if none, type in the word "none."): _____
_____
_____

3. **Conservator:** In the event a court appoints a conservator, guardian of the estate, or guardian of the person for me, I nominate _____
_____ (insert name and address of person nominated) to serve as such conservator or guardian.

   Signed this _____ day of _____, _____.

_____   _____
(Your signature)   (Your social security number)

ACKNOWLEDGMENT

State of _____
(County) of _____

   On this _____ day of _____, _____, before me, personally
appeared _____ (name of principal), who is
personally known to me or provided _____ as identification,
and acknowledged that he or she executed it.

_____
Notary Public

DURABLE POWER OF ATTORNEY FOR HEALTH CARE

WARNING TO PERSON EXECUTING THIS DOCUMENT

This is an important legal document. Before executing this document you should know these important facts.

This document gives the person you designate as your agent (the attorney in fact) the power to make health care decisions for you. Your agent must act consistently with your desires as stated in this document.

Except as you otherwise specify in this document, this document gives your agent the power to consent to your doctor not giving treatment or stopping treatment necessary to keep you alive.

Notwithstanding this document, you have the right to make medical and other health care decisions for yourself so long as you can give informed consent with respect to the particular decision. In addition, no treatment may be given to you over your objection, and health care necessary to keep you alive may not be stopped or withheld if you object at the time.

This document gives your agent authority to consent, to refuse to consent, or to withdraw consent to any care, treatment, service, or procedure to maintain, diagnose or treat a physical or mental condition. This power is subject to any limitations that you include in this document. You may state in this document any types of treatment that you do not desire. In addition, a court can take away the power of your agent to make health care decisions for you if your agent: (1) authorizes anything that is illegal; or (2) acts contrary to your desires as stated in this document.

You have the right to revoke the authority of your agent by notifying your agent or your treating physician, hospital or other health care provider orally or in writing of the revocation.

Your agent has the right to examine your medical records and to consent to their disclosure unless you limit this right in this document.

Unless you otherwise specify in this document, this document gives your agent the power after you die to: (1) authorize an autopsy; (2) donate your body or parts thereof for transplant or therapeutic or educational or scientific purposes; and (3) direct the disposition of your remains.

If there is anything in this document that you do not understand, you should ask an attorney to explain it to you.

I, _____

_____ (insert your name and address),

appoint _____

_____ (insert name, address, and telephone number of agent), as my attorney in fact (agent) for health care decisions. I appoint _____

_____(insert name, address, and telephone number of alternate agent), as my alternative agent for health care decisions. I authorize my agent to make health care decisions for me when I am incapable of making my own health care decisions, with all of the authority permitted under the laws of Tennessee, except as may be limited in the following paragraph. I understand the consequences of appointing an agent for health care.

Special Instructions and Limitations: I direct that my agent comply with the following instructions or limitations (if none, write in the word "none"): _____
_____
_____

In addition, I direct that my agent have authority to make decisions regarding the enforcement of my intentions regarding life-prolonging procedures as stated in any living will I have executed or may execute in the future.

Dated:_____   _____
                                      Signature of Principal

WITNESS STATEMENT

I declare under penalty of perjury under the laws of Tennessee that the person who signed this document is personally known to me to be the principal; that the principal signed this durable power of attorney in my presence; that the principal appears to be of sound mind and under no duress, fraud or undue influence; that I am not the person appointed as attorney in fact by this document; that I am not a health care provider, an employee of a health care provider, the operator of a health care institution nor an employee of an operator of a health care institution; that I am not related to the principal by blood, marriage, or adoption; that, to the best of my knowledge, I do not, at the present time, have a claim against any portion of the estate of the principal upon the principal's death; and that, to the best of my knowledge, I am not entitled to any part of the estate of the principal upon the death of the principal under a will or codicil thereto now existing, or by operation of law.

Witness_____   Witness_____

STATE OF TENNESSEE
COUNTY OF _____

Subscribed, sworn to and acknowledged before me by _____
_____, the declarant, and subscribed and sworn to before me by
_____ and _____, witnesses,
this _____ day of _____, _____.

                              _____
                              Notary Public

My Commission Expires:_____

STATUTORY DURABLE POWER OF ATTORNEY

NOTICE: THE POWERS GRANTED BY THIS DOCUMENT ARE BROAD AND SWEEPING. THEY ARE EXPLAINED IN THE DURABLE POWER OF ATTORNEY ACT, CHAPTER XII, TEXAS PROBATE CODE. IF YOU HAVE ANY QUESTIONS ABOUT THESE POWERS, OBTAIN COMPETENT LEGAL ADVICE. THIS DOCUMENT DOES NOT AUTHORIZE ANYONE TO MAKE MEDICAL AND OTHER HEALTH-CARE DECISIONS FOR YOU. YOU MAY REVOKE THIS POWER OF ATTORNEY IF YOU LATER WISH TO DO SO.

I, _____

_____ (insert your name and address),

appoint _____

_____(insert the name and address of the person appointed) as my agent (attorney-in-fact) to act for me in any lawful way with respect to all of the following powers except for a power that I have crossed out below:

TO WITHHOLD A POWER, YOU MUST CROSS OUT EACH POWER WITHHELD.

Real property transactions;

Tangible personal property transactions;

Stock and bond transactions;

Commodity and option transactions;

Banking and other financial institution transactions;

Business operating transactions;

Insurance and annuity transactions;

Estate, trust, and other beneficiary transactions;

Claims and litigation;

Personal and family maintenance;

Benefits from social security, Medicare, Medicaid, or other governmental programs or civil or military service;

Retirement plan transactions;

Tax matters;

IF NO POWER LISTED ABOVE IS CROSSED OUT, THIS DOCUMENT SHALL BE CONSTRUED AND INTERPRETED AS A GENERAL POWER OF ATTORNEY AND MY AGENT (ATTORNEY IN FACT) SHALL HAVE THE POWER AND AUTHORITY TO PERFORM OR UNDERTAKE ANY ACTION I COULD PERFORM OR UNDERTAKE IF I WERE PERSONALLY PRESENT.

SPECIAL INSTRUCTIONS:

Special instructions applicable to gifts (initial in front of the following sentence to have it apply):

I grant my agent (attorney in fact) the power to apply my property to make gifts, except that the amount of a gift to an individual may not exceed the amount of annual exclusions allowed from the federal gift tax for the calendar year of the gift.

ON THE FOLLOWING LINES YOU MAY GIVE SPECIAL INSTRUCTIONS LIMITING OR EXTENDING THE POWERS GRANTED TO YOUR AGENT.

_____

_____

_____

_____

UNLESS YOU DIRECT OTHERWISE ABOVE, THIS POWER OF ATTORNEY IS EFFECTIVE IMMEDIATELY AND WILL CONTINUE UNTIL IT IS REVOKED.

CHOOSE ONE OF THE FOLLOWING ALTERNATIVES BY CROSSING OUT THE ALTERNATIVE NOT CHOSEN:

(A)   This power of attorney is not affected by my subsequent disability or incapacity.

(B)   This power of attorney becomes effective upon my disability or incapacity.

YOU SHOULD CHOOSE ALTERNATIVE (A) IF THIS POWER OF ATTORNEY IS TO BECOME EFFECTIVE ON THE DATE IT IS EXECUTED.

IF NEITHER (A) NOR (B) IS CROSSED OUT, IT WILL BE ASSUMED THAT YOU CHOSE ALTERNATIVE (A).

If alternative (B) is chosen and a definition o my disability or incapacity is not contained in this power of attorney, I shall be considered disabled or incapacitated for purposes of this power of attorney if a physician certifies in writing at a date later than the date this power of attorney is executed that, based on the physician's medical examination of me, I am mentally incapable of managing my financial affairs. I authorize the physician who examines me for this purpose to disclose my physical or mental condition to another person for purposes of this power of attorney. A third party who accepts this power of attorney is fully protected from any action taken under this power of attorney that is based on the determination made by a physician or my disability or incapacity.

I agree that any third party who receives a copy of this document may act under it. Revocation of the durable power of attorney is not effective as to a third party until the third party receives actual notice of the revocation. I agree to indemnify the third party for any claims that arise against the third party because of reliance on this power of attorney.

If any agent named by me dies, becomes legally disabled, resigns, or refuses to act, I name the following (each to act alone and successively, in the order named) as successor(s) to that agent:

_____.

Signed this _____ day of _____, _____.

_____

(your signature)

State of _____

County of _____

This document was acknowledged before me on _____ (date), by
_____ (name of principal).

_____

(signature of notarial officer)

(Seal, if any, of notary) _____

(printed name)

My commission expires: _____

THE ATTORNEY IN FACT OR AGENT, BY ACCEPTING OR ACTING UNDER THE APPOINTMENT, ASSUMES THE FIDUCIARY AND OTHER LEGAL RESPONSIBILITIES OF AN AGENT.

Durable Power of Attorney for Health Care

INFORMATION CONCERNING THE DURABLE POWER OF ATTORNEY FOR HEALTH CARE

THIS IS AN IMPORTANT LEGAL DOCUMENT. BEFORE SIGNING THIS DOCUMENT, YOU SHOULD KNOW THESE IMPORTANT FACTS:

Except to the extent you state otherwise, this document gives the person you name as your agent the authority to make any and all health care decisions for you in accordance with your wishes, including your religious and moral beliefs, when you are no longer capable of making them yourself. Because "health care" means any treatment, service, or procedure to maintain, diagnose, or treat your physical or mental condition, your agent has the power to make a broad range of health care decisions for you. Your agent may consent, refuse to consent, or withdraw consent to medical treatment and may make decisions about withdrawing or withholding life-sustaining treatment. Your agent may not consent to voluntary inpatient mental health services, convulsive treatment, psychosurgery, or abortion. A physician must comply with your agent's instructions or allow you to be transferred to another physician.

Your agent's authority begins when your doctor certifies that you lack the capacity to make health care decisions.

Your agent is obligated to follow your instructions when making decisions on your behalf. Unless you state otherwise, your agent has the same authority to make decisions about your health care as you would have had.

It is important that you discuss this document with your physician or other health care provider before you sign it to make sure that you understand the nature and range of decisions that may be made on your behalf. If you do not have a physician, you should talk with someone else who is knowledgeable about these issues and can answer your questions. You do not need a lawyer's assistance to complete this document, but if there is anything in this document that you do not understand, you should ask a lawyer to explain it to you.

The person you appoint as agent should be someone you know and trust. The person must be 18 years of age or older or a person under 18 years of age who has had the disabilities of minority removed. If you appoint your health or residential care provider (e.g., your physician or an employee of a home health agency, hospital, nursing home, or residential care home, other than a relative), that person has to choose between acting as your agent or as your health or residential care provider; the law does not permit a person to do both at the same time.

You should inform the person you appoint that you want the person to be your health care agent. You should discuss this document with your agent and your physician and give each a signed copy. You should indicate on the document itself the people and institutions who have signed copies. Your agent is not liable for health care decisions made in good faith on your behalf.

Even after you have signed this document, you have the right to make health care decisions for yourself as long as you are able to do so and treatment cannot be given to you or stopped over your objection. You have the right to revoke the authority granted to your agent by informing your agent or your health or residential care provider orally or in writing or by your execution of a subsequent durable power of attorney for health care. Unless you state otherwise, your appointment of a spouse dissolves on divorce.

This document may not be changed or modified. If you want to make changes in the document, you must make an entirely new one.

You may wish to designate an alternate agent in the event that your agent is unwilling, unable, or ineligible to act as your agent. Any alternate agent you designate has the same authority to make health care decisions for you.

THIS POWER OF ATTORNEY IS NOT VALID UNLESS IT IS SIGNED IN THE PRESENCE OF TWO OR MORE QUALIFIED WITNESSES. THE FOLLOWING PERSONS MAY NOT ACT AS WITNESSES:
   (1)   the person you have designated as your agent;
   (2)   your health or residential care provider or an employee of your health or residential care provider;
   (3)   your spouse;
   (4)   your lawful heirs or beneficiaries named in your will or a deed; or
   (5)   creditors or persons who have a claim against you.

DESIGNATION OF HEALTH CARE AGENT.

I, _____ (insert your name) appoint:
    Name:_____
    Address:_____
                           Phone_____

as my agent to make any and all health care decisions for me, except to the extent I state otherwise in this document. This durable power of attorney for health care takes effect if I become unable to make my own health care decisions and this fact is certified in writing by my physician.

LIMITATIONS ON THE DECISION-MAKING AUTHORITY OF MY AGENT ARE AS FOLLOWS:
_____
_____

DESIGNATION OF ALTERNATE AGENT.

(You are not required to designate an alternate agent but you may do so. An alternate agent may make the same health care decisions as the designated agent if the designated agent is unable or unwilling to act as your agent. If the agent designated is your spouse, the designation is automatically revoked by law if your marriage is dissolved.)

If the person designated as my agent is unable or unwilling to make health care decisions for me, I designate the following persons to serve as my agent to make health care decisions for me as authorized by this document, who serve in the following order:

    A. First Alternate Agent
        Name:_____
        Address:_____
                       Phone_____

    B. Second Alternate Agent
        Name:_____
        Address:_____
                       Phone_____
        The original of this document is kept at_____
_____
_____

The following individuals or institutions have signed copies:

        Name:_____
        Address:_____
_____
        Name:_____
        Address:_____
_____

DURATION.

I understand that this power of attorney exists indefinitely from the date I execute this document unless I establish a shorter time or revoke the power of attorney. If I am unable to make health care decisions for myself when this power of attorney expires, the authority I have granted my agent continues to exist until the time I become able to make health care decisions for myself.

(IF APPLICABLE) This power of attorney ends on the following date:_____

PRIOR DESIGNATIONS REVOKED.

I revoke any prior durable power of attorney for health care.

ACKNOWLEDGMENT OF DISCLOSURE STATEMENT.

I have been provided with a disclosure statement explaining the effect of this document. I have read and understand that information contained in the disclosure statement.

(YOU MUST DATE AND SIGN THIS POWER OF ATTORNEY.)

I sign my name to this durable power of attorney for health care on _____ day of_____,
_____, at _____

(City and State)

_____

(Signature)

_____

(Print Name)

STATEMENT OF WITNESSES.

I declare under penalty of perjury that the principal has identified himself or herself to me, that the principal signed or acknowledged this durable power of attorney in my presence, that I believe the principal to be of sound mind, that the principal has affirmed that the principal is aware of the nature of the document and is signing it voluntarily and free from duress, that the principal requested that I serve as witness to the principal's execution of this document, that I am not the person appointed as agent by this document, and that I am not a provider of health or residential care, an employee of a provider of health or residential care, the operator of a community care facility, or an employee of an operator of a health care facility.

I declare that I am not related to the principal by blood, marriage, or adoption and that to the best of my knowledge I am not entitled to any part of the estate of the principal on the death of the principal under a will or by operation of law.

Witness Signature:_____

Print Name:_____ Date:_____

Address:_____

Witness Signature:_____

Print Name:_____ Date:_____

Address:_____

DIRECTIVE TO PHYSICIANS

Directive made this _____ day of _____ (month, year).

I _____, being of sound mind, wilfully and voluntarily make known my desire that my life shall not be artificially prolonged under the circumstances set forth in this directive.

1. If at any time I should have an incurable or irreversible condition caused by injury, disease, or illness certified to be a terminal condition by two physicians, and if the application of life-sustaining procedures would serve only to artificially postpone the moment of my death, and if my attending physician determines that my death is imminent or will result within a relatively short time without the application of life-sustaining procedures, I direct that those procedures be withheld or withdrawn, and that I be permitted to die naturally.

2. In the absence of my ability to give directions regarding the use of those life-sustaining procedures, it is my intention that this directive be honored by my family and physicians as the final expression of my legal right to refuse medical or surgical treatment and accept the consequences from that refusal.

3. If I have been diagnosed as pregnant and that diagnosis is known to my physician, this directive has no effect during my pregnancy.

4. This directive is in effect until it is revoked.

5. I understand the full import of this directive and I am emotionally and mentally competent to make this directive.

6. I understand that I may revoke this directive at any time.

Signed_____

_____

(City, County, and State of Residence)

I am not related to the declarant by blood or marriage. I would not be entitled to any portion of the declarant's estate on the declarant's death. I am not the attending physician or the declarant or an employee of the attending physician. I am not a patient in the heath care facility in which the declarant is a patient. I have no claim against any portion of the declarant's estate on the declarant's death. Furthermore, if I am an employee of a health care facility in which the declarant is a patient, I am not involved in the financial affairs of the health facility.

Witness_____   Witness_____

SPECIAL POWER OF ATTORNEY

I, _____, of _____, this _____ day of _____, _____, being of sound mind, willfully and voluntarily appoint _____, of _____, as my agent and attorney-in-fact, without substitution, with lawful authority to execute a directive on my behalf under Section 75-2-1105, governing the care and treatment to be administered to or withheld from me at any time after I incur an injury, disease, or illness which renders me unable to give current directions to attending physicians and other providers of medical services.

I have carefully selected my above-named agent with confidence in the belief that this person's familiarity with my desires, beliefs, and attitudes will result in directions to attending physicians and providers of medical services which would probably be the same as I would give if able to do so.

This power of attorney shall be and remain in effect from the time my attending physician certifies that I have incurred a physical or mental condition rendering me unable to give current directions to attending physicians and other providers of medical services as to my care and treatment.

_____
Signature of Principal

State of _____)
County of _____)

On the _____ day of _____, _____, personally appeared before me _____, who duly acknowledged to me that he has read and fully understands the foregoing power of attorney, executed the same of his own volition and for the purposes set forth, and that he was acting under no constraint or undue influence whatsoever.

_____
Notary Public

My commission expires: Residing at:_____

_____

DURABLE POWER OF ATTORNEY FOR HEALTH CARE

INFORMATION CONCERNING THE DURABLE POWER OF ATTORNEY FOR HEALTH CARE

THIS IS AN IMPORTANT LEGAL DOCUMENT. BEFORE SIGNING THIS DOCUMENT, YOU SHOULD KNOW THESE IMPORTANT FACTS:

Except to the extent you state otherwise, this document gives the person you name as your agent the authority to make any and all health care decisions for you when you are no longer capable of making them yourself. "Health care" means any treatment, service or procedure to maintain, diagnose or treat your physical or mental condition. Your agent therefore can have the power to make a broad range of health care decisions for you. Your agent may consent, refuse to consent, or withdraw consent to medical treatment and may make decisions about withdrawing or withholding life-sustaining treatment.

You may state in this document any treatment you do not desire or treatment you want to be sure you receive. Your agent's authority will begin when your doctor certifies that you lack the capacity to make health care decisions. You may attach additional pages if you need more space to complete your statement.

Your agent will be obligated to follow your instructions when making decisions on your behalf. Unless you state otherwise, your agent will have the same authority to make decisions about your health care as you would have had.

It is important that you discuss this document with your physician or other health care providers before you sign it to make sure that you understand the nature and range of decisions which may be made on your behalf. If you do not have a physician, you should talk with someone else who is knowledgeable about these issues and can answer your questions. You do not need a lawyer's assistance to complete this document, but if there is anything in this document that you do not understand, you should ask a lawyer to explain it to you.

The person you appoint as agent should be someone you know and trust and must be at least 18 years old. If you appoint your health or residential care provider (e.g. your physician, or an employee of a home health agency, hospital, nursing home, or residential care home, other than a relative), that person will have to choose between acting as your agent or as you health or residential care provider; the law does not permit a person to do both at the same time.

You should inform the person you appoint that you want him or her to be your health care agent. You should discuss this document with your agent and your physician and give each a signed copy. You should indicate on the document itself the people and institutions who will have signed copies. Your agent will not be liable for health care decisions for yourself as long as you are able to do so, and treatment cannot be given to you or stopped over your objection. You have the right to revoke the authority granted to your agent by informing him or her or your health care provider orally or in writing.

This document may not be changed or modified. If you want to make changes in the document you must make an entirely new one.

You may wish to designate an alternate agent in the event that your agent is unwilling, unable or ineligible to act as your agent. Any alternate agent you designate will have the same authority to make health care decisions for you.

THIS POWER OF ATTORNEY WILL NOT BE VALID UNLESS IT IS SIGNED IN THE PRESENCE OF TWO (2) OR MORE QUALIFIED WITNESSES WHO MUST BOTH BE PRESENT WHEN YOU SIGN OR ACKNOWLEDGE YOUR SIGNATURE. THE FOLLOWING PERSONS MAY *NOT* ACT AS WITNESSES:

— the person you have designated as your agent;
— your health or residential care provider or one of their employees;
— your spouse;

— your lawful heirs or beneficiaries named in your will or a deed;
— creditors or persons who have a claim against you.

I, _____, hereby appoint _____
_____ as my agent to make any and all health care decisions for me, except to the extent I state otherwise in this document. This durable power of attorney for health care shall take effect in the event I become unable to make my own health care decisions.

(a) **STATEMENT OF DESIRES, SPECIAL PROVISIONS, AND LIMITATIONS REGARDING HEALTH CARE DECISIONS.**

Here you may include any specific desires or limitations you deem appropriate, such as when or what life-sustaining measures should be withheld; directions whether to continue or discontinue artificial nutrition and hydration; or instructions to refuse any specific types of treatment that are inconsistent with your religious beliefs or unacceptable to you for any reason.

_____
_____
_____
_____

(attach additional pages as necessary)

(b) **THE SUBJECT OF LIFE-SUSTAINING TREATMENT IS OF PARTICULAR IMPORTANCE.** For your convenience in dealing with that subject, some general statements concerning the withholding or removal of life-sustaining treatment are set forth below. IF YOU AGREE WITH ONE OF THESE STATEMENTS, YOU MAY INCLUDE THE STATEMENT IN THE BLANK SPACE ABOVE:

- If I suffer a conditions from which there is no reasonable prospect of regaining my ability to think and act for myself, I want only care directed to my comfort and dignity, and authorize my agent to decline all treatment (including artificial nutrition and hydration) the primary purpose of which is to prolong my life.
- If I suffer a condition from which there is no reasonable prospect of regaining my ability to think and act for myself, I want care directed to my comfort and dignity and also want artificial nutrition and hydration if needed, but authorize my agent to decline all other treatment the primary purpose of which is to prolong my life.
- I want my life sustained by any reasonable medical measures, regardless of my condition.

In the event the person I appoint above is unable, unwilling or unavailable to act as my health care agent, I hereby appoint _____ of _____ as alternate agent.

I hereby acknowledge that I have been provided with a disclosure statement explaining the effect of this document. I have read and understand the information contained in the disclosure statement.

The original of this document will be kept at _____
_____and the following persons and institutions will have signed copies:
_____
_____

_____ In witness whereof, I have hereunto signed my name this _____ day of _____, _____.

_____

Signature

I declare that the principal appears to be of sound mind and free from duress at the time the durable power of attorney for health care is signed and that the principal has affirmed that he or she is aware of the nature of the document and is signing it freely and voluntarily.

Witness:_____ Address:_____
Witness:_____ Address:_____

State of ombudsman, hospital representative or other authorized person (to be signed only if the principal is in or is being admitted to a hospital, nursing home or residential care home):

I declare that I have personally explained the nature and effect of this durable power of attorney to the principal and that the principal understands the same.

Date:_____
Name:_____ Address:_____

TERMINAL CARE DOCUMENT

To my family, my physician, my lawyer, my clergyman. To any medical facility in whose care I happen to be. To any individual who may become responsible for my health, welfare or affairs.

Death is as much a reality as birth, growth, maturity and old age—it is the one certainty of life. If the time comes when I, _____, can no longer take part in decisions of my own future, let this statement stand as an expression of my wishes, while I am still of sound mind.

If the situation should arise in which I am in a terminal state and there is no reasonable expectation of my recovery, I direct that I be allowed to die a natural death and that my life not be prolonged by extraordinary measures. I do, however, ask that medication be mercifully administered to me to alleviate suffering even though this may shorten my remaining life.

This statement is made after careful consideration and is in accordance with my strong convictions and beliefs. I want the wishes and directions here expressed carried out to the extent permitted by law. Insofar as they are not legally enforceable, I hope that those to whom this will is addressed will regard themselves as morally bound by these provisions.

Signed:_____

Date:_____

Witness:_____ Witness:_____

Copies of this request have been given to: _____
_____
_____

ADVANCE MEDICAL DIRECTIVE

I, _____, willfully and voluntarily make known my desire and hereby declare:

If at any time my attending physician should determine that I have a terminal condition where the application of life-prolonging procedures would serve only to artificially prolong the dying process, I direct that such procedures be withheld or withdrawn, and that I be permitted to die naturally with only the administration of medication or the performance of any medical procedure deemed necessary to provide me with comfort care or to alleviate pain (OPTION: I specifically direct that the following procedures or treatments be provided to me:_____

_____)

In the absence of my ability to give directions regarding the use of such life-prolonging procedures, it is my intention that this advance directive shall be honored by my family and physician as the final expression of my legal right to refuse medical or surgical treatment and accept the consequences of such refusal.

OPTION: APPOINTMENT OF AGENT (CROSS THROUGH IF YOU DO NOT WANT TO APPOINT AN AGENT TO MAKE HEALTH CARE DECISIONS FOR YOU.)

I hereby appoint _____ (primary agent) _____ (address and telephone number), as my agent to make health care decisions on my behalf as authorized in this document. If _____(primary agent) is not reasonably available or is unable or unwilling to act as my agent, then I appoint _____ (successor agent), of _____ _____ (address and telephone number), to serve in that capacity.

I hereby grant to my agent, named above, full power and authority to make health care decisions on my behalf as described below whenever I have been determined to be incapable of making an informed decision about providing, withholding or withdrawing, medical treatment. The phrase "incapable of making an informed decision" means unable to understand the nature, extent and probably consequences of a proposed medical decision or unable to make a rational evaluation of the risks and benefits of a proposed medical decision as compared with the risks and benefits of alternatives to that decision, or unable to communicate such understanding in any way. My agent's authority hereunder is effective as long as I am incapable of making an informed decision.

The determination that I am incapable of making an informed decision shall be made by my attending physician and a second physician or licensed clinical psychologist after a personal examination of me and shall be certified in writing. Such certification shall be required before treatment is withheld or withdrawn, and before, or as soon as reasonably practicable after, treatment is provided, and every 180 days thereafter while the treatment continues.

In exercising the power to make health care decisions on my behalf, my agent shall follow my desires and preferences as stated in this document or as otherwise known to my agent. My agent shall be guided by my medical diagnosis and prognosis and any information provided by my physicians as to the intrusiveness, pain, risks, and side effects associated with treatment or nontreatment. My agent shall not authorize a course of treatment which he knows, or upon reasonable inquiry ought to know, is contrary to my religious beliefs or my basic values, whether expressed orally or in writing. If my agent cannot determine what treatment choice I would have made on my own behalf, then my agent shall make a choice for me based upon what he believes to be in my best interests.

OPTION: POWERS OF MY AGENT (CROSS THROUGH ANY LANGUAGE YOU DO NOT WANT AND ADD ANY LANGUAGE YOU DO WANT.)

The powers of my agent shall include the following:

A. To consent to or refuse or withdraw consent to any type of medical care, treatment, surgical procedure, diagnostic procedure, medication and the use of mechanical or other procedures that affect any bodily function, including, but not limited to , artificial respiration, artificially administered nutrition and hydration, and cardiopulmonary resuscitation. This authorization specifically includes the power to consent to the administration of dosages of pain relieving medication in excess of standard doses in an amount sufficient to relieve pain, even if such medication carries the risk of addiction or inadvertently hastens my death;

B. To request, receive, and review any information, verbal or written, regarding my physical or mental health, including, but not limited to, medical and hospital records, and to consent to the disclosure of this information;

C. To employ and discharge my health care providers;

D. To authorize my admission to or discharge (including transfer to another facility) from any hospital, hospice, nursing home, adult home or other medical care facility; and

E. To take any lawful actions that may be necessary to carry out these decisions, including the granting of releases of liability to medical providers.

Further, my agent shall not be liable for the costs of treatment pursuant to his authorization, based solely on that authorization.

OPTION: APPOINTMENT OF ANOTHER AGENT TO MAKE AN ANATOMICAL GIFT (CROSS THROUGH IF YOU DO NOT WANT TO APPOINT ANOTHER AGENT TO MAKE AN ANATOMICAL GIFT FOR YOU.)

Upon my death, I direct that an anatomical gift of all or any part of my body may be made pursuant to Article 2 (§ 32.1-289 et seq.) of Chapter 8 of Title 32.1 and in accordance with my directions, if any, I hereby appoint _____ as my agent, of _____ (address and telephone number), to make any such anatomical gift following my death. I further direct that _____ _____ _____ (declarant's directions concerning anatomical gift).

This advance directive shall not terminate in the event of my disability.

By signing below, I indicate that I am emotionally and mentally competent to make this advance directive and that I understand the purpose and effect of this document.

_____   _____
(Date)   (Signature of Declarant)

The declarant signed the foregoing advance directive in my presence. I am not the spouse or a blood relative of the declarant.

(Witness) _____   (Witness) _____

MEDICAL POWER OF ATTORNEY

Dated:_____, _____.

    I, _____,
(insert your name and address), hereby appoint_____
_____(insert the name, address, area code and telephone number of the person you wish to designate as your representative) as my representative to act on my behalf to give, withhold or withdraw informed consent to health care decisions in the event that I am not able to do so myself. If my representative is unable, unwilling or disqualified to serve, then I appoint_____
_____ as my successor representative.

    This appointment shall extend to (but not be limited to) decisions relating to medical treatment, surgical treatment, nursing care, medication, hospitalization, care and treatment in a nursing home or other facility, and home health care. The representative appointed by this document is specifically authorized to act on my behalf to consent to, refuse or withdraw any and all medical treatment or diagnostic procedures, if my representative determines that I, if able to do so, would consent to, refuse or withdraw such treatment or procedures. Such authority shall include, but not be limited to, the withholding or withdrawal of life-prolonging intervention when in the opinion of two physicians who have examined me, one of whom is my attending physician, such life-prolonging intervention offers no medical hope of benefit.

    I appoint this representative because I believe this person understands my wishes and values and will act to carry into effect the health care decisions that I would make if I were able to do so, and because I also believe that this person will act in my best interests when my wishes are unknown. It is my intent that my family, my physician and all legal authorities be bound by the decisions that are made by the representative appointed in this document, and it is my intent that these decisions should not be the subject of review by any health care provider, or administrative or judicial agency.

    It is my intent that this document be legally binding and effective. In the event that the law does not recognize this document as legally binding and effective, it is my intent that this document be taken as a formal statement of my desire concerning the method by which any health care decisions should be made on my behalf during any period when I am unable to make such decisions.

    In exercising the authority under this medical power of attorney, my representative shall act consistently with my special directives or limitations as stated below.

SPECIAL DIRECTIVES OR LIMITATIONS ON THIS POWER: (If none, write "none.")

_____
_____
_____

    THIS MEDICAL POWER OF ATTORNEY SHALL BECOME EFFECTIVE ONLY UPON MY INCAPACITY TO GIVE, WITHHOLD OR WITHDRAW INFORMED CONSENT TO MY OWN MEDICAL CARE.

    These directives shall supersede any directives made in any previously executed document concerning my health care.

    X_____
                    Signature of Principal

    I did not sign the principal's signature above. I am at least eighteen years of age and am not related to the principal by blood or marriage. I am not entitled to any portion of the estate of the principal according to the laws of intestate succession of the state of the principal's domicile or to the best of my knowledge under any will or the principal or codicil thereto, or legally responsible for the costs of the principal's medical or other care. I am not the principal's attending physician, nor am I the representative or successor representative of the principal.

WITNESS:_____   DATE:_____

WITNESS:_____   DATE:_____

    STATE OF _____,
    COUNTY OF _____, to-wit:
    I, _____, a Notary Public of said County, do certify that _____
_____, as principal, and _____
and _____, as witnesses, whose names are signed to the writing above bearing
date on the _____ day of _____, _____, have this day acknowledged the same before me.
    Given under my hand this _____ day of _____, _____.
    My commission expires:_____

                   _____
                            Notary Public

STATUTORY POWER OF ATTORNEY

NOTICE: THIS IS AN IMPORTANT DOCUMENT. BEFORE SIGNING THIS DOCUMENT, YOU SHOULD KNOW THESE IMPORTANT FACTS. THE PURPOSE OF THIS POWER OF ATTORNEY IS TO GIVE THE PERSON WHOM YOU DESIGNATE (YOUR "AGENT") BROAD POWERS TO HANDLE YOUR PROPERTY, WHICH MAY INCLUDE POWERS TO PLEDGE, SELL OR OTHERWISE DISPOSE OF ANY REAL OR PERSONAL PROPERTY WITHOUT ADVANCE NOTICE TO YOU OR APPROVAL BY YOU. THE POWERS WILL EXIST * * * AFTER YOU BECOME DISABLED, INCAPACITATED OR INCOMPETENT * * * <u>IF</u> YOU * * * <u>CIRCLE</u> THAT PROVISION. THE POWERS THAT YOU GIVE YOUR AGENT ARE EXPLAINED MORE FULLY IN SECTION 243.10 OF THE WISCONSIN STATUTES. THIS DOCUMENT DOES NOT AUTHORIZE ANYONE TO MAKE MEDICAL OR OTHER HEALTH-CARE DECISIONS FOR YOU. IF THERE IS ANYTHING ABOUT THIS FORM THAT YOU DO NOT UNDERSTAND, YOU SHOULD ASK A LAWYER TO EXPLAIN IT TO YOU.

I _____ (insert your name and address) appoint_____
_____(insert the name and address of the person appointed, or each person appointed, if you want to designate more than one) as my agent to act for me in any lawful way with respect to the powers initialed below. If the person or persons appointed are unable or unwilling to act as my agent, I appoint _____ (insert name and address of alternate person appointed) to act for me in any lawful way with respect to the powers initialed below.

TO GRANT ONE OR MORE OF THE FOLLOWING POWERS, INITIAL THE LINE IN FRONT OF EACH POWER YOU ARE GRANTING.

TO WITHHOLD A POWER, DO NOT INITIAL THE LINE IN FRONT OF IT. YOU MAY, BUT NEED NOT, CROSS OUT EACH POWER WITHHELD.

Initials			Initials		
_____	1.	Real property transactions.	_____	9.	Claims and litigation.
_____	2.	Tangible personal property transactions.	_____	10.	Personal and family maintenance.
_____	3.	Stock and bond transactions.	_____	11.	Benefits from social security, medicare,
_____	4.	Commodity and option transactions.			medicaid or other governmental
_____	5.	Banking and other financial institution			programs or military service.
		transactions.	_____	12.	Retirement plan transactions.
_____	6.	Business operating transactions.	_____	13.	Tax matters.
_____	7.	Insurance and annuity transactions.			
_____	8.	Estate, trust, and other beneficiary transactions.			

SPECIAL INSTRUCTIONS

ON THE FOLLOWING LINES YOU MAY GIVE SPECIAL INSTRUCTIONS LIMITING OR EXTENDING THE POWERS GRANTED TO YOUR AGENT.

_____
_____
_____
_____

This power of attorney will become effective (immediately) (immediately, and is not affected by my subsequent disability, incapacity or incompetency) (when I become disabled, incapacitated or incompetent) <u>CIRCLE</u> ONE.

I agree that any third party who receives a copy of this document may act under it. Revocation of the power of attorney is not effective as to a third party until the third party learns of the revocation. I agree to reimburse the third party for any loss resulting from claims that arise against the third party because of reliance on this power of attorney.

Signed this _____ day of _____, _____.

_____   _____
(Your Signature)   (Your Social Security Number)

State of _____
County of _____
This document was acknowledged before me on _____(date) by
_____ (name of principal).

(seal, if any)

_____
Notary Public

My commission expires: _____

BY ACCEPTING OR ACTING UNDER THE APPOINTMENT, THE AGENT ASSUMES THE FIDUCIARY AND OTHER LEGAL RESPONSIBILITIES OF AN AGENT.

POWER OF ATTORNEY FOR HEALTH CARE

NOTICE TO PERSON MAKING THIS DOCUMENT

YOU HAVE THE RIGHT TO MAKE DECISIONS ABOUT YOUR HEALTH CARE. NO HEALTH CARE MAY BE GIVEN TO YOU OVER YOUR OBJECTION, AND NECESSARY HEALTH CARE MAY NOT BE STOPPED OR WITHHELD IF YOU OBJECT.

BECAUSE YOUR HEALTH CARE PROVIDERS IN SOME CASES MAY NOT HAVE HAD THE OPPORTUNITY TO ESTABLISH A LONG-TERM RELATIONSHIP WITH YOU, THEY ARE OFTEN UNFAMILIAR WITH YOUR BELIEFS AND VALUES AND THE DETAILS OF YOUR FAMILY RELA-TIONSHIPS. THIS POSES A PROBLEM IF YOU BECOME PHYSICALLY OR MENTALLY UNABLE TO MAKE A DECISION ABOUT YOUR HEALTH CARE.

IN ORDER TO AVOID THIS PROBLEM, YOU MAY SIGN THIS DOCUMENT TO SPECIFY THE PER-SON WHOM YOU WANT TO MAKE THOSE DECISIONS PERSONALLY. THAT PERSON IS KNOWN AS YOUR HEALTH CARE AGENT. YOU SHOULD TAKE SOME TIME TO DISCUSS YOUR THOUGHTS AND BELIEFS ABOUT MEDICAL TREATMENT WITH THE PERSON OR PERSONS WHOM YOU HAVE SPECIFIED. YOU MAY STATE IN THIS DOCUMENT ANY TYPES OF HEALTH CARE THAT YOU DO OR DO NOT DESIRE, AND YOU MAY LIMIT THE AUTHORITY OF YOUR HEALTH CARE AGENT. IF YOUR HEALTH CARE AGENT IS UNAWARE OF YOUR DESIRES WITH RESPECT TO A PARTICULAR HEALTH CARE DECISION, HE OR SHE IS REQUIRED TO DETERMINE WHAT WOULD BE IN YOUR BEST INTERESTS IN MAKING THE DECISION.

THIS IS AN IMPORTANT LEGAL DOCUMENT. IT GIVES YOUR AGENT BROAD POWERS TO MAKE HEALTH CARE DECISIONS FOR YOU. IT REVOKES ANY PRIOR POWER OF ATTORNEY FOR HEALTH CARE THAT YOU MAY HAVE MADE. IF YOU WISH TO CHANGE YOUR POWER OF ATTORNEY FOR HEALTH CARE, YOU MAY REVOKE THIS DOCUMENT AT ANY TIME BY DESTROYING IT, BY DIRECTING ANOTHER PERSON TO DESTROY IT IN YOUR PRESENCE, BY SIGNING A WRITTEN AND DATED STATEMENT OR BY STATING THAT IT IS REVOKED IN THE PRESENCE OF TWO WITNESSES. IF YOU REVOKE, YOU SHOULD NOTIFY YOUR AGENT, YOUR HEALTH CARE PROVIDERS AND ANY OTHER PERSON TO WHOM YOU HAVE GIVEN A COPY. IF YOUR AGENT IS YOUR SPOUSE AND YOUR MARRIAGE IS ANNULLED OR YOU ARE DIVORCED AFTER SIGNING THIS DOCUMENT, THE DOCUMENT IS INVALID.

DO NOT SIGN THIS DOCUMENT UNLESS YOU CLEARLY UNDERSTAND IT.

IT IS SUGGESTED THAT YOU KEEP THE ORIGINAL OF THIS DOCUMENT ON FILE WITH YOUR PHYSICIAN.

Document made this _____ day of _____ (month), _____ (year).

CREATION OF POWER OF ATTORNEY FOR HEALTH CARE

I, _____
_____(print name, address and date of birth), being of sound mind, intend by this document to create a power of attorney for health care. My executing this power of attorney for health care is voluntary. Despite the creation of this power of attorney for health care, I expect to be fully informed about and allowed to participate in any health care decision for me, to the extent I am able. For the purposes of this document, "health care decision" means an informed decision to accept, main-tain, discontinue or refuse any care, treatment, service or procedure to maintain, diagnose or treat my physical or mental condition.

DESIGNATION OF HEALTH CARE AGENT

If I am no longer able to make health care decisions for myself, due to my incapacity, I hereby designate
_____
_____(print name, address and telephone number) to be my health care agent for the purpose of making health care decisions on my behalf. If he or she is ever unable or unwilling to do so, I hereby designate _____
_____(print name, address and telephone number) to be my alternate health care agent for the purpose of making health care decisions on my behalf. Neither my

health care agent or my alternate health care agent whom I have designated is my health care provider, an employee of my health care provider, an employee of a health care facility in which I am a patient or a spouse of any of those persons, unless he or she is also my relative. For purposes of this document, "incapacity" exists if 2 physicians or a physician and a psychologist who have personally examined me sign a statement that specifically expresses their opinion that I have a condition that means that I am unable to receive and evaluate information effectively or to communicate decisions to such an extent that I lack the capacity to manage my health care decisions. A copy of that statement must be attached to this document.

GENERAL STATEMENT OF AUTHORITY GRANTED

Unless I have specified otherwise in this document, if I ever have incapacity I instruct my health care provider to obtain the health care decision of my health care agent, if I need treatment, for all of my health care and treatment. I have discussed my desires thoroughly with my health care agent and believe that he or she understands my philosophy regarding the health care decisions I would make if I were able. I desire that my wishes be carried out through the authority given to my health care agent under this document.

If I am unable, due to my incapacity, to make a health care decision, my health care agent is instructed to make the health care decision for me, but my health care agent should try to discuss with me any specific proposed health care if I am able to communicate in any manner, including blinking my eyes. If this communication cannot be made, my health care agent shall base his or her decision on any health care choices that I have expressed prior to the time of the decision. If I have not expressed a health care choice about the health care in question and communication cannot be made, my health care agent shall base his or her health care decision on what he or she believes to be in my best interest.

LIMITATIONS ON MENTAL HEALTH TREATMENT

My health care agent may not admit or commit me on an inpatient basis to an institution for mental diseases, an intermediate care facility for the mentally retarded, a state treatment facility or a treatment facility. My health care agent may not consent to experimental mental health research or psychosurgery, electroconvulsive treatment or drastic mental health treatment procedures for me.

ADMISSION TO NURSING HOMES OR
COMMUNITY-BASED RESIDENTIAL FACILITIES

My health care agent may admit me to a nursing home or community-based residential facility for short-term stays for recuperative care or respite care.

If I have checked "Yes" to the following, my health care agent may admit me for a purpose other than recuperative care or respite care, but if I have checked "No" to the following, my health care agent may not so admit me:

1. A nursing home — Yes_____ No_____
2. A community-based residential facility — Yes_____ No_____

If I have not checked either "Yes" or "No" immediately above, my health care agent may only admit me for short-term stays for recuperative or respite care.

PROVISION OF A FEEDING TUBE

If I have checked "Yes" to the following, my health care agent may have a feeding tube withheld or withdrawn from me, unless my physician has advised that, in his or her professional judgment, this will cause me pain or will reduce my comfort. If I have checked "No" to the following, my health care agent may not have a feeding tube withheld or withdrawn from me.

My health care agent may not have orally ingested nutrition or hydration withheld or withdrawn from me unless provision of the nutrition or hydration is medically contraindicated.

Withhold or withdraw a feeding tube — Yes_____ No_____

If I have not checked either "Yes" or "No" immediately above, my health care agent may not have a feeding tube withdrawn from me.

HEALTH CARE DECISIONS FOR PREGNANT WOMEN

If I have checked "Yes" to the following, my health care agent may make health care decisions for me even if my agent knows I am pregnant. If I have checked "No" to the following, my health care agent may not make health care decisions for me if my health care agent knows I am pregnant.

Health care decision if I am pregnant — Yes_____ No_____
If I have not checked either "Yes" or "No" immediately above, my health care agent may not make health care decisions for me if my health care agent knows I am pregnant.

STATEMENT OF DESIRES, SPECIAL PROVISIONS OR LIMITATIONS

In exercising authority under this document, my health care agent shall act consistently with my following stated desires, if any, and is subject to any special provisions or limitations that I specify. The following are specific desires, provisions or limitation that I wish to state (add more items if needed):

1)_____
2)_____
3)_____

INSPECTION AND DISCLOSURE OF INFORMATION
RELATING TO MY PHYSICAL OR MENTAL HEALTH

Subject to any limitations in this document, my health care agent has the authority to do all of the following:

(a)   Request, review and receive any information, verbal or written, regarding my physical or mental health, including medical and hospital records.
(b)   Execute on my behalf any documents that may be required in order to obtain this information.
(c)   Consent to the disclosure of this information.

(The principal and the witnesses all must sign the document at the same time.)

SIGNATURE OF PRINCIPAL
(person creating the power of attorney for health care)

_____   _____
Signature   Date
(The signing of this document by the principal revokes all previous powers of attorney for health care documents.)

STATEMENT OF WITNESSES

I know the principal personally and I believe him or her to be of sound mind and at least 18 years of age. I believe that his or her execution of this power of attorney for health care is voluntary. I am at least 18 years of age, am not related to the principal by blood, marriage or adoption and am not directly financially responsible for the principal's health care. I am not a health care provider who is serving the principal at this time, an employee of the health care provider, other than a chaplain or a social worker, or an employee, other than a chaplain or a social worker, of an inpatient health care facility in which the declarant is a patient. I am not the principal's health care agent. To the best of my knowledge, I am not entitled to and do not have a claim on the principal's estate.

Witness No. 1:   Witness No. 2:

(print) Name_____   (print) Name_____
Address:_____   Address:_____

_____   _____
Signature   Signature

Date:_____   Date:_____

STATEMENT OF HEALTH CARE AGENT AND ALTERNATE HEALTH CARE AGENT

I understand that _____ (name of principal) has designated me to be his or her health care agent or alternate health care agent if he or she is ever found to have incapacity and unable to make health care decisions himself or herself. _____ (name of principal) has discussed his or her desires regarding health care decisions with me.

_____   _____
Agent's signature   Alternate's signature
Address:_____   Address:_____

Failure to execute a power of attorney for health care document under chapter 155 of the Wisconsin Statutes creates no presumption about the intent of any individual with regard to his or her health care decisions.

This power of attorney for health care is executed as provided in chapter 155 of the Wisconsin Statutes.

DECLARATION TO PHYSICIANS

1. I, _____, being of sound mind, voluntarily state my desire that my dying may not be prolonged under the circumstances specified in this document. Under those circumstances, I direct that I be permitted to die naturally. If I am unable to give directions regarding the use of life-sustaining procedures or feeding tubes, I intend that my family and physician honor this document as the final expression of my legal right to refuse medical or surgical treatment and to accept the consequences from this refusal.

2. If I have a TERMINAL CONDITION, as determined by 2 physicians who have personally examined me, I do not want my dying to be artificially prolonged and I do not want life-sustaining procedures to be used. In addition, if I have such a terminal condition, the following are my directions regarding the use of feeding tubes (check only one):

    a. Use feeding tubes if I have a terminal condition ❏

    b. Do not use feeding tubes if I have a terminal condition ❏

    c. If I have not checked either box, feeding tubes will be used. ❏

3. If I am in a PERSISTENT VEGETATIVE STATE, as determined by 2 physicians who have personally examined me, the following are my directions regarding the use of life-sustaining procedures and feeding tubes:

    a. Check only one: Use life-sustaining procedures if I am in a persistent vegetative state ❏

                      Do not use life-sustaining procedures if I am in a persistent vegetative state ❏

                      If I have not checked either box, life-sustaining procedures will be used. ❏

    b. Check only one: Use feeding tubes if I am in a persistent vegetative state ❏

                      Do not use feeding tubes if I am in a persistent vegetative state ❏

                      If I have not checked either box, feeding tubes will be used. ❏

4. By law, this document cannot be used to authorize: a) withholding or withdrawal of any medication, procedure or feeding tube if to do so would cause me pain or reduce my comfort; and b) withholding or withdrawal of nutrition or hydration that is administered to me through means other than a feeding tube unless, in my physician's opinion, this administration is medically contraindicated.

5. If I have been diagnosed as pregnant and my physician knows of this diagnosis, this document has no effect during the course of my pregnancy.

Signed_____ Date_____
Address_____

I know the person signing this document personally and I believe him or her to be of sound mind. I am not related to the person signing this document by blood, marriage or adoption, and am not entitled to and do not have a claim on any portion of the person's estate and am not otherwise restricted by law from being a witness.

Witness_____

Witness_____

This document is executed as provided in chapter 154, Wisconsin Statutes.

LIMITED POWER OF ATTORNEY

I, _____

_____ (your name and address), do hereby grant a limited

and specific power of attorney to _____

_____ (your agent's name and address), as

my attorney-in-fact (agent), giving said agent the full power and authority to undertake and

perform the following acts on my behalf to the same extent as if I had done so personally:

The authority of my agent shall include such incidental acts as are reasonable and necessary to carry out and perform the authorities and duties stated herein.

My agent agrees to accept this appointment subject to its terms, and agrees to act in a fiduciary capacity consistent with my best interest, as my agent in his or her discretion deems appropriate, and I hereby ratify all such acts of my agent.

This power of attorney may be revoked by me at any time, and will automatically be revoked by my death; PROVIDED that any person relying on this power of attorney before or after my death shall have full rights to accept the granted authority of my agent until receipt of actual notice of revocation.

Signed this _____ day of _____, _____.

_____
Signature

INDEX

A

advance directive for health care, *See* living will.
agent, 5
Alabama, 27, 30, 40, 72
Alaska, 19, 23, 30, 31, 40, 76
Arizona, 27, 30, 40, 78
Arkansas, 40
attorney at law, 5
attorney-in-fact, 6
attorneys, 9-14
autopsy, 30

C

California, 19, 23, 30, 41, 80, 82
California Power of Attorney Handbook, 41
case reporters, 17
child care power of attorney, 8, 35, 70, 137
code, 16
Colorado, 19, 23, 41, 86
Connecticut, 19, 23, 30, 31, 41, 89

D

Delaware, 30, 42, 91
digests, 17
District of Columbia, 30, 42, 96
durable power of attorney, 6, 19, 22, 59

E

execute, 6

F

financial power of attorney, 6, 19-28
Florida, 27, 30, 31, 42, 98
Florida Power of Attorney Handbook, 42
food and water, 33

G

general power of attorney, 6
Georgia, 19, 24, 30, 31, 43, 99, 104

H

Hawaii, 27, 30, 43, 106
health care power of attorney, 7, 29-33
How to Write Your Own Living Will, 8, 33
hydration, *See* food and water.

I

Idaho, 30, 43, 107
Illinois, 19, 23, 25, 30, 31, 44, 111, 117
incapacity, 6, 22
incompetency, *See* incapacity.
Indiana, 19, 23, 25, 30, 31, 44, 121
Iowa, 30, 44, 123

K

Kansas, 30, 45, 124
Kentucky, 45

L

law libraries, 16
lawyers, *See* attorneys.
legal encyclopedia, 18
*Legal Malpractice and Other Claims against Your
    Lawyer*, 14
legal research, 16
life-prolonging procedures, 29, 33
limited power of attorney, 6, 20, 210
living wills, 7, 33
Louisiana, 27, 45

M

Maine, 19, 25, 30, 46, 126, 127
Maryland, 30, 46, 130
Massachusetts, 30, 46, 134
Michigan, 36, 47, 137
Minnesota, 19, 23, 25, 30, 47, 138, 140
Mississippi, 30, 47, 141
Missouri, 27, 48
Montana, 19, 23, 25, 48, 143

N

Nebraska, 19, 23, 26, 30, 48, 145, 146
Nevada, 27, 30, 49, 148
New Hampshire, 27, 30, 49, 152
New Jersey, 49
New Mexico, 19, 23, 26, 30, 32, 49, 154, 157
New York, 19, 23, 26, 30, 50, 160, 167, 170, 171
New York Power of Attorney Handbook, 50
North Carolina, 19, 23, 26, 30, 50, 172, 174
North Dakota, 30, 50, 177
nutrition, *See* food and water.

O

Ohio, 27, 51
Oklahoma, 30, 32, 51, 182
Oregon, 27, 30, 32, 51, 186
organ donation, 30

P

Pennsylvania, 27, 51
power of attorney for child care, 8, 35, 70, 137
practice manuals, 17
principal, 6

R

real estate, 20
revoking a power of attorney, 36, 71
Rhode Island, 52

S

South Carolina, 30, 52, 188
South Dakota, 52
special power of attorney, *See* limited power of
    attorney.
springing power of attorney, 6
state laws, 16, 39-55
statutes, 16

T

Tennessee, 19, 23, 26, 30, 53, 191, 192
terminology, 5
Texas, 19, 23, 26, 30, 53, 194, 196
third parties, 15

U

Utah, 27, 30, 53, 199

V

Vermont, 30, 54, 200
Virginia, 27, 30, 54, 202

W

Washington, 54
West Virginia, 30, 54, 204
Wisconsin, 19, 23, 27, 30, 55, 205, 206
Wyoming, 55

Your #1 Source for Real World Legal Information...

SPHINX® PUBLISHING
A Division of Sourcebooks, Inc.®

- Written by lawyers
- Simple English explanation of the law
- Forms and instructions included

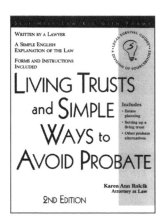

LIVING TRUSTS & SIMPLE WAYS TO AVOID PROBATE, 2ND EDITION

Explains how probate works and what a living trust can do that a will cannot. Illustrates simple ways to avoid probate and save hundreds of dollars.

176 pages; $19.95; ISBN 1-57071-336-7

HOW TO MAKE YOUR OWN WILL

Valid in 50 states, this book contains 14 different legal forms that will help you put your financial affairs in order. Also discusses inheritance laws.

144 pages; $12.95; ISBN 1-57071-228-X

HOW TO WRITE YOUR OWN LIVING WILL

Step-by-step guide to writing living wills in all 50 states and the District of Columbia, complete with necessary forms.

160 pages; $9.95; ISBN 1-57071-167-4

See the following order form for books written specifically for California, Florida, Georgia, Illinois, Massachusetts, Michigan, Minnesota, New York, North Carolina, Pennsylvania, and Texas! *Coming soon—Ohio and New Jersey!*

What our customers say about our books:

"It couldn't be more clear for the lay person." —R.D.

"I want you to know I really appreciate your book. It has saved me a lot of time and money." —L.T.

"Your real estate contracts book has saved me nearly $12,000.00 in closing costs over the past year." —A.B.

"...many of the legal questions that I have had over the years were answered clearly and concisely through your plain English interpretation of the law." —C.E.H.

"If there weren't people out there like you I'd be lost. You have the best books of this type out there." —S.B.

"...your forms and directions are easy to follow." —C.V.M.

Sphinx Publishing's Legal Survival Guides
are directly available from the Sourcebooks, Inc., or from your local bookstores.
For credit card orders call 1–800–43–BRIGHT, write P.O. Box 372, Naperville, IL 60566,
or fax 630-961-2168

SPHINX® PUBLISHING'S NATIONAL TITLES
Valid in All 50 States

LEGAL SURVIVAL IN BUSINESS

How to Form a Limited Liability Company (April)	$19.95
How to Form Your Own Corporation (2E)	$19.95
How to Form Your Own Partnership	$19.95
How to Register Your Own Copyright (2E)	$19.95
How to Register Your Own Trademark (2E)	$19.95
Most Valuable Business Legal Forms You'll Ever Need (2E)	$19.95
Most Valuable Corporate Forms You'll Ever Need (2E)	$24.95
Software Law (with diskette)	$29.95

LEGAL SURVIVAL IN COURT

Crime Victim's Guide to Justice	$19.95
Debtors' Rights (3E)	$12.95
Defend Yourself against Criminal Charges	$19.95
Grandparents' Rights (2E)	$19.95
Help Your Lawyer Win Your Case	$12.95
Jurors' Rights (2E)	$9.95
Legal Malpractice and Other Claims against Your Lawyer (2E) (June)	$18.95
Legal Research Made Easy (2E)	$14.95
Simple Ways to Protect Yourself from Lawsuits	$24.95
Victims' Rights	$12.95
Winning Your Personal Injury Claim	$19.95

LEGAL SURVIVAL IN REAL ESTATE

How to Buy a Condominium or Townhome	$16.95
How to Negotiate Real Estate Contracts (3E)	$16.95
How to Negotiate Real Estate Leases (3E)	$16.95
Successful Real Estate Brokerage Management	$19.95

LEGAL SURVIVAL IN PERSONAL AFFAIRS

How to File Your Own Bankruptcy (4E)	$19.95
How to File Your Own Divorce (3E)	$19.95
How to Make Your Own Will	$12.95
How to Write Your Own Living Will	$9.95
How to Write Your Own Premarital Agreement (2E)	$19.95
How to Win Your Unemployment Compensation Claim	$19.95
Living Trusts and Simple Ways to Avoid Probate (2E)	$19.95
Neighbors' Rights	$12.95
The Power of Attorney Handbook (3E)	$19.95
Simple Ways to Protect Yourself from Lawsuits	$24.95
Social Security Benefits Handbook (2E)	$14.95
Unmarried Parents' Rights	$19.95
U.S.A. Immigration Guide (3E)	$19.95
Guia de Inmigracion a Estados Unidos (2E) (May)	$19.95

Legal Survival Guides are directly available from Sourcebooks, Inc., or from your local bookstores.

For credit card orders call 1–800–43-BRIGHT, write P.O. Box 372, Naperville, IL 60566, or fax 630-961-2168

SPHINX® PUBLISHING ORDER FORM

BILL TO:		SHIP TO:	
Phone #	Terms	F.O.B. Chicago, IL	Ship Date

Charge my: ☐ VISA ☐ MasterCard ☐ American Express

☐ **Money Order or Personal Check**

Credit Card Number ☐☐☐☐☐☐☐☐☐☐☐☐☐☐☐☐

Expiration Date ☐☐☐☐

Qty	ISBN	Title	Retail	Ext.
		SPHINX PUBLISHING NATIONAL TITLES		
____	1-57071-166-6	Crime Victim's Guide to Justice	$19.95	____
____	1-57071-342-1	Debtors' Rights (3E)	$12.95	____
____	1-57071-162-3	Defend Yourself against Criminal Charges	$19.95	____
____	1-57248-082-3	Grandparents' Rights (2E)	$19.95	____
____	1-57248-087-4	Guia de Inmigracion a Estados Unidos (2E) (May)	$19.95	____
____	1-57248-021-1	Help Your Lawyer Win Your Case	$12.95	____
____	1-57071-164-X	How to Buy a Condominium or Townhome	$16.95	____
____	1-57071-223-9	How to File Your Own Bankruptcy (4E)	$19.95	____
____	1-57071-224-7	How to File Your Own Divorce (3E)	$19.95	____
____	1-57248-083-1	How to Form a Limited Liability Company (April)	$19.95	____
____	1-57071-227-1	How to Form Your Own Corporation (2E)	$19.95	____
____	1-57071-343-X	How to Form Your Own Partnership	$19.95	____
____	1-57071-228-X	How to Make Your Own Will	$12.95	____
____	1-57071-331-6	How to Negotiate Real Estate Contracts (3E)	$16.95	____
____	1-57071-332-4	How to Negotiate Real Estate Leases (3E)	$16.95	____
____	1-57071-225-5	How to Register Your Own Copyright (2E)	$19.95	____
____	1-57071-226-3	How to Register Your Own Trademark (2E)	$19.95	____
____	1-57071-349-9	How to Win Your Unemployment Compensation Claim	$19.95	____
____	1-57071-167-4	How to Write Your Own Living Will	$9.95	____
____	1-57071-344-8	How to Write Your Own Premarital Agreement (2E)	$19.95	____
____	1-57071-333-2	Jurors' Rights (2E)	$9.95	____
____	1-57248-090-4	Legal Malpractice and Other Claims against...(2E) (June)	$18.95	____
____	1-57071-400-2	Legal Research Made Easy (2E)	$14.95	____
____	1-57071-336-7	Living Trusts and Simple Ways to Avoid Probate (2E)	$19.95	____
____	1-57071-345-6	Most Valuable Bus. Legal Forms You'll Ever Need (2E)	$19.95	____
____	1-57071-346-4	Most Valuable Corporate Forms You'll Ever Need (2E)	$24.95	____

Qty	ISBN	Title	Retail	Ext.
____	1-57248-089-0	Neighbors' Rights	$12.95	____
____	1-57071-348-0	The Power of Attorney Handbook (3E)	$19.95	____
____	1-57248-020-3	Simple Ways to Protect Yourself from Lawsuits	$24.95	____
____	1-57071-337-5	Social Security Benefits Handbook (2E)	$14.95	____
____	1-57071-163-1	Software Law (w/diskette)	$29.95	____
____	0-913825-86-7	Successful Real Estate Brokerage Mgmt.	$19.95	____
____	1-57071-399-5	Unmarried Parents' Rights	$19.95	____
____	1-57071-354-5	U.S.A. Immigration Guide (3E)	$19.95	____
____	0-913825-82-4	Victims' Rights	$12.95	____
____	1-57071-165-8	Winning Your Personal Injury Claim	$19.95	____
		CALIFORNIA TITLES		
____	1-57071-360-X	CA Power of Attorney Handbook	$12.95	____
____	1-57071-355-3	How to File for Divorce in CA	$19.95	____
____	1-57071-356-1	How to Make a CA Will	$12.95	____
____	1-57071-408-8	How to Probate an Estate in CA (April)	$19.95	____
____	1-57071-357-X	How to Start a Business in CA	$16.95	____
____	1-57071-358-8	How to Win in Small Claims Court in CA	$14.95	____
____	1-57071-359-6	Landlords' Rights and Duties in CA	$19.95	____
		FLORIDA TITLES		
____	1-57071-363-4	Florida Power of Attorney Handbook (2E)	$12.95	____
____	1-57248-093-9	How to File for Divorce in FL (6E) (July)	$21.95	____
____	1-57248-086-6	How to Form a Limited Liability Co. in FL (April)	$19.95	____
____	1-57071-401-0	How to Form a Partnership in FL	$19.95	____
____	1-57071-380-4	How to Form a Corporation in FL (4E)	$19.95	____
____	1-57071-361-8	How to Make a FL Will (5E)	$12.95	____
____	1-57248-088-2	How to Modify Your FL Divorce Judgement (4E) (May)	$22.95	____
____	*Form Continued on Following Page*		**SUBTOTAL**	____

To order, call Sourcebooks at 1-800-43-BRIGHT or FAX (630)961-2168 (Bookstores, libraries, wholesalers—please call for discount)

SPHINX® PUBLISHING ORDER FORM

Qty	ISBN	Title	Retail	Ext.
		FLORIDA TITLES (CONT'D)		
_____	1-57071-364-2	How to Probate an Estate in FL (3E)	$24.95	_____
_____	1-57248-081-5	How to Start a Business in FL (5E) (March)	$16.95	_____
_____	1-57071-362-6	How to Win in Small Claims Court in FL (6E)	$14.95	_____
_____	1-57071-335-9	Landlords' Rights and Duties in FL (7E)	$19.95	_____
_____	1-57071-334-0	Land Trusts in FL (5E)	$24.95	_____
_____	0-913825-73-5	Women's Legal Rights in FL	$19.95	_____
		GEORGIA TITLES		
_____	1-57071-376-6	How to File for Divorce in GA (3E)	$19.95	_____
_____	1-57248-075-0	How to Make a GA Will (3E)	$12.95	_____
_____	1-57248-076-9	How to Start a Business in Georgia (3E)	$16.95	_____
		ILLINOIS TITLES		
_____	1-57071-405-3	How to File for Divorce in IL (2E)	$19.95	_____
_____	1-57071-415-0	How to Make an IL Will (2E)	$12.95	_____
_____	1-57071-416-9	How to Start a Business in IL (2E)	$16.95	_____
_____	1-57248-078-5	Landlords' Rights & Duties in IL (February)	$19.95	_____
		MASSACHUSETTS TITLES		
_____	1-57071-329-4	How to File for Divorce in MA (2E)	$19.95	_____
_____	1-57248-050-5	How to Make a MA Will	$9.95	_____
_____	1-57248-053-X	How to Probate an Estate in MA	$19.95	_____
_____	1-57248-054-8	How to Start a Business in MA	$16.95	_____
_____	1-57248-055-6	Landlords' Rights and Duties in MA	$19.95	_____
		MICHIGAN TITLES		
_____	1-57071-409-6	How to File for Divorce in MI (2E)	$19.95	_____
_____	1-57248-077-7	How to Make a MI Will (2E)	$12.95	_____
_____	1-57071-407-X	How to Start a Business in MI (2E)	$16.95	_____
		MINNESOTA TITLES		
_____	1-57248-039-4	How to File for Divorce in MN	$19.95	_____
_____	1-57248-040-8	How to Form a Simple Corporation in MN	$19.95	_____
_____	1-57248-037-8	How to Make a MN Will	$9.95	_____
_____	1-57248-038-6	How to Start a Business in MN	$16.95	_____
		NEW YORK TITLES		

Qty	ISBN	Title	Retail	Ext.
_____	1-57071-184-4	How to File for Divorce in NY (March)	$19.95	_____
_____	1-57248-095-5	How to Make a NY Will (2E)	$12.95	_____
_____	1-57071-185-2	How to Start a Business in NY	$16.95	_____
_____	1-57071-187-9	How to Win in Small Claims Court in NY	$14.95	_____
_____	1-57071-186-0	Landlords' Rights and Duties in NY (March)	$19.95	_____
_____	1-57071-188-7	New York Power of Attorney Handbook	$19.95	_____
		NORTH CAROLINA TITLES		
_____	1-57071-326-X	How to File for Divorce in NC (2E)	$19.95	_____
_____	1-57071-327-8	How to Make a NC Will (2E)	$12.95	_____
_____	1-57248-096-3	How to Start a Business in NC (2E)	$16.95	_____
_____	1-57248-091-2	Landlords' Rights & Duties in NC (June)	$19.95	_____
		PENNSYLVANIA TITLES		
_____	1-57071-177-1	How to File for Divorce in PA	$19.95	_____
_____	1-57248-094-7	How to Make a PA Will (2E)	$12.95	_____
_____	1-57071-178-X	How to Start a Business in PA	$16.95	_____
_____	1-57071-179-8	Landlords' Rights and Duties in PA (June)	$19.95	_____
		TEXAS TITLES		
_____	1-57071-330-8	How to File for Divorce in TX (2E)	$19.95	_____
_____	1-57248-009-2	How to Form a Simple Corporation in TX	$19.95	_____
_____	1-57071-417-7	How to Make a TX Will (2E)	$12.95	_____
_____	1-57071-418-5	How to Probate an Estate in TX (2E)	$19.95	_____
_____	1-57071-365-0	How to Start a Business in TX (2E)	$16.95	_____
_____	1-57248-012-2	How to Win in Small Claims Court in TX	$14.95	_____
_____	1-57248-011-4	Landlords' Rights and Duties in TX	$19.95	_____

SUBTOTAL THIS PAGE _____

SUBTOTAL PREVIOUS PAGE _____

Illinois residents add 6.75% sales tax
Florida residents add 6% state sales tax plus applicable discretionary surtax _____

Shipping— $4.00 for 1st book, $1.00 each additional _____

TOTAL _____